E 457.2 .H69 2011

Hogan, Jackie, 1967-

Lincoln, Inc.

DATE DUE

GAYLORD   PRINTED IN U.S.A.

Lincoln, Inc.

Lincoln, Inc.

Selling the Sixteenth President in Contemporary America

Jackie Hogan

ROWMAN & LITTLEFIELD PUBLISHERS, INC.
Lanham • Boulder • New York • Toronto • Plymouth, UK

Published by Rowman & Littlefield Publishers, Inc.
A wholly owned subsidiary of The Rowman & Littlefield Publishing Group, Inc.
4501 Forbes Boulevard, Suite 200, Lanham, Maryland 20706
http://www.rowmanlittlefield.com

Estover Road, Plymouth PL6 7PY, United Kingdom

Distributed by National Book Network

British Library Cataloguing in Publication Information Available

Library of Congress Cataloging-in-Publication Data
Hogan, Jackie, 1967–
    Lincoln, Inc. : selling the sixteenth president in contemporary America / Jackie Hogan.
        p. cm.
    Includes bibliographical references and index.
    ISBN 978-1-4422-0954-1 (cloth : alk. paper) — ISBN 978-1-4422-0956-5 (electronic)
    1. Lincoln, Abraham, 1809–1865—Influence. 2. Lincoln, Abraham, 1809–1865—Public opinion. 3. Lincoln, Abraham, 1809–1865—Miscellanea. 4. Public opinion—United States. 5. Market segmentation—United States. I. Title.
    E457.2.H69 2011
    973.7092—dc23   2011024065

∞™ The paper used in this publication meets the minimum requirements of American National Standard for Information Sciences—Permanence of Paper for Printed Library Materials, ANSI/NISO Z39.48-1992.

Printed in the United States of America

To Marilyn Hogan
with love and gratitude.
Thank you for sharing my Lincoln journey.

Contents

Acknowledgments

$\mathcal{W}$hen I began my journey into *Lincoln, Inc.*, I had no idea how many miles I would travel, how many libraries and museums I would haunt, and how many Lincoln enthusiasts I would meet along the way. I would like to thank the many teachers, librarians, museum staff, professional historians, and history buffs who have shared their insights with me over the last three years. In particular, I would like to thank the organizers and participants at the University of Indiana's Lincoln Institute, the Lincoln on the Circuit workshop, and the Horace Mann Institute at the Abraham Lincoln Presidential Library and Museum. I also extend my thanks to Bradley University for supporting my sabbatical research on Lincoln, and to the Bradley library staff for their able assistance in locating rare and hard-to-find texts. Thanks to Sarah Stanton and Jin Yu for their able shepherding of the publication process, and to David Grazian at the University of Pennsylvania, whose perceptive comments helped guide my revisions. Finally, I extend my warmest thanks to my family and friends who have given me their unflagging enthusiasm and support, despite hearing more about Lincoln than they ever wanted to know.

· 1 ·

Lincoln, Inc.:
Selling the Sixteenth President

$\mathcal{A}$s many before me have observed, more books have been written about Abraham Lincoln than about any other American. This, however, is not one of them. This book is not so much about Lincoln as it is about *us*. It is about the ways we as Americans think about, talk about, and represent Lincoln; the ways we use him in our political, ideological, personal, and national struggles; and the ways we simultaneously deify and commercially exploit him. In short, this is a book about the ways Abraham Lincoln is packaged and sold in the marketplace of American ideas.

Let me state at the outset that this is not an exercise in debunking myths about Lincoln, although such myths are abundant and certainly worth scrutinizing. I leave it to my colleagues across the academy to debate the veracity of claims about Lincoln's political philosophy, his religious convictions, his views on race, his sexual orientation, his physical and mental health, and the legacy of his life and works. Nor is this an attempt to knock a most revered American hero off his pedestal. While Lincoln is often called our greatest president, I am less interested in proving or disproving the man's greatness than in understanding why we see Lincoln the way we do.

As a journalist noted shortly after Lincoln's assassination, one of the great tragedies of his untimely death was that it forevermore "made it impossible to speak the truth of Abraham Lincoln."[1] In the years since that fateful night at Ford's Theatre, fact and legend have become so intertwined in the Lincoln story that it now may be impossible for us to know the man as he really was. Instead, we are largely limited to twenty-first-century interpretations of what twentieth-century historians wrote about nineteenth-century recollections of the man. We are reduced to standing in a historical hall of mirrors, trying to discern the original from its countless reflections. Lincoln has

1

become what postmodern theorists call a simulacrum: a copy of a copy of a copy, so far removed from the original that the original is no longer knowable.

It is crucial to remember that the voluminous scholarship on the sixteenth president reveals more than historical facts. I argue that the stories of our nation's "great men" (and the few women who are fortunate enough to be remembered by history) provide us with much more than simply the details of their remarkable lives. They provide us with a vision of the nation itself—a vision of the nation's perceived values, virtues, and aspirations, its fears, its fantasies, its dirty little secrets. Such stories serve as discourses of national identity.[2] So, in a very real sense, constructions of Lincoln—whether in books, museums, school pageants, or even mattress advertisements—are symbolic constructions of the nation. In learning about Lincoln, we learn about ourselves, about who we are and who we wish we could be.

SELLING ABRAHAM LINCOLN

The packaging and selling of Abraham Lincoln is not a recent development. In fact, during Lincoln's lifetime he was actively "branded" and marketed to the voting public, much as political candidates are promoted today. Like many politicians in mid-nineteenth-century America, Lincoln shied away from public self-promotion, but his supporters deftly crafted his political image nonetheless. To admirers, he was Honest Abe, Old Abe, even Father Abraham. In his first presidential bid, he was dubbed the Rail Splitter, a moniker that accentuated his humble pioneer origins and his strong work ethic. In the lead-up to the Illinois state Republican convention of 1860, supporters journeyed to an old Lincoln family homestead to locate some of the fence rails their candidate was said to have split as a young man. They dramatically paraded two of the rails onto the convention floor as a testament to the grit and vigor of their Everyman, and later even cut up and sold fragments of the rails to raise money for Lincoln's campaign.[3] The rail-splitter image proved a popular one, and when the complex political horse-trading at the national Republican convention in Chicago came to an end, Abraham Lincoln had secured his party's nomination for president. To improve the chances of this underdog candidate, one supporter commissioned an artist to paint a portrait of Lincoln that would be "good looking, whether the original would justify it or not."[4] The selling of Abraham Lincoln had begun.

Even before Lincoln took the White House, his opponents were chipping away at his homespun, man-of-the people image. He was a closet abolitionist, they said, a traitor to his nation and his race, a vulgarian, a buffoon. Negative characterizations only intensified when he assumed the presidency and the Civil War began. In the Confederate press, Lincoln was a tyrant, a brute, a bloodthirsty invader.[5] In the North, abolitionists portrayed him as being soft on slavery, while critics of the war lambasted him for sacrificing Union soldiers to liberate Southern slaves. The best that some Northern supporters could manage to say of him was that he was a man of integrity and good intentions despite his woeful mismanagement of national affairs. With such friends, Lincoln hardly needed enemies.

When the tides turned in the Civil War and Union victory appeared inevitable, Lincoln's image took on a new luster, at least in the North. As one contemporary put it, during the closing phases of his reelection campaign, even his fiercest former critics were "all skedaddling for the Lincoln train."[6] His assassination, coming as it did amid the euphoria of Union victory but before the messy business of Reconstruction, helped secure his position as the preeminent American martyr. His murder on Good Friday of 1865 inspired parallels with Jesus Christ and put him on a path to becoming the patron saint of the nation. The selling of the sixteenth president had entered a new phase, a phase in which Lincoln the man would become less important than Lincoln the image, the symbol, the embodiment of cherished national ideals.

As scholars Merrill Peterson and Barry Schwartz have documented, Lincoln's image has changed dramatically over time.[7] Although Lincoln had been a controversial and often unpopular president, in the days immediately following his death, public sentiments were almost uniformly positive, at least outside of the South. In countless eulogies, sermons, and poems, in editorials and political speeches, and, later, in paintings and public monuments, Lincoln was venerated as the Great Emancipator, the savior of the Union, a man of humble origins and lofty ideals. There was little tolerance for dissenting opinion: in cities across the nation, those who spoke ill of the slain president were set upon by angry mobs or imprisoned by outraged judges.[8]

In the cross-country funeral procession that covered some 1,700 miles over twelve days, Lincoln's body was viewed by an estimated one million people, with each city along the route trying to outmourn its predecessors with extravagant displays of black crepe and torchlight marches, of dirges, tolling bells, and fainting mourners. So began the hagiography of Abraham Lincoln. As Lincoln was sanctified in memorial works of art, idiosyncrasy and controversy were stripped from the man, leaving only the most idealized qualities behind. Typical of the genre, John Sartain's 1865 engraving, *Abraham Lincoln the Martyr Victorious*, shows Lincoln being welcomed into heaven by George Washington and a host of winged angels. In 1865, writers such as Walt Whitman and Julia Ward Howe depicted Lincoln as a beloved and steadfast leader.[9] In public statuary such as the *Freedmen's Monument* in Washington, D.C., (1876) and Augustus Saint-Gaudens's *Abraham Lincoln: The*

Man in Lincoln Park, Chicago (1887), Lincoln is positioned as a defender of liberty and a dignified statesman. Many early biographies likewise seemed less concerned with historical accuracy and complexity than with crystallizing the image of a hero worthy of the nation's veneration. Perhaps most notably, Josiah G. Holland's best-selling *Life of Abraham Lincoln* (1866) portrayed Lincoln as an exemplar of Christian virtue—honest, humble, self-sacrificing, compassionate, brave, and industrious.

The nation would wait two decades for more multidimensional representations of Lincoln. Lincoln's former law partner, William Herndon, and his former presidential secretaries, John Nicolay and John Hay, published detailed biographies of Lincoln in 1889 and 1890, respectively, and journalist Ida Tarbell's biography of Lincoln was serialized by *McClure's* magazine in 1895. Unlike previous biographical elegies, these works were grounded in written documents and firsthand accounts of those who had known Abraham Lincoln. The man who emerged from such works was the "folklore Lincoln,"[10] the Lincoln who lives most vividly in the popular imagination today—a frontier farm boy, a teller of tales, a precocious autodidact, a natural-born leader, a tenderhearted friend, a man of courage, honesty, and integrity, a devoted father and long-suffering husband who had been traumatized by the deaths of his mother, his sister, and his first love, Ann Rutledge.

Many of the "facts" presented in these accounts have since been challenged, and certain details (particularly his alleged romance with Ann Rutledge, his reputed rejection of traditional Christianity, and his possibly illegitimate birth) scandalized the American public when they were first published. After subsisting for two decades on an "epic Lincoln,"[11] most readers had little appetite for details that challenged their idealized image of the martyr president. Ultimately, public discourse came to embrace both sides of the Lincoln narrative: both the "folklore Lincoln," the plainspoken man from the prairies, and the "epic Lincoln," the heroic statesman, commander, and martyr. The tension between these two very different Lincolns did not undermine his status as national hero. Quite the contrary, the complex image of Lincoln seems to have offered a little something for everyone. In the years since his death, Lincoln's name and image have been usefully appropriated by myriad, often competing interests: Democrats and Republicans, socialists and corporate executives, deists and evangelists, peace activists and war hawks, the civil rights movement and the Ku Klux Klan.

Because of the complexity and malleability of Lincoln's image, each faction has been able to fashion him into the champion of their cause. In a sense, each faction has remade Lincoln in their own image. This tendency has been particularly apparent in recent years in the political rhetoric of both the Republican and Democratic parties. In defense of President George W. Bush's post-9/11 curtailment of civil liberties, for example, his Republican supporters invoked an authoritarian Lincoln who, in the midst of the Civil War, suspended the writ of habeas corpus, placed limits on free speech, and established military tribunals for perceived enemies of the state. The Democrats, by contrast, presented quite a different Lincoln to the American people during the 2008 presidential election. Barack Obama's Lincoln was a man of reason, moderation, and compassion, a man committed to racial and social justice, a proponent of equal opportunity for all. In the century and a half since his death, Abraham Lincoln has become a recognizable brand, whose name and image imbue diverse causes with qualities like integrity, wisdom, and unimpeachable Americanness.

Lincoln's appeal has not been lost on commercial entities. As early as the first decade of the twentieth century, businesses were using Lincoln's name and image for financial gain. Among the most prominent and long-lived were the Lincoln National Life Insurance Company founded in 1905 and the Lincoln Motor Company established in 1917. But countless Lincoln-themed businesses can be found across the nation today, from the Abe Lincoln Gun Club in Springfield, Illinois, to Honest Abe's Pest Control in Eatontown, New Jersey, and Ruthie's Lincoln Freeze drive-in in Hodgenville, Kentucky. In communities with deeper historical connections to the sixteenth president, his name and image are ubiquitous, with banks, restaurants, mobile-home parks, and strip malls, among many others, riding Mr. Lincoln's coattails.

Of course, the most obvious example of the commodification of the sixteenth president is the thriving market in Lincoln collectibles, or Lincolniana, ranging from plastic kitsch to professionally authenticated Lincoln relics. A casual browse through a Lincoln souvenir shop reveals that virtually no object is too mundane or too profane to be adorned with Lincoln's image. There are the usual caps, T-shirts, and key chains, but also playing cards, bobble heads, and shot glasses (despite Lincoln's reputation as a teetotaler). However, the real money is to be made (and spent) in the realm of genuine historical artifacts: Lincoln's handwritten documents, his personal items, and even parts of the man himself, usually his hair or blood. The lucrative trade in Lincolniana dates back at least to the turn of the twentieth century. By the 1909 centennial of Lincoln's birth, his signature could command $1,000, roughly twice the average American's salary at that time.[12] The going rate for a lock of his hair was $330.[13] In 2008, a letter in Lincoln's hand sold for a staggering $3.4 million, surpassing the record for any American manuscript ever sold at auction.[14] At the low end of the market, souvenir manufacturers and retailers profit from the trade in Lincolniana; at the high end, dealers, auction houses, publishers of collector's guides, and even talented forgers cash in on the Lincoln image.[15]

Currently, however, perhaps no single economic sector has so firm a hold on Lincoln's name and image as the tourism industry. Lincoln was born in Kentucky, moved to Indiana as a child, and spent most of his adult life in Illinois. In these three states, the Lincoln industry is at its apex. Lincoln historical sites abound. These include, most prominently, what some Lincoln devotees call the "big three": the Lincoln birthplace in Hodgenville, Kentucky; the Lincoln boyhood home near Lincoln City, Indiana; and the Lincoln home in Springfield, Illinois. In 2005, a fourth site was added to this must-see list: the Abraham Lincoln Presidential Library and Museum (ALPLM) in Springfield, Illinois. Far more plentiful are sites where Abraham Lincoln visited briefly, or where one of his family members, one of his friends, or perhaps a friend of a friend once lived or worked. County courthouses where Lincoln argued a case, a hotel or historic house where Lincoln spent the night, and the birthplaces of Lincoln's friends, family, and even biographers are all among what might be called the secondary Lincoln sites.

Then there are the tertiary sites, or what might be more accurately described as the hypothetical Lincoln sites. There is the cottage in Bement, Illinois, where Lincoln *may* have met with Stephen A. Douglas to set the terms of their celebrated 1858 debates; the park in Harrodsburg, Kentucky, where Lincoln's parents *may* have wed; and the cemetery inside the Lincoln boyhood site in Indiana where Lincoln's mother, Nancy Hanks Lincoln, *may* be buried. Typically such sites are marketed as genuine and indisputable Lincoln historic sites, with such straightforward names as "the Nancy Hanks Lincoln Gravesite." Only visitors who take the time to read the small print on historical markers or to ask the right questions will learn that the ground they are treading may not actually be what the marketing implies. Yes, Lincoln's mother was probably buried in the vicinity of today's fenced-off cemetery (the fence lending the site an air of sacred authenticity), but no one really knows where, and the weathered headstone was actually a twentieth-century addition.[16]

But Lincoln historic sites, from the big three to the hypothetical, are only part of the story here. Lincoln events, ranging from lectures and conferences to festivals, theatrical productions, art shows, and historical reenactments, generate substantial revenue and publicity for communities that, in many cases, are in decline. Lincoln offers the double promise of bringing much-needed cash to struggling local economies while at the same time promoting community pride and a sense of national belonging among people who have been sidelined by globalization and the associated decline of traditional employment sectors such as agriculture and manufacturing.

The other leading branch of the Lincoln industry, one that is more national, and indeed international, in scope, is Lincoln scholarship. Encompassing an estimated 15,000 books, along with documentary films, museum exhibits, and countless pamphlets and articles, the field of Lincoln scholarship is incalculably vast.[17] So much so, in fact, that some Lincoln enthusiasts have to look for guidance from volumes such as Michael Burkhimer's (2003) *100 Essential Lincoln Books*. The field includes both professional scholars and amateur historians whose reputations, careers, book royalties, and speaker's fees are tied to the Lincoln brand. Even in the years immediately following his death, prominent speakers could earn $2,500 per engagement for their reflections on the martyr president.[18] Today, top-tier Lincoln scholars can command $50,000 for a single lecture.

I do not wish to imply that all Lincoln scholars or museum curators or Lincolniana dealers or towns that draw on Lincoln's fame are somehow simply exploiting Lincoln in cynical, self-serving ways. There is no reason why commercial or career interests cannot merge with genuine admiration for Abraham Lincoln, with pride in one's Lincoln connections, with a desire to share knowledge of his life and achievements with others. Nowhere is this clearer than among the nation's schoolteachers.

By the turn of the twentieth century, Lincoln had become a mainstay of school curricula.[19] Didactic biographies, such as William M. Thayer's *The Pioneer Boy, and How He Became President* (1863) and Horatio Alger's *Abraham Lincoln, the Backwoods Boy* (1883), were employed to instill morality, strength of character, and a strong work ethic in American children. While the books may have changed, teachers today still find in Lincoln an American exemplar, a model of honor, determination, and civic virtue, a man who overcame adversity, unpopularity, and personal tragedy to lead the nation through the fiery crucible of civil war. Teachers' dedication to the study and teaching of Lincoln and their willingness to share their curricular innovations with colleagues could hardly be called self-serving. While inventive Lincoln lessons may win teachers professional kudos, educators' rewards for teaching Lincoln are less tangible than the rewards of professional Lincoln scholars, documentarians, or tourism operators. The teacher's Lincoln is the Lincoln of higher purposes, a vehicle for the transmission of knowledge, the building of character, and the protection of essential American values.

Whether Lincoln is "sold" for financial gain, for political and ideological purposes, or more generally to protect and sustain neighborhood and nation, every American iteration of Lincoln reflects widely circulating notions of Americanness. Carefully examining today's Lincoln, we gain insight into national self-conceptions, into our communal norms, values, and preoccupations. Two centuries after his birth, Lincoln has become a Rorschach test onto which Americans project their highest hopes and loftiest ideals.

Each chapter of this book explores one aspect of "Lincoln, Inc.," the use of the sixteenth president for political, ideological, or financial gain in contemporary America. In chapter 2, "Mr. Lincoln's Coattails," I examine the use of Lincoln for economic gain. First I discuss the branding of Lincoln by businesses and manufacturers who trade on his image. Then I look specifically at the thriving world of Lincoln tourism and the "little lies" that help sustain it.

In chapter 3, "Packaging the President," I analyze representations of Lincoln in best-selling biographies from 1866 to 2006. I highlight the ways that the selective use of quotations and anecdotes and the selective omission of unpalatable details create an almost flawless "mythic Lincoln." I then consider the ways that Lincoln detractors construct him as the antithesis of American values and virtues, as a kind of biographer's Bizarro Lincoln.

In chapter 4, "Telling Fictions: Lincoln in Literature, Television, and Film," I examine representations of Lincoln in historical fiction, tales of suspense, romance novels, and works of science fiction/fantasy. Whether fictional accounts portray Lincoln as an earnest backwoodsman, a frontier heartthrob, or an axe-wielding vampire slayer, such tales can be read as texts of desire and reflections of changing social contexts. They are "telling" fictions because they mirror (or *tell* us) the fears and fascinations of the time period in which they are produced. Fiction molds Lincoln into an infinitely flexible hero for all ages.

In chapter 5, "What Would Lincoln Do?" I analyze the use of Lincoln for political and ideological gain. I begin with the use of Lincoln in twenty-first-century party politics, giving close attention to the 2008 presidential race. I then examine what Richard Carwardine has called the "unseemly tussle over [Lincoln's] soul"[20]—that is, competing claims about Lincoln's religious beliefs—and what such contestations reveal about the role of religion in the public sphere today. Finally, I consider the use of Lincoln in the ever-contentious debates about homosexuality, abortion, and race relations.

In chapter 6, "*A* Is for Abe: Teaching Lincoln," I examine the place of Lincoln in American education today. I interview teachers from across the nation about the promises and pitfalls of teaching Lincoln. I then analyze both classroom materials and children's books for representations of Abraham Lincoln, paying careful attention to what today's lessons in Lincoln leave out of the discussion. I argue that the topics educators and authors avoid reveal a great deal about national priorities and national taboos.

In chapter 7, "Lincoln under Glass," I examine representations of Lincoln in museums and traveling exhibits throughout the Lincoln heartland and Washington, D.C. I identify the overarching themes in such displays, discuss the delicate balance between Lincoln education and Lincoln veneration, and consider the reception of the conventional Lincoln narrative by museumgoers. The chapter gives special attention to the ways that museum representations of Lincoln are grounded in the economic realities of the competitive edutainment marketplace.

Finally, in chapter 8, "Selling Lincoln: Who Do We Think We Are?" I examine the ways that representations of Lincoln, and of certain "anti-

Lincolns," reflect popular notions about the American character. I began this book by asserting that stories of our national heroes are actually stories about who we think we are. By examining the ways Lincoln is "sold" today, we gain a keener understanding of American national identity. In our constructions of Lincoln, we can see the nation at its best—an idealized America. But if we look carefully, we can also see the strains of inequality and exclusion just beneath the glossy surface.

After Abraham Lincoln drew his last breath, Edwin Stanton, Lincoln's secretary of war, is reputed to have said, "Now he belongs to the ages."[21] Time has proven him right. Lincoln belongs to our age as much as he belonged to the Civil War era, as much as he belonged to the Progressive era, the New Deal era or the Cold War era. Each age finds in Lincoln what it needs: inspiration, hope, and an idealized reflection of itself.

AN OUTSIDER'S PERSPECTIVE ON LINCOLN

In this book, I develop what I call an outsider's perspective on Lincoln. Of course, I do not wish to imply that the social sciences are somehow marginal disciplines. In fact, historians and social scientists are increasingly engaged in fruitful exchanges of theory and method that enrich our understanding of human experience. Rather, I employ the term *outsider's perspective* because I am not a member of the scholarly Lincoln fraternity (and I use the term *fraternity* quite intentionally because, with a few notable exceptions, the Lincoln field is still largely dominated by male academicians). I am not a historian. I am not interested in weighing in on debates about what Lincoln really thought or did or said. And I have no intention of becoming a career Lincoln specialist. Rather, I am a social scientist examining Lincoln as a powerful and enduring national icon. As such, I bring a social scientist's tool kit to my analysis.

I am certainly not the first sociologist to analyze Lincoln's enduring role in American society. Barry Schwartz, for example, offers a compelling discussion of the topic, drawing on the work of nineteenth-century sociologist Emile Durkheim.[22] However, my approach to Lincoln representations is strongly grounded in critical theory and the scholarship on gender, race, and nationalism. In addition, I utilize many of the techniques and perspectives of cultural studies, along with those drawn from the fields of semiotics and critical discourse analysis, although I do not adopt any of these approaches in a wholesale manner.

I draw insights from the literature on social constructivism, which suggests that our understandings of the world are profoundly shaped by cultural factors. While I do not adopt the most extreme position on social construction, the notion that nothing is real or that reality has been obliterated,[23] I do contend that as social creatures we humans interpret our experiences through collectively constructed lenses, through our systems of cultural representation, principally language and image. The way we interpret (and "construct") reality therefore reflects shared perceptions. Not surprisingly, then, Lincoln is perceived and constructed differently by different groups—Northerners and Southerners, liberals and conservatives, agnostics and believers—and his image is constantly changing along with the nation's changing values, ideals, and material circumstances.[24] But Lincoln's image not only mirrors our society, it helps shape our society. To paraphrase Barry Schwartz, Lincoln serves both as a model *of* society and as a model *for* society.[25] Lincoln is held up as a national exemplar—model worker, model family man, model statesman, and model citizen—and we are encouraged to follow in his footsteps. In this way, representations of Lincoln, and of all our great national heroes, guide our actions and shape our lives in significant ways.

I am by no means suggesting that representations of Lincoln determine whether some people are rich or poor, powerful or marginalized. The argument here is rather that the stories all nations tell themselves about their cherished heroes encourage people to view the world, and act in the world, in ways that confer advantages and disadvantages on certain groups. Neither am I subscribing to a false consciousness model in which calculating elites manipulate Lincoln's image for their own purposes, namely to placate and control the masses. This is too simplistic. Certainly there are many readily verifiable cases of those in power using Lincoln's image to legitimize their authority, and we will discuss some of them here. But Lincoln has also been appropriated and repackaged by more marginal groups for the purposes of resistance and critique. So rather than a top-down model of Lincoln propaganda being imposed on the gullible masses, I suggest that Lincoln's image has been and continues to be constructed through complex negotiations of meaning among a range of individuals and institutions.

My approach to Lincoln will no doubt rankle traditional scholars and devotees of the sixteenth president. I intend no disrespect to those for whom the study of Lincoln is a passion, a profession, or both, as I intend no disrespect to Lincoln himself. Rather, I aim here to use an outsider's perspective on Lincoln to notice things that might otherwise be overlooked, and to say the things that Lincoln insiders might be reluctant to say. To this end, I conclude each chapter with this outsider's perspective. In my analysis of Lincoln representations, I draw on social scientific theories and concepts but avoid the kind of professional jargon that obscures meaning for all but the initiated. My intent is not to water down the social scientific perspective but to use it as it should be used, to help shed light on the human experience, specifically to help shed light on the uses, and perhaps abuses, of Abraham Lincoln.

• 2 •

Mr. Lincoln's Coattails: Marketing, Memorabilia, and Presidential Tourism

*I*n a March 1860 address at New Haven, Connecticut, Abraham Lincoln declared, "I don't believe in a law to prevent a man from getting rich; it would do more harm than good."[1] Little could he have known, however, that one day an entire industry would grow up around his name and image.

The trade in Lincoln products and services is so vast and so diverse it would be impossible to calculate its net revenues. Just a browse around the gift shop of any Lincoln historic site provides a snapshot of the low end of the Lincoln souvenir market: Lincoln pencil sharpener, $2.95; Lincoln magnet, $8.95; Lincoln bobble-head doll, $12.95; Lincoln cross-stitch kit, $24.00; Gettysburg Address necktie, $29.99; and a seemingly infinite array of books, bookmarks, posters, postcards, stickers, paperweights, caps, T-shirts, mugs, and tote bags (see figure 2.1). For the well-heeled visitor, there are "limited edition" and special-order items to be had: a bronze bust of Lincoln for $1,500, a set of Lincoln presidential china for $1,730, or perhaps a full-size Lincoln Replica Bed for $4,999.[2]

To collectors of authentic Lincoln artifacts, however, such souvenirs pale in comparison to genuine historical "relics," principally documents, photographs, and personal items associated with Lincoln. *The Rail Splitter*, a journal and auction service for collectors of Lincolniana, lists items ranging from shards of Lincoln's White House china to fragments of marble from his tomb, ribbons from his funeral procession, and images and papers that can be linked with the sixteenth president in some way. Among the more modestly priced articles recently listed is a print autographed by Isaac Diller, the "son of Lincoln's druggist," valued at $250 to $300. In the top tier are papers written and signed in Lincoln's hand, which list for thousands and even tens of thousands of dollars.[3] Sotheby's 2008 sale of a Lincoln letter for $3.4 million,

Figure 2.1. Typical Lincoln memorabilia: Lincoln bobble-head doll. *Photo by Matthew Behnke*

and Christie's 2009 sale of his handwritten reelection acceptance speech for $3.44 million, are indicators of the bull market in Lincolniana as the nation celebrated the 2009 bicentennial of Lincoln's birth.[4]

BRANDING LINCOLN

In addition to purveyors of Lincoln collectibles, a substantial number of businesses trade on Lincoln's name and image. Today large firms, including the Lincoln Financial Group, Lincoln Motors, and Lincoln Educational Services Corporation, capitalize on positive perceptions of the martyr president (which is ironic, since Lincoln's own business ventures failed so miserably, leaving him with crippling debts). Likewise, a host of small businesses attempt to ride Mr. Lincoln's coattails to success, particularly in locations with historical connections to the Civil War president. In the surrounds of Springfield, Illinois, Lincoln's home for most of his adult life, a cab company, a car wash, a caterer, a chiropractic clinic, a clock shop, a gas station, a heating and air-conditioning contractor, several hotels and restaurants, a landscaper, a Tae Kwon Do studio, and a veterinary clinic, among other enterprises, have adopted Lincoln's name and often his likeness. In and around this city with a population of roughly 116,000, at least ninety-eight businesses (and a public toilet block) are named for its most famous resident.

Businesses large and small also employ Lincoln in advertising. In 2002, the Lincoln Financial Group launched a multimillion-dollar ad campaign featuring an Abraham Lincoln impersonator. In television and print ads, the faux Lincoln is shown guiding and protecting the company's patrons. In one television spot, Lincoln works as a gondolier for a retired couple on holiday in Venice, with the slogan, "Retirement. It's a lot more enjoyable when Lincoln's looking out for you."[5] While some have criticized this ad campaign for trivializing the president's life and legacy, the use of Lincoln here makes sense given the nature and the history of the company. In 1905, Lincoln's sole surviving son Robert Todd Lincoln granted the corporation permission to use his father's name and image,[6] and today the organization proudly proclaims that they "built a company in honor of his name, and spent the last 105 years living up to it."[7] For a financial services company, Lincoln's name, with its associations of dignity, integrity, and discernment, is a bankable commodity, or as one advertising executive put it, a "unique and ownable" asset.[8]

Even businesses with no connections to Lincoln capitalize on his image. Each year on Presidents Day, Honest Abe can be found hawking everything from furniture and carpets to hot tubs and SUVs, with slogans like, "Honestly, you can't beat these prices!" Recently, Lincoln has featured in national promotional campaigns for car insurance, diet soft drinks, sleeping pills, and a cable television show, among others. In a Diet Mountain Dew ad, Lincoln is a testosterone-pumped pro wrestler; in a Geico insurance ad, he finds himself unable to lie to his wife when she asks, "Does this dress make my backside look big?" And in a $100 million ad campaign by the makers of the sleep aid Rozerem, he plays chess with a talking beaver.[9] Even the popular political comedy program *The Colbert Report*, with a wink at the widespread use of Lincoln as a poster boy for American patriotism, has promoted itself with the tagline, "It's what Lincoln would have watched."

Clearly, Abraham Lincoln is widely commodified today, whether through the trade in Lincolniana or the use of his name and image for promotional purposes. However, nowhere is the commercialization of Lincoln more intense and more visible than in the realm of Lincoln tourism.

ON THE ROAD WITH LINCOLN

Let us begin our tour in the Lincoln heartland: Kentucky, his birthplace; Indiana, his boyhood home; and Illinois, his home for most of his adult life. The 2,200-mile "Lincoln Heritage Trail" runs through these three states, stopping at more than fifty Lincoln sites along the way. These include, most famously, the "big three" Lincoln sites: the Abraham Lincoln Birthplace National Historic Site, the Lincoln Boyhood National Memorial, and the Lincoln Home National Historic Site, all run by the National Park Service (NPS). Other sites of primary significance include the Knob Creek Farm in Hodgenville, Kentucky, where Lincoln spent his early years; Lincoln's New Salem, a reconstruction of the village Lincoln called home as a young man; and Lincoln's law offices and his tomb in Springfield, Illinois. The newest and highest-profile Lincoln site in the heartland is the Abraham Lincoln Presidential Library and Museum (ALPLM) in Springfield, which opened in 2005, arguably making Springfield the unrivaled epicenter of Lincoln veneration.

Far more plentiful, however, are what might be termed secondary Lincoln sites, locations where Lincoln once visited or conducted business, or sites associated with Lincoln's family, friends, and acquaintances. Among many such sites are the Kentucky estate of Henry Clay, Lincoln's political role model; the Lincoln Pioneer Village in Rockport, Indiana, a collection of newly constructed buildings in the style of Lincoln's era; and the Ratcliff Inn in Carmi, Illinois, where Lincoln once stayed in 1840.

The Lincoln Heritage Trail also encompasses a number of tertiary sites, including sites with only tangential connections to Lincoln or no discernable connection at all. Mammoth Cave in Kentucky; a historic Mormon settlement in Illinois; and Santa Claus Land (now Holiday World and Splashin' Safari) in Santa Claus, Indiana, are among these. Off the Heritage Trail itself, a multitude of tourist sites trade on Lincoln's fame, from the "Lincoln Jamboree" stage show in Hodgenville, Kentucky, to the many Lincoln-shaped corn mazes that are carved out of fields across the Midwest every fall. Here, for a few dollars, visitors are invited to literally "get inside Lincoln's head."

As varied as such sites are, they are united by the material realities of tourism: Lincoln's name and image pull in visitors who, ideally, open their pocketbooks for admissions tickets, souvenirs, and hospitality services. And the payoff from Lincoln tourism is potentially quite substantial. The Abraham Lincoln Presidential Library and Museum attracted more than one million visitors in its first two years of operation, with its on-site gift shop generating a million dollars in sales after only three months.[10] Lincoln's tomb, the Lincoln home, and Lincoln's New Salem each attract in excess of 200,000 visitors annually, and even lesser-known sites, such as the Bloomington, Illinois, mansion of David Davis, Lincoln's longtime friend and associate, can host around 50,000 visitors each year.[11]

It is little wonder, then, that tourism promotional offices throughout the Lincoln heartland feature Lincoln prominently in their advertising campaigns. Even communities without a strong historical connection to Lincoln forge profitable links with his image. In 2008, for instance, the Heritage Corridor Convention and Visitor's Bureau in northern Illinois distributed *Abe's Travel Scrapbook*, a glossy seventy-seven-page brochure featuring a Lincoln impersonator enjoying the many amenities of the region, a region with few actual links to the sixteenth president. We see snapshots of the imitation Abe browsing in a bookshop, checking into a hotel, riding a mountain bike, and even playing miniature golf. "We do not know for a fact that Lincoln would have enjoyed water parks, auto racing, upscale shopping or a round of golf," the pamphlet explains. "But we know that Lincoln loved his home state . . . [and] that he would want others to see some of the places his constituents called home."[12]

In the absence of any actual historical connections to Lincoln, businesses in the Lincoln heartland can still cash in on the martyr president's fame just by employing his image. Although it is unlikely that Lincoln counted burritos among his favorite foods, the logo of Springfield's El Presidente Burritos and Baja Grill features a likeness of Lincoln in a sombrero. In an even more extreme illustration of the commodification of Lincoln's image, one hotel billboard on the interstate highway near Bowling Green, Kentucky, consists of a portrait of Lincoln in front of a U.S. flag and the slogan, "Lincoln never slept here, but you can!"

Potential profits are sizeable outside the Lincoln heartland as well. During the recent Lincoln bicentennial, businesses in the Washington, D.C. area offered a wide range of Lincoln-themed packages. The trendy Mie N Yu restaurant in Georgetown was promoting Lincoln-themed cocktails such as the "Abe-hat-tan." The storied Willard Intercontinental Hotel was selling tickets to a restaging of Lincoln's second inaugural ball for $165. And the Madison Hotel offered a "Lincoln Bedroom" package including bed and breakfast for two, a reproduction of the Gettysburg Address, a copy of Doris Kearns Goodwin's *Team of Rivals*, and a set of commemorative towels embroidered with "I slept in the Lincoln Bedroom," for $809 per night.

Lincoln's Golden Years: 2008–2010

Of course, Lincoln tourism and the commodification of Lincoln are nothing new. As the nation celebrated the centennial of Lincoln's birth in 1909, the

Evansville (IN) Courier ran a political cartoon showing customers browsing at a newsstand where every last publication carried Lincoln's name and likeness. In this atmosphere of Lincoln-mania, it is perhaps not surprising that Lincoln's autograph could fetch roughly twice the annual salary of the average American at the time.

Similarly, with the confluence of three historic events, the first decade of the twenty-first century saw an intensification of interest in all things Lincoln. First, in anticipation of the February 2009 bicentenary of Lincoln's birth, the Abraham Lincoln Bicentennial Commission designated February 2008 through February 2010 as the official Lincoln Bicentennial period. With its mandate to help facilitate and publicize bicentennial events around the nation, the commission helped keep Lincoln in the news by publicizing new commemorative stamps and coins, rededicating the Lincoln Monument, and promoting conferences, publications, exhibitions, and a diverse range of Lincoln productions both across the nation and abroad.

Coinciding with such bicentennial publicity, another historic event turned the eyes of the nation toward the Lincoln heartland—the 2008 presidential race. In February 2007, Barack Obama announced his presidential bid on the grounds of the Old State Capitol in Springfield, Illinois, the site of Lincoln's pivotal "house divided" speech of 1858. Referring to Lincoln as "a tall, gangly, self-made . . . lawyer" from Illinois, and peppering his speech with some of Lincoln's most well-known phrases, Obama seemed to invite comparisons between himself and Lincoln. Throughout the protracted campaign and well after Obama's 2008 victory, such comparisons were frequently made, an issue we will explore further in chapter 5.

Finally, 2008 marked the sesquicentennial of the famed Lincoln-Douglas debates. Between August and October of 1858, Lincoln faced Stephen A. Douglas in a series of seven debates held throughout the state of Illinois, as the two men vied for a seat in the U.S. Senate. Although Lincoln ultimately lost the election, the debates brought him to the attention of a national audience and thus served as a springboard to his successful bid for the presidency in 1860. In 2008, communities across Illinois commemorated the historic debates with lectures, performances, exhibits, and festivals. A Lincoln and Douglas "Reunion Tour" was heavily promoted by the Illinois Bureau of Tourism. Its website included three-day Lincoln-Douglas getaway itineraries, complete with hotel reservation forms and links to attractions and events billed as "presidential fun," although tourists likely had to strain to discern connections between the revered president and the Mattoon Bagelfest or the "R" Pizza Farm (the "only farm in the St. Louis area where pizza is grown!").[13] An examination of the ways that one Illinois community marked the debate sesquicentennial illustrates the far-reaching effects of Lincoln promotion.

Lincoln and Douglas met in Freeport, Illinois, in August 1858 for their second senatorial debate. The debate is most remembered for the exchange in which Lincoln forced Douglas to acknowledge that "the people of a Territory can, by lawful means, exclude slavery from their limits prior to the formation of a State constitution," regardless of the Supreme Court's *Dred Scott* decision, which declared that territorial authorities did not have this power.[14] This position came to be known as the Freeport Doctrine. Although Douglas won the Illinois Senate race, his comments in Freeport turned proslavery Southern Democrats against him, making it virtually impossible for him to win the 1860 presidential race.

Freeport, Illinois celebrated the 150th anniversary of the debates with a full slate of activities over six days. Events included, among others, three public exhibits, two parades, two films, a food and music festival, a full-length play, a costume ball, a Debate Square dedication ceremony, and a Lincoln and Douglas "reunion" performance. Most of the activities were scheduled over the Labor Day weekend, which allowed local hotels to offer "Debate Weekend" packages complete with lodging, special access passes to events, and commemorative souvenirs. Although most events were free and open to the public, the economic impact of the celebration was not insubstantial.

The Freeport Visitor's Bureau reported that visitors to the area more than doubled during the celebrations, and, conservatively estimated, the events generated more than $500,000 in additional revenue for the Freeport area.[15] Area hotels were booked to near capacity, tickets to the Grand Ball and the community theater production of *Mrs. Lincoln* were in short supply, and patrons at local restaurants waited in lines that at times stretched out of doors and spilled onto crowded sidewalks. Some local merchants sold out of Lincoln-Douglas souvenirs, and vendors on Debate Square were doing a brisk trade in stovepipe hats, Lincoln figurines, and commemorative medallions. As the late-summer thermometer rose, enterprising teens hawked bottled water out of overloaded coolers, while local service groups raised money selling bratwurst and sodas. On every corner, it seemed, eager consumers were opening their wallets to celebrate the city's place in the Lincoln legend.

Besides this most visible economic activity, the debate celebrations presented a favorable marketing opportunity for local businesses and organizations. While ads in the local paper used Lincoln's image to sell everything from potato chips to used cars, the lengthy Sesquicentennial Parade provided ample occasion for promoting local interests. Typical of small-town parades in the nation's midsection, area marching bands, Boy Scouts, military veterans, firefighters, and Shriners in minicars were all well represented. Likewise, businesses ranging from banks and realtors to a scrap metal company seized the chance for some free advertising, as did politicians and advocacy groups.

Lincoln symbolism was freely employed. The Humane Society delegation included a golden retriever in a stovepipe hat; the Cancer Association carried a sign with the Lincoln-inspired slogan, "Let us abolish cancer"; and the local hotel association float featured a tall black hat atop an antique bed.

Other signs of Lincoln's economic impact were evident both along the parade route and throughout the city of Freeport. In anticipation of the sesquicentennial events, the city undertook an ambitious urban beautification program. By 2008, a serious and prolonged economic downturn had taken its toll on the city, leaving many older buildings abandoned or in a state of disrepair. A 1992 sculpture of *Lincoln and Douglas in Debate* by artist Lily Tolpo stood in a rather barren downtown lot near the railroad tracks. With funding from city and state agencies and individual and corporate donors, Freeport set about tidying, repainting, and landscaping the area.[16] Light poles in the neighborhood were adorned with red, white, and blue banners bearing donors' names, and patriotic bunting hung from seemingly every building, including some that were clearly long abandoned. Most notably, the block around Tolpo's Lincoln-Douglas sculpture was transformed into a leafy park with extensive signage explaining the historical significance of the location. One plaque offered positive publicity for the commercial and individual sponsors of the Debate Square Improvement Project, from the biggest donors, dubbed the "President's Cabinet," to the more modest contributors, the "Rail Splitters."

All this economic activity centered on Lincoln is by no means merely a calculating attempt to turn a profit. On the contrary, communities like Freeport have more than money invested in the image of Lincoln. In communities that have been left behind by the dynamics of globalization—communities where jobs have evaporated, businesses have closed, and tax revenues have dropped—local pride suffers. As unemployment rises and young people leave in ever larger numbers to seek opportunities elsewhere, those who remain seek to shore up both their material resources and their collective identity. Emphasizing the community's connection with the great moments and great figures of national history is one way of doing so.

During Freeport's debate sesquicentennial celebrations, community pride was palpable. Signage in Debate Square reminded visitors that the debate gave Freeport "a place in our nation's history," for it was the Freeport debate that put Lincoln on the road to the presidency. As the chair of the sesquicentennial committee declared during the dedication of Debate Square, "Without Freeport, there would be no Lincoln." Local news coverage echoed and expanded on this theme. The Freeport debate "turned out to be a crucial factor in the fate of this nation," one reporter asserted. From Freeport, there "evolved a national voice that eventually took form in an Emancipation

Proclamation, a document that holds historical significance right up there with the Declaration of Independence and the Constitution of the United States."[17] In other words, although one-fifth of Freeport's children live in poverty today, although families there earn 25 percent less than the average family in Illinois, and although both the unemployment rate and the crime rate in Freeport are high compared with state and national figures, the community has good reason to be proud.[18]

Throughout the debate celebrations, Freeport's role in the abolition of slavery and the promotion of racial equality was a favorite theme of speakers and audience members alike. On the eve of the debate reunion, an Abraham Lincoln reenactor was given a thunderous round of applause when he declared that Freeport had always held firm in its antislavery sentiment. He proceeded to commend the community for continuing to work toward racial equality today. Keynote speaker and renowned Lincoln scholar Harold Holzer was likewise enthusiastically received when he asserted that Freeport had played a pivotal role in the battle to rid the nation of the evil of slavery. Even a placard in Debate Square reminded visitors that although Douglas attempted to incite racism in Freeport, he was unable to do so.

It is worth noting that only weeks after the dedication of Debate Square a large-scale installation celebrating Freeport's African-American history was erected on a nearby site. While African Americans account for approximately 14 percent of the community's residents, Abbie Reese, the artist who spearheaded the *Untold Stories* exhibit, observed that little work has been done to preserve or celebrate Freeport's African-American heritage.[19] Few African Americans or other ethnoracial minorities were visible among the spectators and key players at Freeport's sesquicentennial events.[20] Organizers did include a reenactor portraying Frederick Douglass, the famed black abolitionist, but some spectators seemed uncertain of just who he was. One observer in the crowd referred to him as "Frederick Stephens, or Stephens-something. You know, the black guy." Although the Frederick Douglass reenactor played only a marginal role in the weekend celebrations, he was warmly received by the crowds. Community pride was clearly bound up not only with Freeport's Lincoln connections, but with notions of Freeport's role in promoting racial equality.

The Lincoln-Douglas Reunion Tour demonstrates how community and regional pride intersects with the full flowering of Lincoln's commodification. Countless other smaller-scale projects reveal the same dynamic. Free lectures and performances at public libraries and schools, reenactments at local historical societies, and other similar events may not generate much revenue for the organizers, but they are enmeshed in a web of economic activity nonetheless. Typically, speakers, performers, and Lincoln reenactors are paid for their appearances, and they may also take the opportunity to promote their books, CDs, DVDs, or other products at the venue. In addition, because Lincoln is so revered in American public life, Lincoln events typically garner positive publicity for sponsoring organizations, publicity that could conceivably boost donations, membership fees, or sales for the sponsor. Finally, beyond mere dollars and cents, Lincoln events and Lincoln sites enjoy glory by association. Because of Lincoln's place in the national pantheon, a Lincoln connection promises respect, honor, and acclaim.

The Little Lies of Lincoln Tourism

With Lincoln connections promising both glory and monetary gain, it is little wonder that tourist sites sometimes stake competing claims on the martyr president. For instance, both the Lincoln boyhood site in Indiana and Lincoln's New Salem in Illinois claim to be the place where Lincoln spent his "formative years." Numerous sites in Kentucky, Illinois, and Indiana claim to be the place where Lincoln developed his strength of character and commitment to equality. The Lincoln home site claims Springfield as "the city that Lincoln truly called home," while the Kentucky Department of Tourism gives prominent place to Lincoln's own proclamation that he was, in fact, a Kentuckian. Lincoln's New Salem in rural Illinois reinforces its claims on Lincoln with hints of the supernatural. An introductory video at the site tells visitors that the village sprang up out of the wilderness shortly before Lincoln arrived and withered away shortly after he left, almost as if it were put there to nurture the great man. And the Lincoln birthplace site reminds its visitors that Kentucky is really "where it all began."

Each site emphasizes the depth and authenticity of its Lincoln connections. In some cases, these are well documented. In others, evidence is stretched to meet local needs, disclaimers are buried in fine print and footnotes, and obfuscating language leaves visitors under misapprehensions about the significance of what they have seen. Such devices might be called the "little white lies" of Lincoln tourism. I borrow the term from anthropologist Edward Bruner, who discusses what he calls the "little white lies of historical reconstruction."[21] In order to make the tourist's experience safe and enjoyable, he explains, historical sites everywhere make adjustments to the physical environment. Electric lights and heating, paved walkways, wheelchair ramps, and modern restrooms are now common features of what are promoted as "authentic" Lincoln-era sites. While visitors at such sites may enjoy "stepping back in time" (as many tourism pamphlets promise), they no doubt also appreciate being able to step back into the present when they need to use a toilet. It can be argued that such "little white lies" do no harm, and they make the visitor's experience more pleasurable. The same argument can be made for other little lies of interpretation, like giving visitors the impression that an artifact is genuine when it is a reproduction, or using terms like "traditional story" for claims that are unsubstantiated by evidence. It is these little lies that we examine next.

Across the Lincoln heartland and at Lincoln sites in and around Washington, D.C., visitors clearly yearn for authenticity. Guides are asked repeatedly whether certain artifacts are "real," whether Lincoln himself actually owned, touched, or used certain objects, and even whether particular trees were standing when Lincoln passed by. For their part, guides seem to understand this quest for authenticity. As a guide at the newly restored President Lincoln's Cottage in Washington, D.C., told a group of visitors, "When you're holding this handrail, know that Lincoln held the same one. You're walking in Lincoln's footsteps in the truest sense." Hushed reverence is the typical response when visitors are invited to gaze upon or even touch a genuine Lincoln artifact—almost as if some microscopic trace of the great man remains, as if some of Lincoln's greatness might be imparted to those who seek him with a pure heart.

Sites with less well-documented Lincoln connections often strain somewhat to establish any genuine link with the great man. The Stephenson County Historical Society Museum in Illinois displays a wooden gavel with a certificate attesting that it was made from an "elm tree that was planted and cherished by the hand of Abraham Lincoln." At Bryant Cottage in Bement, Illinois, a guide relates the "traditional story" that Lincoln and Stephen Douglas met there to agree on terms for their now famous debates. Although she admits that there is little documentary evidence of the meeting, she reassures visitors that scholars "haven't been able to disprove" that it occurred.

Even the nation's leading Lincoln sites promote certain little white lies. At the Lincoln boyhood site in Indiana, considerable space is dedicated to Lincoln's genealogy, complete with images of his forebears. A painted portrait identified as Nancy Hanks Lincoln, the president's mother, bears a striking resemblance to Lincoln himself—so much so that one visitor was overheard exclaiming, "He looks just like her!" The small print reveals, however, that since no images of Lincoln's mother exist, this portrait is simply one artist's best guess at her appearance. Likewise, visitors strolling from this introductory gallery to the marker for Lincoln's boyhood cabin will walk by the site signposted as the "Nancy Hanks Lincoln Gravesite." While the weathered headstone and iron fence surrounding the site lend it an air of hallowed authenticity, a careful reading of NPS interpretive materials reveals that the exact location of the grave is uncertain, and the headstone was only added to the site in the twentieth century.

Figure 2.2. Classical temple at the Abraham Lincoln Birthplace National Historic Site. *Courtesy of the Author*

Likewise, at the Lincoln birthplace site in Kentucky, a tiny log cabin stands ensconced in a Doric-style temple of granite and marble (see figure 2.2), the following words inscribed above the entrance: "Here over *the log cabin where Abraham Lincoln was born*, destined to preserve the union and to free the slave, a grateful people have dedicated this memorial to unity, peace and brotherhood among the states" (emphasis added). A notice prohibiting flash photography and food, "for the protection of resources," and a guard posted within the temple add to the impression that one is approaching a sacred historical treasure.

Visitors would be forgiven for believing that they have seen the actual cabin where Lincoln was born. But, again, a careful reading of NPS interpretive material reveals that the cabin is only "symbolic"; that is, it is a fake. As James Loewen detailed in his 1999 book, *Lies across America: What Our Historic Sites Get Wrong*, the original Lincoln family cabin was most likely dismantled and its timbers recycled long before Lincoln became famous.[22] But in 1895 a businessman bought the land where the Lincolns once lived and built a cabin there in the hopes of attracting tourists. When the venture fell flat for lack of visitors, the entrepreneur disassembled the structure and took it on the road to various expositions, marketing it as Lincoln's authentic birthplace cabin. Eventually the sham cabin was reerected on the Kentucky site. But when the grand temple was built to house the structure, it was decided that the cabin was too large to fit comfortably inside. So ultimately the logs were lopped off, and a smaller version of the cabin was erected inside the memorial building.[23]

Writing a decade ago, Loewen asserted that the NPS "pretends the cabin is real."[24] By 2008, however, it was clear that some attempts had been made to inform the public of the structure's actual origins. Visitors who buy the twelve-dollar guidebook to NPS Lincoln sites or spend sufficient time carefully examining displays in the visitor center can find detailed factual accounts of the cabin's history. However, many tourists skip the guidebook and visitor center altogether to go straight to the temple itself, where no such explanations are offered. Little wonder, then, that many visitors can be overheard expressing wonder and admiration that the whole extended Lincoln family actually lived in this tiny structure.

It would be overly simplistic to blame visitors' misperceptions of the cabin's authenticity on the NPS alone. After all, the notion of Lincoln's humble log-cabin birth are deeply ingrained in the American imagination, and the rough-hewn cabin housed in the temple closely accords with popular images of Lincoln's early life. No doubt, even with more visible disclaimers, many visitors would see what they expect to see: tangible proof that even the lowliest citizen can rise to the top of American society. After all, as much as the site is a temple to a single man, it is a temple to the American Dream. Some might argue that little white lies are justifiable and tolerable if they help sustain that dream.

Other prominent Lincoln sites purvey their own little lies. In spring of 2008, the U.S. Congress designated forty-two counties in central Illinois as the Abraham Lincoln National Heritage Area. An organization known as the Looking for Lincoln Coalition was launched to help preserve, develop, and market Lincoln sites within the heritage area. As part of this effort, the coalition has sponsored "Looking for Lincoln" signs and pamphlets throughout the region, which offer visitors the opportunity to "walk the floors where Lincoln walked," to "spend time with the spirit of Lincoln," and of course to buy souvenirs "to help you remember your time in the Land of Lincoln."[25]

Even the Abraham Lincoln Presidential Library and Museum displays Looking for Lincoln placards encouraging visitors to "See the real thing!" at locations throughout the Lincoln heartland. Each placard presents a description of a Lincoln site, complete with brief travel directions to the attraction. Curiously, however, many of the "real" sites listed are actually reproductions themselves. Almost all of the "historic" buildings now standing at Lincoln's New Salem, for instance, were erected between 1919 and 1941 with an eye toward drawing in tourists and creating local jobs.[26] Having such sites promoted as the "real thing" in the nation's premier Lincoln museum no doubt fosters a public misperception about these sites.[27]

In communities throughout central Illinois, eye-catching Looking for Lincoln signs draw visitors' attention to local Lincoln connections (see figure 2.3). However, the signs themselves are not without their own little white lies. At the entrance to the David Davis Mansion in Bloomington, for instance, the Looking for Lincoln sign declares in large, boldface type that "Abraham Lincoln sometimes stayed at the Davis home." Only visitors who read the less conspicuous print below will learn that Lincoln actually visited an earlier home nearby. The mansion currently open to tourists was only completed after Lincoln's death.

Similarly, Looking for Lincoln promotes Oakland Cemetery in Petersburg, Illinois, as the final resting place of Ann Rutledge, the young woman "reputed to be Lincoln's sweetheart."[28] Only the word *reputed* hints at the heated debate around the issue of Lincoln's possible romance with Ann Rutledge. Based on hearsay accounts long after Lincoln's death, and ignoring the absence of a single piece of documentary evidence (a letter, say, between the lovers or their family members mentioning the match), Lincoln's former law partner and biographer William Herndon controversially claimed that Ann Rutledge was Lincoln's one true love. The romance is now so firmly

Figure 2.3. Looking for Lincoln historical marker, Springfield, Illinois. *Courtesy of the Author*

entrenched in Lincoln folklore that the young woman's grave is a popular stop on the Lincoln tourism trail. However, the little white lie of the Ann Rutledge gravesite turns out to be not so little after all, for there is convincing evidence that she is not buried there.

When Ann Rutledge died in 1835 at the tender age of twenty-two, her body was laid to rest in New Salem's Concord Cemetery.[29] There it remained in relative obscurity until Samuel Montgomery, an undertaker and part owner of the Oakland Cemetery in nearby Petersburg, came up with a plan to increase business. He would relocate Ann's remains to his own cemetery and erect a monument to her that would serve both as a tourist site and a way to sell more cemetery plots. Although Ann's original unmarked gravesite was excavated, little could be recovered—two bones, a lock of hair, some buttons, and scraps of ribbon and lace. Of these, it appears, only the two bones made their way to the new plot in Oakland Cemetery. Yet the grand headstone in place today bears an inscription that reads, in part, "I am Ann Rutledge who sleep beneath these weeds, Beloved of Abraham Lincoln." While the burial site and perhaps the entire tale of romance may be fabrications, the economic impact of Lincoln tourism on small-town Petersburg, population 2,207, is very real indeed.

How can we account for the little (or not so little) white lies of Lincoln tourism? The most obvious explanation is that they make the tourist experience more pleasurable. The tourism industry operates on the reasonable assumption that tourists do not generally want to experience sorrow and guilt, they do not want their deeply held beliefs challenged, and they do not want to be confronted with controversies and complex historical arguments. Rather, they want the kind of simple, pleasing stories that make them feel good about their trip and, not coincidentally, make them repeat customers and eager consumers of gift-store merchandise. When the Abraham Lincoln Presidential Library and Museum was under construction, consultants from the tourism industry reportedly advised curators to tone down, or even eliminate, coverage of the brutalities of slavery.[30] The public would be horrified, they said, and horrified patrons do not make for a successful tourist venture. So one principle behind the little white lies of Lincoln tourism is simple: make the tourists happy, and they will spend more money.

Beyond the economic imperative, however, the little lies of Lincoln tourism have the potential to reaffirm individual and collective identities. Those who visit Lincoln sites do so for a variety of reasons. Among others, there are the Lincoln and Civil War enthusiasts who offer detailed explanations of everything from Confederate sidearms to Lincoln's shoe size to polite passersby, thereby asserting their own status as experts. Likewise, there are those with personal connections to Lincoln, who can be overheard telling companions of a great-great-grandfather who fought in the Civil War or a long-ago relative who had tea with Mary Lincoln. Such connections provide individuals with honor by association. Then there are the visitors who seem only mildly curious, those who perhaps happened to be in the area with some time to kill. While they may not use the opportunity to assert themselves as experts or persons of distinction, to visit such a site is, in a sense, to worship at the national altar, to affirm one's commitment to the ideals that both Abraham Lincoln and the nation that bore him are thought to embody—qualities like honesty, humility, ingenuity, godliness, and hard work. Little white lies that gloss over complexities or ignore documentary evidence in favor of popular Lincoln lore help sustain the gratifying stories we weave for ourselves as individuals, as communities, and as a nation. Simply put, the little white lies of Lincoln tourism make us feel better—both about Lincoln and about ourselves.

AN OUTSIDER'S PERSPECTIVE ON LINCOLN: COMMODIFICATION, SIMULATION, AND RIDING THE RAIL SPLITTER'S COATTAILS

Whether in Lincoln knickknacks, genuine Lincoln artifacts, Lincoln-themed businesses, Lincoln advertisements, or Lincoln tourism, Abraham Lincoln is commodified in countless ways across the nation today. But the real question is whether this commodification in any way diminishes or sullies the Great Emancipator.

It could be argued that the widespread commercial use of Lincoln is simply a reflection of the American people's esteem for a national hero. According to this logic, whether Lincoln adorns Mount Rushmore or a souvenir shot glass, the effect is the same. His name and image remind us of our shared ideals, the ideals Lincoln seems to have both embodied and died to preserve. We can draw useful insights here from sociologist Emile Durkheim's studies of religion. Durkheim argued that religion brings communities closer together in two important ways: it provides an opportunity to articulate shared norms and values, and it engages people in collective action. From this Durkheimian perspective, the veneration of Abraham Lincoln, as a kind of civil religion, serves these same purposes. It allows us to reflect on our national ideals through certain rituals like visiting Lincoln sites or celebrating Lincoln's birthday. Durkheim, were he alive today, might even suggest that in Abraham Lincoln the American people have created a god in their own image. Invoking Lincoln, in whatever form he takes today, could therefore be seen as an act of national self-worship that serves to bind us all closer together.[31]

By contrast, others will consider the commercialization of Lincoln to be disrespectful and distasteful. Eyebrows were undoubtedly raised when Lincoln's Waffle Shop opened just steps from the Washington, D.C. house where the martyr president drew his last breath.[32] From this moral vantage point, cashing in on the most thoroughly sanctified of American presidents is a desecration, something akin to using the image of Jesus to sell toilet paper or vodka. From this perspective, those who sell Lincoln for material gain are no different from the would-be grave robbers who, in 1876, attempted to steal Lincoln's remains and hold them for ransom.[33]

Beyond such moral objections, however, the often casually maligned work of postmodern and Marxist theorists offers another way of looking at the commodification of Lincoln. According to postmodern theorists such as Jean Baudrillard, we now live in a world dominated by simulacra—that is, copies of copies of copies. We increasingly experience our world through the lens of the mass media and inhabit carefully engineered physical environments—gated communities with their cookie-cutter houses; orderly, climate-controlled shopping malls; or Disney-style theme parks that immerse visitors in an elaborate world of make believe.[34] Baudrillard, among others, finds this manic simulation troubling on several counts, two of which concern us here. The first is that in the process of reproducing copies of copies, we eventually lose the original. The second is that, eventually, the original is considered inferior to the copies.[35]

Let us first examine how this can be applied to a masterpiece of the art world, Leonardo da Vinci's famed *Mona Lisa*. While the painting itself hangs in the Louvre in Paris, it is one of the most widely reproduced and parodied images in contemporary popular culture, almost as instantly recognizable as Mickey Mouse or the golden arches. While it is impossible, of course, to see the original "Mona Lisa"—the actual model is now long dead—and although only visitors to the Louvre can view the original painting, most of us have seen the *Mona Lisa*'s enigmatic smile in art history books or on posters, T-shirts, and calendars. It can be argued that exposure to countless reproductions of the painting in a sense obliterates the original artwork. That is, we come to the painting with a whole set of preconceptions and associations that prevent us from seeing the painting in all its subtlety and complexity. The actual painting may, in fact, prove a disappointment to visitors, many of whom can be overheard complaining that it is "so small" or "too dark."[36] Clearly, the reproductions of the painting have become so ubiquitous that the original pales by comparison.

Now, to apply this same argument to Lincoln, postmodern theorists in Baudrillard's camp would argue that the frequent and indiscriminate use of Lincoln's name and image strips Lincoln of all substance and nuance and renders him an empty sign. In other words, Lincoln the man becomes little more than an arbitrary symbol standing for concepts such as "honesty," "courage," or "all-American." Ironically, then, an overexposure to Lincoln's image may make it more difficult for us to know and understand the historical Lincoln. Furthermore, as idealized, sanitized, and rather bland versions of Lincoln come to dominate the public imagination, it becomes increasingly difficult to introduce any complexity or controversy into the discussion of Abraham Lincoln. Any less-than-ideal Lincoln would only be a disappointment to a public reared on myth and endless, squeaky-clean simulation.

Further insight into the commodification of Lincoln can be drawn from Marxist theory. In Karl Marx's formulation, commodification (or commoditization) is the shift from use value to exchange value. In other words, commodification occurs when we go from valuing something for its use (for instance, eating the corn we grow) to valuing it for what it will get us in exchange (say, seven dollars per bushel). This process is a key part of capitalism, and Marx argues that it eventually infects all aspects of social life, as everything from politics and art to family and sex get real or metaphorical price tags attached to them. From a Marxist theoretical perspective, commodification is deeply troubling because it perverts natural human relations, making even the most intimate dealings subject to cost-benefit calculations and, ultimately, to various forms of exploitation. Furthermore, fixating on exchange value prevents us from seeing the inherent value of the people, things, and phenomena that are being commodified. From this perspective, the commodification of Abraham Lincoln is highly problematic. In commodifying Lincoln, there is the danger that he will become valued principally for the payoffs his name and image can deliver. If this is the case, it will become increasingly difficult for us to understand, and learn from, Lincoln.

In sum, the social sciences provide us with two very different views of Lincoln's commodification. On the one hand, any and all commodification of the Great Emancipator is a form of veneration, not only of the man but of the nation as a whole. On the other, commodifying Lincoln transforms him into a hollow symbol that is endlessly and callously exploited. Both perspectives provide insights into the ways that we use Lincoln today, and both require us to ask ourselves some uncomfortable questions. In commodifying Lincoln—whether to sell bobble heads or sleeping pills, life insurance or hotel rooms—are we losing Lincoln? And if we lose Lincoln, our own Father Abraham, will we lose something of ourselves?

· 3 ·

Packaging the President:
Lincoln Biographies

$\mathscr{I}$n his classic essay on "civil religion" in the United States, sociologist Robert Bellah noted that Abraham Lincoln both embodied and promulgated some of the most deeply cherished conceptions of American national identity.[1] Lincoln's life was a vivid illustration of the rewards of the Puritan ethics of hard work, self-discipline, and moderation; his words reaffirmed the sacred mission of God's "almost chosen people"; and his Good Friday assassination transformed him into a national martyr, even a national demigod. As we venerate Lincoln, therefore, we are venerating the nation itself. As Progressive intellectual Herbert Croly remarked, Americans "disguise flattery of themselves under the form of reverence for [Lincoln]."[2] If the veneration of Lincoln is an act of national self-worship, then Lincoln scholarship provides the religion's doctrinal texts.

The field of Lincoln publications is almost incalculably vast. There are estimated to be 15,000 Lincoln books in circulation. To put that in perspective, if you were somehow able to read one Lincoln book per day—a daunting task given that many of them top seven hundred pages—it would take you roughly forty years to reach the end of your Lincoln library. Of course, by that time, you would have another forty years' worth of books awaiting you, a Sisyphean challenge for even the most devoted Lincoln scholar. More daunting yet is the fact that for every Lincoln book that makes its way to market, numerous scholarly journal articles are published. In the last twenty years alone, academic articles with significant Lincoln content have been published at the rate of roughly one per week, nearly double those focused on George Washington, Lincoln's perennial competitor in the "greatest American president" stakes.[3] Add to these scholarly books and articles a host of pamphlets, periodicals, and news coverage (not to mention the realm of Lincoln fiction), and the massive scope of the Lincoln publishing industry becomes clear.

Some scholars have suggested that Lincoln's prominence in the world of publishing is waning. Barry Schwartz, for instance, asserts that there is generally less interest in Lincoln now than in the early twentieth century. He adds that "even the slight rise in Lincoln books during the last twenty-five years occurs against a background of long-term decline."[4] However, an analysis of listings in the WorldCat database of publications worldwide reveals an overall increase in Lincoln publications over the past 140 years.[5] As figure 3.1 demonstrates, temporary and relatively minor decreases have been seen roughly every thirty years. However, the more pronounced decline between 1960 and 1985 has been followed by a dramatic surge in Lincoln publications through the first decade of the twenty-first century.

Lincoln scholarship runs the gamut from traditional biographies, to narrowly focused analyses of such topics as Lincoln's health or marriage, to explorations of contemporary moral and political issues through a Lincolnian lens. Although as early as 1936 historian James G. Randall asked his colleagues to consider whether the "Lincoln theme" had been exhausted,[6] recent publications suggest that Lincoln remains a mine of untold treasures for earnest scholars. Even a cursory sampling of recent titles reveals the perceived value and appeal of Lincoln content: "Abraham Lincoln and the Global Economy"; "On Abortion: A Lincolnian Perspective"; "Lincoln's Craniofacial Microsomia: Three-Dimensional Laser Scanning of 2 Lincoln Life Masks"; or *Lincoln's Table: A President's Culinary Journey from Cabin to Cosmopolitan*, with its recipes for "Young Abe's Gingerbread Men" and "Rail Splitter" corn muffins.[7] It is even possible to find an "Acupuncture Diagnosis of Abraham Lincoln," in which the author suggests that Lincoln's "sluggish colon points to Yang-Ming channel pair manifestation."[8]

It is a truism of the publishing industry that there will always be an eager audience for publications about dogs, doctors, and Lincoln, conventional wisdom that inspired Richard Grayson's 2001 book, *Lincoln's Doctor's Dog*. No doubt the wealth of Lincoln titles both reflects and further fuels widespread interest in the sixteenth president. While Lincoln's marketability may help authors' book sales, however, it is crucial to acknowledge that complex factors shape any scholar's choice of topic: among them, unanswered questions about the topic, the availability of materials to study, institutional support for the topic, personal interest in the topic, and, yes, marketability. It would be presumptuous in the extreme to make any generalizations about scholars' motivations for studying Lincoln, particularly since I myself have chosen to write a Lincoln-themed book. What I can do, however, is examine the works Lincoln scholars produce for patterns of meaning. Are there any consistent themes running through the Lincoln scholarship? What are the leading

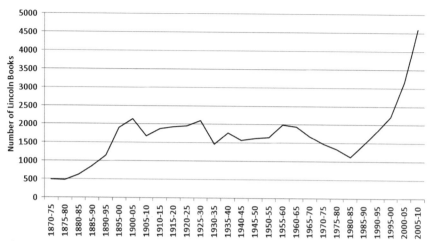

Figure 3.1. Number of Lincoln Books Published Worldwide: 1870–2010.

points of contention? And to what extent has Lincoln scholarship changed over time? In answering these questions, among others, we will better understand not only the ways scholars "package" Lincoln, but also the ways such constructions serve commercial, political, and broader cultural purposes.

In this chapter I examine twenty prominent Lincoln biographies published between 1866 and 2006, from accounts written in the first decades after Lincoln's death by those who knew him, to more recent volumes focusing on themes as diverse as his psychology, his political acumen, his moral values, and his sexuality.[9] This is not a statistically representative sample of the many thousands of Lincoln publications in circulation, and for this reason I make no claims of statistical significance. Nonetheless, I argue that the analysis of prominent biographies gives us insight into both scholarly and popular understandings of Lincoln. On the one hand, we can reason that the most widely read biographies will most profoundly shape national perceptions of Lincoln, and on the other hand it may be that certain biographies are commercially successful precisely *because* they either confirm or radically challenge cherished assumptions about Lincoln.

In the course of my analysis, I coded more than 10,000 pages of text for recurring quotations, anecdotes, and themes. Of course all Lincoln biographies can be expected to include much of the same material. Because certain names, dates, events, quotations, and the like are part of the historical record, they are consistently included in any telling of Lincoln's life story. There is nothing remarkable in that fact. What is of interest, however, is the way certain details are shaded by authors to make them appear more or less significant, more or less certain, more positive or more negative. So it is that, from the same historical record, authors have created subtly or even dramatically different visions of Abraham Lincoln.

In an analogy that would have been well understood in the Civil War era, Lincoln biographers are like patchwork quilt makers. They all begin with the same myriad fragments of his life, scraps of every hue and texture. But every maker combines these fragments in different ways, creating different designs, emphasizing different shades, and choosing which fragments to leave out altogether. However, when we see certain designs emerging again and again, such patterns tell us something about what we as a nation expect to see, what we *want* to see in accounts of Lincoln's life.

"AMONG THE NOBLEST OF THE NATION'S TREASURES": THEMES IN LINCOLN BIOGRAPHIES

In a detailed analysis of the ways Lincoln's image has changed since his death, historian Merrill Peterson identified five main tropes in representations of Lincoln: Lincoln as the "Savior of the Union," as the "Great Emancipator," as a "Man of the People," as the "First American," and as a "Self-Made Man."[10] While Barry Schwartz has argued that only one of these, the "Great Emancipator," is dominant today, my analysis suggests greater complexity than this.[11] Out of a list of two hundred themes that appeared in more than one of the twenty biographies in my sample, seven were most prominent: Lincoln's humor, his godliness, his achievements as a self-made man, his battles with depression, his honesty, his physical strength and stature, and his humble origins (see figure 3.2).[12]

Reflected in this portrait of Lincoln are our national self-conceptions. Americans have long conceived of their nation as youthful and robust, friendly, forthright, and reverent, a land of opportunity where even the humblest born can rise to the top.[13] Even Lincoln's much-discussed bouts of depression have a

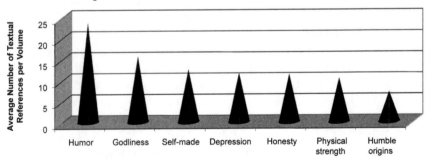

Figure 3.2. Themes in All Lincoln Biographies.

parallel in national narratives. At the level of national symbolism, Lincoln had to triumph over his inner darkness to fulfill his divinely sanctioned mission just as the nation itself had to struggle to subdue the frontier, civil rebellion, and foreign competitors to fulfill its Manifest Destiny.[14] Such triumph over adversity seems simply to prove the mettle of the man and the fortitude of the nation.

It is also clear, however, that the relative importance of these fundamental themes has changed over time in Lincoln biographies (see figure 3.3). Certainly Lincoln's renowned wit and storytelling have been featured consistently in his biographies. Most notably, Lincoln's humor is a significant preoccupation of early twentieth-century biographers such as Ida Tarbell and Carl Sandburg, whose portrayals of Lincoln as a folk hero are now firmly ingrained in the national imagination. These writers were reacting against earlier hagiographic biographies by authors such as Josiah Holland who gave readers a straitlaced, pious, and rather dour Lincoln. In Holland's florid nineteenth-century prose, Lincoln was "the tree which rose so high, and spread its leaves so broadly, and bore such golden fruit, and then fell before the blast because it was so heavy and so high." Lincoln was "simple, unpretending, sympathetic with all humanity, and reverent toward God . . . among the noblest of the nation's treasures."[15] Such elegiac descriptions stand in stark contrast to Tarbell's observation that "people liked him . . . because he was 'good company.' He loved to talk, to tell stories, to discuss, to play games. Wherever he went he brightened things, made them more interesting."[16]

Tales of Lincoln's wit and humor remain a prominent part of Lincoln biographies today. His godliness, his honesty, and his physical strength, however, have noticeably decreased in significance over time. The most likely explanation for this shift of emphasis lies in changing social conditions. With increased secularization of American life over the last century, reverence toward God and traditional Christian virtues, such as honesty, may be seen as less essential traits for a national hero than they were in the nineteenth century.

Likewise, with the thorough industrialization of American society and the attendant transition from physical labor to intellectual labor, Lincoln's size and strength have declined in importance. In nineteenth- and early twentieth-century biographies, Lincoln appeared to have almost superhuman strength. As biographer William Thayer observed in 1882, Lincoln "was not only a giant in stature, but a giant in strength. . . . He could carry a load to which the strength of three ordinary men would scarcely be equal."[17] At the turn of the century, Ida Tarbell likewise emphasized his stature and muscularity. "Lincoln was twenty-two years old," she wrote, "almost six feet four inches in height, and weighed nearly one hundred and eighty pounds. There was not an ounce of extra flesh on his body, nothing but hard, sinewy muscle, and if he had gripped your hand you would have known that he could crush

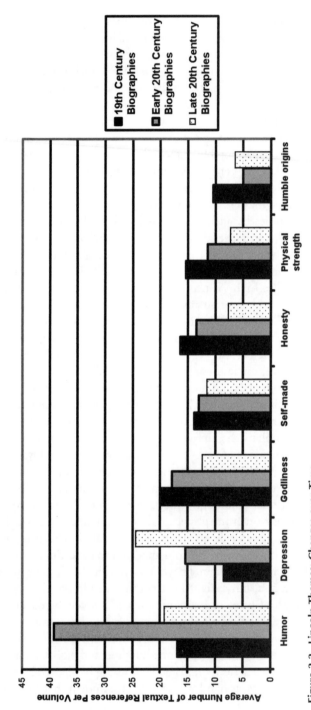

Figure 3.3. Lincoln Themes: Changes over Time

it if he wished."[18] But, of course, he would not have wished to crush anyone's hand, for Tarbell's Lincoln was a gentle giant, a man whose sheer physical power was moderated by self-restraint and kindheartedness.

Lincoln's rise from a humble log cabin to the White House, and his constant drive toward self-improvement even without the benefits of a formal education or advantageous social connections, feature prominently in Lincoln biographies from every period. Such a consistent emphasis on Lincoln as a self-made man reveals the enduring salience of the American Dream. The notion that with hard work and self-discipline anyone can rise up through the ranks of American society has been a staple of national narratives since the very birth of the nation. American literature, drama, and film are replete with protagonists who rise from rags to riches, from obscurity to fame. In a sense, Lincoln offers comforting proof that all our labors and self-denial will pay off in the end. Just as Lincoln rose, we can rise. The American Dream is alive and well.

While some themes, such as Lincoln's godliness and strength, have decreased in significance over time, and some, such as his humor and his achievements as a self-made man, have remained prominent over time, Lincoln's struggle with depression has been gaining attention in recent biographies. The tendency in nineteenth-century hagiographic biographies was to simply omit controversial material. Lincoln's unorthodox religious views and the details of his reportedly stormy marital relationship—regularly included in twentieth-century biographies—rarely appear in nineteenth-century texts.[19] Likewise, Lincoln's bouts of depression, or "melancholy," receive little attention in early biographies. By the early to mid-twentieth century, however, biographers had transformed Lincoln into a romantic hero, a man of both superhuman strength, as noted earlier, and heightened emotional sensitivity. His capacity for deep suffering and his seemingly natural empathy for all living things served only to make him more perfect, indeed rather Christlike.

In the late twentieth century, biographers began to treat Lincoln's depressive episodes more analytically. Instead of presenting Lincoln's melancholy as an outward manifestation of inner perfection, biographers began to speculate about both the origins and consequences of Lincoln's temperament. Did the loss of his mother and sister early in life scar him emotionally? Did strained relations with an overly strict father drive him to seek the external validation of political office? Did his frontier experiences of brutality and grinding poverty help shape his policies on slavery? Biographers posing such questions in recent decades have increasingly placed Lincoln on the analyst's couch.

This more intensive focus on Lincoln's psychological makeup no doubt reflects late twentieth-century mainstreaming of certain principles from the fields of psychology and psychoanalysis. It is now generally taken for granted that early childhood trauma or familial dysfunction can leave deep and lasting imprints and lead to psychological disturbances such as depression, anxiety, or even posttraumatic stress disorder. It is therefore not surprising that biographers attempt to unlock the many mysteries of Lincoln using these now common psychological keys. Two additional factors undoubtedly contribute to the increased psychologizing in Lincoln biographies. The first is the heightened introspection of the so-called "me generation" of the late twentieth century, with its drive toward self-awareness and its cults of personality.[20] The second factor is the partial destigmatization of depression in the late twentieth century. With advertisements for antidepressants filling television screens and magazine pages across the nation, and books with titles such as *Prozac Nation* topping best-seller lists, it is evident that depression has come out of the closet in recent years.[21]

Even in the fickle realm of politics, depression is no longer a fatal career liability. In 1972, public opinion forced Senator Thomas Eagleton to resign as the Democratic vice presidential nominee when it was revealed that he had been treated for depression. By contrast, in 2006, U.S. representative Patrick Kennedy handily won reelection after openly discussing his treatment for depression, alcoholism, *and* prescription drug addiction. While depression has certainly not been entirely destigmatized, changing attitudes toward the illness have allowed Lincoln's recent biographers to more openly discuss his depressive tendencies. One recent biographer has even suggested that Lincoln's melancholy was the source of his greatness, a topic to which I return in chapter 5.[22]

HOGS, BOOKS, AND INDIANS: ANECDOTES IN LINCOLN BIOGRAPHIES

Just as prominent themes in Lincoln biographies help to reveal both perceptions of Lincoln and national self-conceptions, recurring anecdotes in Lincoln biographies offer insight into the ways Lincoln is constructed as a national exemplar. Of course, all biographers work from a finite set of materials, so it is not surprising that the same major events are included in most Lincoln biographies: the young Lincoln's journey from his birthplace in Kentucky to his boyhood in Indiana and his adult life in Illinois, his first run for elective office, his marriage, his legal career, his rise to the presidency, and so on. More revealing is the inclusion of less pivotal, more mundane details of his life, such as the day he rescued a hog mired in the mud, or the times he walked miles to borrow a book or return a slight overcharge to a customer. I would argue that such details are not simply included to add color to Lincoln biographies, but rather that these particular details construct Lincoln in very specific, and overwhelmingly positive, ways.

Perhaps the most obvious trend revealed by an analysis of recurring Lincoln anecdotes is that anecdotes emphasizing positive aspects of Lincoln's character are much more common than anecdotes that reveal less than ideal aspects of his character or behavior (see figure 3.4). For instance, 90 percent of all biographies note Lincoln's kindness toward animals—his rescue of a dog, a hog, or a baby bird and his profound remorse after shooting a turkey. Such anecdotes reinforce the notion of Lincoln as kindhearted and empathetic toward all living creatures. However, only 35 percent of biographies include the fact that as a young man Lincoln worked slaughtering hogs and in some accounts even sewed the hogs' eyelids shut to better drive them to market. Similarly, while three-quarters of biographies emphasize that Lincoln served as a captain in the Black Hawk War without ever shedding blood, and most of those note that he bravely defended an "old Indian" who wandered into camp during the conflict, few biographies include the fact that Lincoln was arrested briefly during that war for unlawfully discharging his firearm in camp. The fact that Lincoln provided legal defense for slave owners, and reports that he penned a so-called "infidel pamphlet" challenging some of the basic tenets of Christianity, are likewise often overlooked by biographers. The inclusion of any inglorious details might disrupt the flawless veneer of the Lincoln image as it has been cultivated since his death.

Rather, most recurring anecdotes serve to reinforce the idealized image of Lincoln. Lincoln biographies seldom fail to note his impoverished childhood and his drive toward self-betterment through study. The dominant image is that of a gangly boy in tattered clothes living in a rough-hewn, dirt-floor cabin, toiling over borrowed books by the light of a dying fire. The more vivid the description of deprivation, the more awe inspiring Lincoln's journey to immortality seems to be.

Other recurring anecdotes further serve to gild the proverbial lily. Lincoln's virility is reconfirmed through reports of his participation in various wrestling matches and his romance with Ann Rutledge. His magnanimity is illustrated through his interactions with Edwin Stanton. As a prominent attorney, Stanton had not only refused to allow Lincoln to assist with the high-profile McCormick reaper case, but he had also branded Lincoln a "long armed ape."[23] Yet, in spite of suffering this stinging personal insult, Lincoln later appointed Stanton secretary of war. Lincoln's famed honesty is affirmed through countless anecdotes from his days as a businessman, a lawyer, and a politician. And his ingenuity is commonly illustrated through two incidents. As a young man, Lincoln is said to have cleverly saved a heavily laden flatboat on the Sangamon River, and as a defense attorney he famously won his client's freedom by using an almanac to refute a witness's testimony about having seen the crime committed by the light of the moon.

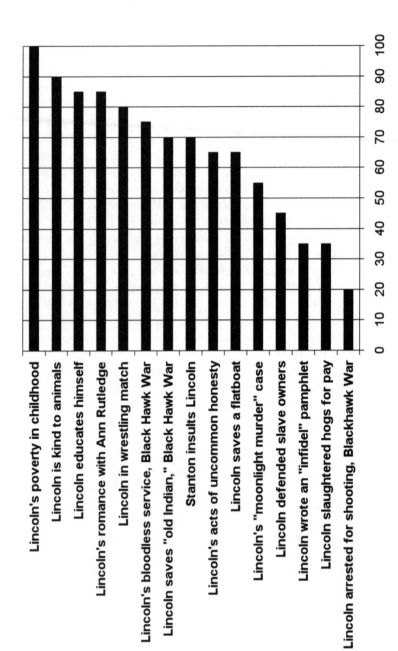

Figure 3.4. Lincoln Anecdotes in All Biographies

Not surprisingly, the relative importance of certain anecdotes to the construction of Lincoln's image has changed over time (see figure 3.5). A number of shifts in emphasis stand out here. First, we see that anecdotes illustrating Lincoln's honesty and practical ingenuity have decreased over time, perhaps reflecting a general decline in the perceived importance of these traits. In addition, while biographers in all periods have made efforts to stress Lincoln's kindness toward animals, we see that nineteenth-century biographers were much more likely to also mention him slaughtering hogs. Such a shift reflects the changing nature of human-animal relations in the twentieth century: most Americans today have little contact with livestock or butchery, many have intense emotional attachments to pets (now sometimes called "animal companions"), and there is now a widespread injunction against cruelty to animals.[24] Perhaps most prominently, we see that Lincoln's admirable performance in the Black Hawk War has been mentioned less and less as public sentiments about the Indian wars have shifted from general approval to critique and disapproval.

Finally, we see that Lincoln's alleged romance with Ann Rutledge has had a prominent place in twentieth-century biographies. In recent years, it has even served to affirm Lincoln's heterosexuality in the face of assertions that he was gay. By contrast, Victorian notions of propriety no doubt discouraged many nineteenth-century biographers from including such material. Indeed, when Lincoln's former law partner William Herndon first brought the alleged relationship to light in a public lecture in 1866, he was castigated in the press for bringing shame on the great martyr's memory.[25]

THE QUOTES MAKETH THE MAN:
LINCOLN IN HIS OWN WORDS

Because Lincoln died without writing a memoir, we will never know how he would have framed his own life story. But, in a sense, we *can* know Lincoln through his own words. Biographers typically pepper their texts rather liberally with Lincoln quotations, invoking the presence of the great man himself.

Certain quotations are virtually compulsory in Lincoln biographies: "A house divided against itself cannot stand," "The mystic chords of memory" and the "better angels of our nature," "Government of the people, by the people, for the people," "With malice toward none, with charity for all." And, of course, Lincoln's characterization of America as "the last best hope of earth." These words, from Lincoln's most famous speeches, appear in up to 90 percent of the biographies in the sample. However, in addition to taking passages from Lincoln's greatest speeches, biographers quote from Lincoln's

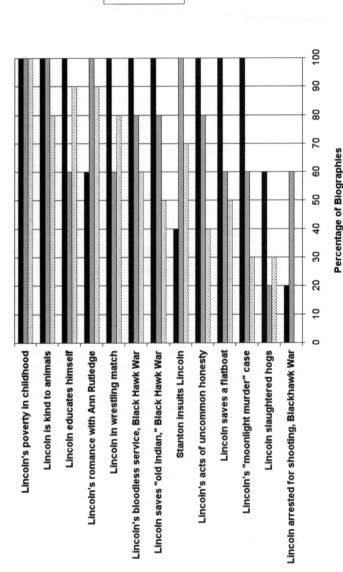

Figure 3.5. Lincoln Anecdotes: Change over Time

letters, legal papers, and minor speeches, from records of meetings, and even from recollections of personal conversations.

Scholars have analyzed Lincoln's words in minute detail for insight into his political philosophy, his religious beliefs, his character, his executive skills, his rhetorical gifts, and his inner conflicts, among other things. However, I would argue that the repetition of Lincoln's words can tell us at least as much about ourselves as it tells us about Lincoln. We must always remember that biographers choose which quotations to include and which to leave out. Such choices both reflect and shape prevailing views of Lincoln and, by extension, prevailing views of the nation itself.

While biographers draw most heavily on quotations from Lincoln's major speeches, approximately forty quotations from a variety of sources appear in more than one of the biographies in our sample. Let us leave aside Lincoln's most well-known pronouncements, which other scholars have analyzed so thoroughly, to examine the ways Lincoln is constructed through some less common quotations.[26] With even a cursory glance at figure 3.6, it is clear that quotations that cast Lincoln in a positive light—as hardworking, reverent, self-sacrificing, and firmly antislavery—are more commonly included in biographies than quotations that could be interpreted as heretical or racist. For instance, roughly two-thirds of the biographies analyzed include Lincoln's concise summary of his early years. "[I]t is a great piece of folly to attempt to make anything out of my early life," he told his first biographer in the midst of the 1860 presidential campaign. "It can all be condensed into a single sentence, and that sentence you will find in Gray's *Elegy*: 'The short and simple annals of the poor.'"

Of course this quote establishes that Lincoln came from humble beginnings and that he identified with the poor and downtrodden. It suggests that he was modest and plainspoken, but it also demonstrates that he was well read. In addition, the frequent repetition of this quote both reflects and reinforces the enduring importance of the American Dream in national self-conceptions. The quote reminds us that in this land of opportunity a child born into obscurity and poverty can rise to the very pinnacle of society. Whether or not this is true, it is a notion that comforts and sustains us as a nation.

Likewise, more than half of the biographies in the current sample include Lincoln's references to a divine Being, a merciful Maker, and the perfect plans of the Almighty. Far fewer biographers choose to include Lincoln's stated doubts about the afterlife, his declaration that he was not a Christian, or his alleged description of Christ as a "bastard." It must be noted that the first three of these quotations are from written sources, while the last three are from oral recollections. Some biographers may consider the latter less reliable and choose to exclude them on that basis. Nonetheless, the overall effect of such choices is

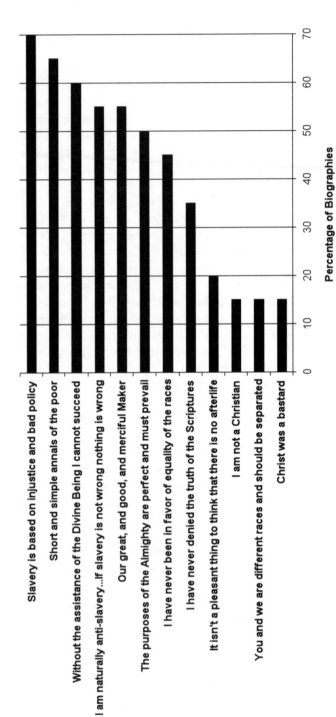

Figure 3.6. Lincoln Quotations in All Biographies

to portray Lincoln as a stalwart Christian, a portrayal that accords with long-standing and widespread notions of America as a community of Christians.

Just as Lincoln's own words are used to characterize him as a Christian and an exemplar of the American Dream, they are used as proof that he was staunchly antislavery. His assertions that slavery was "based on injustice and bad policy," and that he was "naturally antislavery," feature prominently in the biographies. Far fewer texts include quotations in which Lincoln denies advocating equality between blacks and whites and asserts that due to insurmountable natural differences, the races should be separated. For most of his political career, his favored solution to slavery was "colonization," the removal of slaves and their descendants to all-black colonies to be established in Africa, Central and South America, or the Caribbean. Because Lincoln was a longtime and very public advocate of colonization, biographers could certainly reproduce his numerous statements on the topic, but most choose to downplay or omit such materials in their accounts of Lincoln's life.

Even those biographers who include such references are careful to note that while by today's standards Lincoln's statements may seem prejudicial, by the standards of his time and place they were remarkably progressive. One recent biographer urged readers to "remember that [Lincoln was] talking to a deeply prejudiced white audience, in an environment in which racial stereotypes [were] part of the common culture."[27] In other words, Lincoln had to play to a racist crowd, but that does not mean that he really believed the things he said. To suggest that Lincoln was committed to racial separatism and an inevitable racial hierarchy would undermine the hallowed image of the Great Emancipator and the principle of racial equality that he has come to represent.

Although Lincoln did not bequeath his life story to us in his own hand, biographers have used his words to portray him as a pious, self-sacrificing opponent of slavery and the quintessential self-made man. Such portrayals are a reflection of our national self-image. In our long-standing national narratives, we are a deeply religious nation, an altruistic nation, a nation of freedom and opportunity where all men regardless of class or race can succeed.[28] And Honest Abe Lincoln, the Rail Splitter, the Great Emancipator, is our national exemplar.

LINCOLN LOVERS AND LINCOLN HATERS: DISPUTATIONS IN LINCOLN BIOGRAPHIES

Some will undoubtedly argue that identifying such conventional portrayals of Abraham Lincoln is of little value—that it is only natural for all Lincoln biographies to contain common themes and quotations because all biographers are working from the same raw material. Yet there exists a subset of Lincoln biographies that contain few of these conventional elements: biographies by Lincoln detractors.

One recent example from the field of anti-Lincoln writings, Thomas DiLorenzo's (2006) *Lincoln Unmasked: What You're Not Supposed to Know about Dishonest Abe*, seeks to debunk common assumptions about Lincoln. While the author does not discuss Lincoln's humor, his melancholy, or his physical strength, he tackles all of the other major themes identified above (see figure 3.2). As the title of the volume suggests, the author asserts that Lincoln was fundamentally dishonest, a typical politician who would say anything to get elected and then cash in on his elective office. He further notes that Lincoln never professed Christian faith and only used biblical allusions to curry favor with a God-fearing electorate. As for the notion that Lincoln was a poor backwoods boy who became an exemplar of the American self-made man, DiLorenzo charges that from early in his career, Lincoln was little more than a corporate stooge and an influence peddler who cared less about lofty ideals than about lining his own pockets.

Not surprisingly, then, DiLorenzo deploys none of the favorable anecdotes discussed above. Reading an anti-Lincoln tract makes it all the clearer how important such anecdotes and quotations are to the maintenance of a positive Lincoln image in most biographies. Tales of Lincoln growing up poor, rescuing helpless animals, falling in love, saving a flatboat, wrestling a bully, or forgiving a rival humanize Lincoln and render him both sympathetic and admirable. Such homey anecdotes have no place in works that challenge widespread perceptions of Lincoln's greatness.

Likewise, Lincoln's best-known words and noblest sentiments receive little play in DiLorenzo's critical biography. Only one of Lincoln's most memorable quotes, discussed above, is included, "with malice toward none, with charity toward [*sic*] all."[29] And this is deployed only to prove Lincoln's hypocrisy in his prosecution of a brutal and merciless war against the Confederacy. Rather, DiLorenzo chooses to focus on Lincoln's more controversial statements: "I have no purpose to introduce political and social equality between the white and black races," "You and we are different races. We have between us a broader difference than exists between almost any other two races. . . . It is better for us both, therefore, to be separate," and "There is a natural disgust in the minds of nearly all white people, to the idea of an indiscriminate amalgamation of the white and black races."[30] So while critical biographers do selectively use Lincoln's own words, these words are used in evidence against him, to raise questions about his character, his integrity, and his motivations.

DiLorenzo is at pains to demonstrate that many respectable scholars share his negative assessment of Lincoln. He lists more than seventy-five such scholars by name and praises many of them in his text. By contrast, he heaps scorn on the "Lincoln idolaters," the "Lincoln cultists," and mainstream

Lincoln biographers whom he asserts "tend to be cover-up artists, court historians, gatekeepers, and propagandists more than genuine scholars."[31] Their goals are simple and insidious, he asserts. On one level, they glorify Lincoln for ideological purposes—either to indoctrinate Americans into fighting and dying for a militarist-expansionist state or to win support for bloated social welfare programs. And in more practical terms, they glorify Lincoln to win fame and fortune, tenure, book contracts, and lecture tours. What DiLorenzo does not acknowledge, however, is that anti-Lincoln authors are at least as vulnerable to charges of allowing ideological and even monetary considerations to shape their interpretations of Lincoln's life. In a sense, all of us who write about Lincoln are participants in the literary branch of Lincoln, Inc. All of us contribute to the packaging of the sixteenth president.

AN OUTSIDER'S PERSPECTIVE ON LINCOLN: FRAMING THE SIXTEENTH PRESIDENT

Early in the twentieth century, linguistic anthropologists suggested that the language we use not only reflects our perceptions of the world but helps shape our perceptions. In two frequently cited examples, researchers asserted that speaking a language with a large number of words for various types of snow or subtle color variations actually allows individuals to better perceive such subtleties.[32] While the validity of these rather simple examples has been challenged, more recent research by neuroscientists and cognitive psychologists confirms that the language we use does indeed shape our perceptions of the world around us. Lera Boroditsky of Stanford University reports that in linguistic systems with gendered nouns, people perceive common objects differently depending on the grammatical gender ascribed to them.[33] For instance, while Spanish speakers are likely to describe a bridge as "strong, sturdy and towering," German speakers are more likely to describe the *same* bridge as "beautiful, elegant, and slender." *Bridge* is masculine in Spanish (*el puente*) but feminine in German (*die brucke*), and thus Spanish speakers attribute more masculine traits to the bridge, while German speakers perceive its more feminine traits. Boroditsky found consistent results across many languages, including an artificial language she created for the purposes of the experiment.[34]

Such findings shed light on the ways humans construct reality. Yes, we live in a physical world of objects and sensations and beings, but as we interpret sensory data we also order that data in very particular ways, imposing meaning and structure on the world. Writing in 1974, sociologist Erving Goffman suggested that we interpret our experiences through a kind of filter, or "framework," of concepts and associations that allow us to quickly and efficiently make sense of—and act in—the world.[35] In more recent years, scholars scrutinizing mass media, social movements, and political rhetoric, among other phenomena, have analyzed the ways these interpretive frames shape public opinion, public policy, and public action, sometimes through the quite conscious management (or manipulation) of public discourses.[36]

In this age of twenty-four-hour news outlets, we can readily observe politicians, corporations, and activists attempting to promulgate a consistent set of metaphors, labels, and pared-down "talking points" on a particular issue. Controlling vocabulary and imagery (in other words, controlling frames of reference) is a crucial step toward controlling the direction of public debate. As Entman puts it, "To frame is to select some aspects of a perceived reality and make them more salient in a communicating text in such a way as to promote a particular problem definition, causal interpretation, moral evaluation, and/or treatment recommendation for the item described."[37] The framing of issues, events, and values is central to the ways we understand and act in the world.

We can usefully apply the principles of frame analysis to constructions of Abraham Lincoln. The oft-repeated words and images, anecdotes, and events of the Lincoln narrative create interpretive frames that shape our perceptions of Lincoln. The overwhelmingly positive and heroic representations found in mainstream biographies not only serve as a framework for understanding Lincoln but also shape the kinds of questions we ask about him, the kinds of conversations we have about him, and the kinds of books that subsequently get written about him. Moreover, specific Lincoln stories are stitched together by what social scientists call metanarratives, overarching narrative themes that direct our attention to seemingly universal truths and values. In the Lincoln story, these include, among other themes, meritocratic individualism; progress through struggle; the nobility of self-sacrifice; the triumph of democracy, freedom, and equality; and the inviolability of the nation.[38] While some biographers may consciously weave such themes through their studies of Lincoln, others are no doubt unaware that in simply building on existing scholarship they almost inevitably repeat many of the same value claims that have dominated Lincoln biographies since his death.

Through this conventional framing of the Lincoln narrative the American audience is constantly reminded that we belong to a national "moral community," with shared values and priorities and shared "common sense" understandings of the natural social order.[39] And, although biographies may not explicitly direct us to live our lives as Lincoln lived his, they carry powerful implicit messages about what is right and good and natural and true: that in America, the best and the brightest will rise to the top; that as we triumph over adversity we become stronger and advance both as individuals and as a nation; that individuals must be willing to sacrifice for the general good; that as a nation, we are moving steadily toward higher forms of democracy and social justice; and that despite internal struggles and divides, we are now, and ever shall be, one nation—nurturing the same ideals, working toward the same goals, and worshipping the same heroes.

On the one hand, such metanarratives may promote social solidarity by smoothing over differences and encouraging the acceptance of certain values and rules of conduct. However, from the perspective of critical theory, the unchallenged repetition of such themes both reflects imbalances of power and helps perpetuate them.[40] The notion that the most deserving among us rise to the top legitimates the authority of our political, cultural, and economic elites, making us perhaps less likely to question their pronouncements. The notion that as a nation we are constantly progressing toward more perfect democracy and greater equity may hinder much-needed political reform and blind us to the real and persistent social barriers that hamper the progress of marginalized groups within the nation. Similarly, the notion that everyone can achieve the American Dream if only they try hard enough may lead us to assume that disadvantaged and disenfranchised groups are simply not trying hard enough, an assumption that might discourage us from trying to understand and combat systemic inequalities. And the notion that above all else the nation must be safeguarded and preserved at all costs ultimately serves the interests of the state. Citizens who embrace this message of national devotion will be less likely to challenge governmental authority when they are called upon to sacrifice their property, their liberties, and even their lives for the good of the nation.

The danger of such dominant and largely unquestioned frames in the Lincoln narrative is that they potentially stifle meaningful debate. As we will see in subsequent chapters, certain questions about Lincoln are almost unaskable today—"Was he a racist?" or "Was he gay?," for instance. Scholars who challenge the dominant discourses by raising such issues are often quickly dismissed by the academy. So the conventional framing of the Lincoln story may prevent us from understanding the man and his age in all their complexity. There is a broader issue at work, however, for the metanarratives described here do not simply run through our Lincoln stories. We can find similar overarching themes in stories of our other national heroes, past and present. We can find them in our Hollywood films, at our political rallies, on inspirational bumper stickers, and in recruiting campaigns for the armed services. We see them in our sitcoms, where seemingly ordinary Americans happily labor toward our communal ideals. We find them in ads for beer, frozen vegetables, and homeowners insurance, where products are wrapped in red, white, and blue. They are so ubiquitous that they are almost unassailable. To be sure, when conventional narratives inhibit full and honest discussion of Lincoln's life and times, it is an opportunity lost. But far graver are the consequences when widely circulating metanarratives impede examination of the very nature of our society today.

Ideas such as meritocratic individualism, nationalism, and inevitable progress form a kind of ideological scaffolding that envelops and constrains debate on all manner of vital social issues. Should we go to war? Should we extend health care to all within our borders? Should we allow stem cell research? Should we curtail immigration? The way we talk about and think about all these issues is shaped by largely invisible frameworks of ideas and associations. Seldom do we ponder why our deliberations about war are so wedded to the concepts of freedom, democracy, and national devotion (even when the particular conflict may have little to do with such principles). Seldom do we question why we think and talk the way we do about momentous national decisions. The discourses simply strike us as natural, commonsensical. People of course take many different stances on such issues, but they generally draw on the same metanarratives. In the highly polarized debate over abortion, for instance, we see a woman's individual "right to choose" on one side and a fetus's individual "right to life" on the other side. Even when working toward opposite goals, both sides refer to the same metanarrative of individual rights and freedoms.

Social theorists disagree about how such frameworks are created. Some suggest that powerful elites build the frames to suit their own interests and that the masses are more or less unaware of the ideological cages in which they live. Others contend that masses and elites alike contribute chunks of meaning to this scaffolding and then attempt to use it to support their own positions (which is my own take on the matter). But even those of us who see narrative frames as collectively constructed acknowledge that the groups with the most resources at their disposal (for instance, the rich, the politically connected) have more power to reshape these frames through their own prominent contributions of meaning. The examination of narrative and ideological frames is more than some abstract intellectual parlor game. History shows us that those who most effectively bolster and employ such frames often exert potent influence over human events. Arguably, for instance, by pulling from the narrative of the "triumph of democracy" and expanding it to encompass the notion of "spreading democracy," Theodore Roosevelt paved the path to American imperialism (a path that some say we have never left and that many others admit we stray onto from time to time even today).[41] Over the ensuing one hundred years, "spreading democracy" has become a firm fixture in our national conversations about such issues as foreign policy and armed conflict. It is a largely unexamined, taken-for-granted value that helps sway our decisions.

Whether we are trying to understand and learn from Lincoln or trying to make the kinds of monumental decisions that every nation must make, if we fail to scrutinize the words and images, the narratives and "frames," that shape our thoughts and action, we fail to use every tool at our disposal to face up to history, to the present, and to the future. If we are unable or unwilling to recognize the ways we construct reality, we will remain ever baffled at seeing the bridge as delicate and slender while others insist it is solid and stout.

· *4* ·

Telling Fictions: Lincoln in Literature, Television, and Film

$\mathcal{T}$he story begins as so many Lincoln stories before it have begun: the log cabin, the frontier wilderness, the loving mother doomed to die before her time, and one strapping, striving lad, Abraham Lincoln. But in this gothic narrative, young Abe discovers a horrifying secret lurking in the Indiana woods.

> Abe didn't say a word. He made straight for his journal and wrote down a single sentence. One that would radically alter the course of his life, and bring the fledgling nation to the brink of collapse. "I hereby resolve to kill every vampire in America."[1]

Abraham Lincoln appears in a dizzying array of fictional works, including novels, television productions, films, and plays. The works range from embellished biographical accounts such as Gore Vidal's *Lincoln* and John Ford's *Young Mr. Lincoln*, to fantastical odysseys and biting political satires.[2] In Seth Grahame-Smith's *Abraham Lincoln: Vampire Hunter* (quoted above), Lincoln battles mounting legions of the undead; in *Star Trek*: "The Savage Curtain," he risks his life to teach a powerful alien that good must triumph over evil; in *Night at the Museum: Battle of the Smithsonian*, he saves the world from domination by a megalomaniacal Egyptian pharaoh; and in *Abraham Lincoln's Big Gay Dance Party*, he champions gay rights and free speech between campy dance numbers.[3]

Lincoln is sometimes the primary focus of such fictional narratives, and at other times he serves as a supporting character. But, almost without exception, wherever the fictional Abraham Lincoln appears, he is a hero. He is America at its best, humanity at its best, mature manhood at its best. He is a figure onto which both authors and audiences can project their hopes and ideals. In this sense, fictional treatments of Abraham Lincoln are "telling fictions." If we look carefully, these stories reflect back to us (or *tell* us) our collective desires and fears.

FROM SENTIMENTALITY TO SENSATIONALISM: THE EVOLUTION OF THE FICTIONAL LINCOLN

To date, Lincoln has appeared as a character in countless novels, plays, and short stories, as well as in more than 250 television and film productions in the United States alone.[4] We can find him in fictional texts dating to just after the Civil War, and best-selling novels and big-budget films still continue to feature fictional Lincolns. In the last chapter, we saw that representations of Lincoln in biographies have changed over time in accordance with changing tastes, values, and ways of life. Likewise, over the past 150 years, fictional representations of Lincoln have changed. Indeed, the transformation of the fictional Lincoln has been even more dramatic than shifts in the biographer's Lincoln.

Going back to some of the earliest fictional representations of Lincoln, in novels such as Henry Ward Beecher's 1867 *Norwood* and Edward Eggleston's 1888 *The Graysons*, Lincoln was "a saintly and sentimentalized figure, a heroic individual without flaws or personal demons."[5] However, the twentieth century saw both a growing number of fictional Lincolns and more complexity and diversity in representations of the sixteenth president. We can still find the sentimentalized, heroic Lincoln in recent films and novels, but we will also find the conflicted Lincoln, the cunning Lincoln, the macho Lincoln, and even the sexy Lincoln.

For the purposes of analysis, it is possible to identify five broad genres of film and literature featuring fictional representations of Lincoln: biographical fiction/biopic, period suspense, contemporary suspense, romance, and science fiction/fantasy.[6] While these are the most common genres in which fictional Lincolns are found as principal characters, Lincoln (and fictional characters who dress up as Lincoln) may also be found in a vast range of other genres, from action-adventure (Arnold Schwarzenegger's *Kindergarten Cop*), to socially conscious satire (Spike Lee's *Bamboozled*), to revisionist historical fiction (Thomas Dixon's *The Clansman* and D. W. Griffith's *The Birth of a Nation*), to light comedy (*Bill and Ted's Excellent Adventure*).[7] Such multifarious depictions, though fascinating, are unfortunately beyond the scope of this chapter. Instead, let us focus on representations of Lincoln in the five key genres listed above. Of central concern is not only how Lincoln is represented in each genre but also what such representations tell us about our collective fantasies and fascinations.

LINCOLN IN BIOGRAPHICAL FICTION:
THE SIXTEENTH PRESIDENT AS BOY SCOUT

According to American Boy Scout law, a scout is "trustworthy, loyal, helpful, friendly, courteous, kind, obedient, cheerful, thrifty, brave, clean and reverent."[8] With a few notable qualifications, this aptly characterizes Abraham Lincoln in works of biographical fiction. Let us take as our examples Gore Vidal's (1984) novel—later a television miniseries—*Lincoln*; William Safire's (1988) *Freedom: A Novel of Abraham Lincoln and the Civil War*; Richard Slotkin's (2000) *Abe: A Novel*; and John Ford's biopic *Young Mr. Lincoln* (1939), starring Henry Fonda in the title role.

Slotkin's *Abe* and Ford's *Young Mr. Lincoln* both cover Lincoln's early life, ending with his early adulthood in Illinois, and yet the two works provide a neat contrast that demonstrates the ways that Lincoln's image has changed over time in American fiction and film. In 1939, Henry Fonda portrayed a humble, patriotic, god-fearing Lincoln who chops wood for a needy client, falls in love with a beautiful girl, and calms an angry mob with good humor and a Bible verse. A man of the frontier, he is not afraid to use his strength and size in defense of justice. "By jing, I said listen to me!" he tells a lynch mob. "I can lick any man here, hands down." But with his towering stature and his obvious moral authority, no man steps forward to challenge him. He is compassionate and self-deprecating, aiding a poor widow and describing himself as "just a sorta' jack-legged lawyer." He is "plain Abraham Lincoln," a good American who knows "what's right and what's wrong" and stands up for truth and human dignity.

Similarly, Slotkin's young Abe has an innate and well-calibrated moral compass. Upon first reading the Declaration of Independence as a boy, he is immediately struck by the hypocrisy and immorality of slavery and its utter incompatibility with the democratic principles proclaimed in that foundational document.[9] He also has a deep sense of honor and propriety. He dutifully turns over all his hard-earned wages to his father, is quick to defend the modesty of women, and, despite his powerful heterosexual desire, refuses to patronize prostitutes whom he suspects of plying their trade under duress.[10] He is strong and brave and resourceful. He is "worth any three men with an ax in his hands," he can "whup" even the most imposing opponent in a fair fight, and in a harrowing flatboat journey down the Mississippi, he repeatedly saves his companions from certain death.[11] "You saved our hash a dozen times or more," says a grateful fellow traveler.[12] He has a fierce natural intelligence and a burning ambition to escape the small-minded confines of frontier society to make something of himself. He is firm in his convictions that American democratic government is "the most perfect that ever was" and that the great American republic is a place "where a man who knows things can become anything he wants."[13]

This fictional Abe befriends a local Indian who teaches him to "listen" to nature and have compassion for all living creatures.[14] Young Lincoln is stirred by the cause of equal rights for women and blacks and is sickened by the inhumanity of slavery.[15] He abhors the injustice of a "Gov'ment that says men are equal in their rights then lets them make niggers of the rest [and] sell men women children like they was hogs."[16] After spending time with a runaway slave and witnessing the horrors of the New Orleans slave markets, Lincoln champions the humanity of blacks and works desperately to prevent a slave from being sold "down the river" to a life of hard labor on plantations in the Deep South.[17]

Slotkin's Abe is an exemplar of manhood, of morality, and of the great American Dream. Like Henry Fonda's "Young Mr. Lincoln," he is a Boy Scout in thought, word, and deed. And yet while Henry Fonda's 1939 Lincoln is a man of flawless virtue, Slotkin's Lincoln, coming to the page in the year 2000, is a man of passions and imperfections. Despite pledging never to be a "man of blood," in a fit of "blood-rage" he savagely beats a bully.[18] Despite his deep respect for women and his strong sense of sexual propriety, he loses his virginity to a "clean" and willing prostitute.[19] He furthermore commits what some of his fellows see as "blasphemy" by subtly questioning the existence of God in a debate on slavery.[20] Biographical fiction from the latter half of the twentieth century and into the twenty-first century is more likely than earlier texts to expose some cracks in the perfect veneer of the mythic Lincoln.

Gore Vidal's (1984) *Lincoln* and William Safire's (1988) *Freedom* are consistent with this trend. Both novels concentrate on Lincoln's presidential years, and both present Lincoln through the eyes of his friends and his enemies. This narrative structure creates a more multidimensional Lincoln, a man who is "a saint" to some and an ignorant, weak buffoon to others, "a well-meaning but inadequate man."[21] Nonetheless, despite offering many conflicting opinions of the sixteenth president in their novels, both Vidal and Safire suggest certain basic truths: that Lincoln was intelligent, politically astute, ambitious, honorable (though not above manipulating circumstances for certain political and military ends), brave, moderate in habits and beliefs, compassionate, and good humored.

In Safire's novel, this overwhelmingly positive and idealized view of Lincoln is presented through the fictionalized diary of presidential secretary John Hay. Entries from the behind-the-scenes diary are peppered throughout the novel, providing the reader with what appears to be the most candid and most accurate perspective on Lincoln. It is John Hay's words that seem to capture Safire's own view of Lincoln:

I respect him, I admire him, I even love him, and it will be my goal in life to make certain the world knows what a great man he is, but I also know he is neither the lovable Lincoln of the funny stories and Western ways, nor the hateful dictator-baboon of the newspaper legends. He is a hardened man who gives in at the edges but will not give an inch on his central idea, who knows how to say no, who puts the fervor of the Declaration of Independence ahead of the compromises of the constitution, and who is looking for a general who is willing to take and inflict heavy casualties to save the Union.[22]

The Lincoln of Safire and Vidal is a political and military hero whose personal flaws only serve to make him more heroic. He is "a man of powerful passions when it comes to women," one character observes in Vidal's novel, but also a man with "powerful control over himself." Yes, he patronizes prostitutes and even contracts syphilis, but he has also "saved the honor of more women than any other man I ever knew. The way they would fling themselves at him."[23] He is a man of his times who does not question the assumption that blacks and whites are inherently different and "the colored race [is] inferior to the white."[24] Nonetheless, he is a tireless champion of the notion that even inferior men deserve to enjoy the fruits of their own labor. And although he does not come to the presidency with a plan to abolish slavery (for he believes he lacks the constitutional authority to do so), he does everything in his power to preserve the Union and prevent the further spread of slavery. So Lincoln in these biographical novels is not an angel; he is not an abolitionist or a champion of black equality. He is flawed, and yet despite his flaws he dedicates his life to higher constitutional and divine principles. One underlying lesson of such novels is that heroes are not people without flaws; they are people who rise to greatness despite their flaws.

Safire, Vidal, and Slotkin all take great pains to ground their narratives in documented historical facts. Readers of such biographical fiction find the real people, places, and events of Lincoln's life as well as countless everyday details of nineteenth-century life—the food, clothing, landscapes, labor, and pastimes of Lincoln's age. Typically, biographical novels about Lincoln also include many of his most famous quotations—"If slavery is not wrong, then nothing is wrong," "better angels of our nature," "with malice toward none"—as well as appendices with notes about authenticity and sources. Safire's mammoth volume, spanning more than 1,400 pages divided into nine "books" and 165 chapters, concludes with almost 200 pages of "sources and commentary." The inclusion of such material in biographical fiction lends an air of authenticity to the narrative construction of Abraham Lincoln as Boy Scout in chief.

LINCOLN IN PERIOD SUSPENSE:
THE MACGUFFIN PRESIDENT

Perhaps more than any filmmaker before him, Alfred Hitchcock popularized the "MacGuffin," a plot element that drives the action of the narrative while actually having little substance. In a spy movie, the MacGuffin might be mysterious and never-explained "top-secret files"; in an adventure novel it might be a legendary treasure. The characters may or may not reach their goal, and in fact sometimes the MacGuffin itself is almost entirely forgotten in the end, but it nonetheless serves to bring together the characters of the narrative in an atmosphere of heightened tension. In suspense novels set during the Civil War era, President Lincoln often serves as the MacGuffin. Villains conspire against him and intrigue swirls around him, but Lincoln himself is typically less a living, breathing character than a bland and distant abstraction.

Among many period suspense novels and films featuring Abraham Lincoln, let us consider David Robertson's (1997) novel *Booth*; Steven Wilson's (2008) *President Lincoln's Spy*; three young-adult novels, Anna Myers's (2005) *Assassin*, Ann Rinaldi's (1999) *An Acquaintance with Darkness*, and Gary Blackwood's (2005) *Second Sight*; and Robert Redford's (2010) period film *The Conspirator*. All of these suspense narratives revolve around plots to assassinate Abraham Lincoln. As the title of Robertson's novel suggests, *Booth* explores the conspiracy from the perspective of the assassin John Wilkes Booth. *President Lincoln's Spy* centers on a separate group of fictional villains conspiring against the president. The three young-adult novels feature naive adolescents who unwittingly stumble into plots against Lincoln, and *The Conspirator* explores the trial of Mary Surratt, the only woman charged in the conspiracy to assassinate Lincoln. While portrayals of Lincoln's enemies vary a great deal in these narratives, representations of Lincoln himself are conventional and insipid.

Perhaps most striking in this pool of suspense narratives is the representation of John Wilkes Booth. In the young-adult novels, he is handsome, charming, and charismatic, but also a callous womanizer, an unapologetic racist, and a staunch defender of slavery. Blacks are an inferior race, he believes, and "the colored man is better off as a slave."[25] Significantly, all of these novels suggest that Booth was mentally unstable. He was "a devil," driven by irrational "blind fury" against Lincoln, and even Booth himself wonders whether he might be "destined for insanity" like his father.[26] He paces a boardinghouse parlor, "disheveled, angry. Like an alien thing . . . his eyes burning . . . ranting and swearing" like a "madman."[27] He "reminds you very much of a caged animal, the way he paces nervously . . . the slightly wild, slightly dangerous look in his eyes."[28] The young adult's Booth is part demon, part beast, and unambiguously pathological.

By contrast, in Robertson's *Booth*, Lincoln's assassin is a largely sympathetic character. He grows up in a family that befriends "Christian, Jew and Muslim" alike; he finds slavery distasteful and even defends his black driver against a racist insult.[29] He harbors no personal antipathy for Lincoln and even finds him "a gentleman, and very captivating in his person."[30] Nonetheless, he becomes convinced that the only way to stop the bloody war is to assassinate Lincoln. Robertson's Booth is a man of powerful passions and tragic flaws. With his deeply romantic nature, he is drawn to the noble and vulnerable Mary Surratt, but his love ultimately destroys her. A star of the stage, he suffers from delusions of grandeur and believes that by eliminating Lincoln he will become the savior of the South, "a type of Christ."[31] Even in this more nuanced and sympathetic portrayal, Booth appears mentally unbalanced. Certainly his friends believe his assassination plans to be "insane dreams . . . incredible madness," even as they are drawn into the plot.[32] In Robertson's novel, Booth is not so much a "devil" as a gifted but deeply troubled man whose mania leads not only to his own downfall but to the downfall of the fundamentally good people who are attracted to him.

Similarly varied representations of Lincoln's enemies are found in *President Lincoln's Spy* and in *The Conspirator*. In *President Lincoln's Spy*, a noble and headstrong captain in the Union army is recruited to infiltrate a group of conspirators, Dickensian villains of the seediest variety. There is the brutal career criminal with his "shaggy black hair . . . his thick body . . . misshapen knuckles . . . heavy chin and battered nose." His plot against Lincoln is driven by racial hatred and his belief that "Lincoln and those other nigger lovers want this country overrun by those black bastards."[33] There is the dissipated lawyer dabbling in crime to pay his gambling debts. There are insatiably greedy war profiteers, several corrupt bureaucrats, and a little, bespectacled, clubfooted poet who is good at heart but easily manipulated into treachery by his criminal associates. In contrast to these traitors, the Union captain is intelligent, forthright, courageous, and fiercely patriotic. "This is for Lincoln!" he exclaims as he punches one of the villains in the face.[34] In this period suspense novel, good and evil are starkly delineated.

In Redford's *The Conspirator*, on the other hand, there is a blurry line between villain and victim. The film centers on the trial of Mary Surratt, accused conspirator in the assassination of President Lincoln. Her young lawyer, Frederick Aiken, doubts her innocence and has qualms about taking the case. However, when he realizes that powerful forces within the government are conspiring to deny her a fair hearing and ensure a conviction, he mounts an earnest defense. Throughout the film, Surratt's role in the conspiracy is uncertain. She may or may not have been a party to the assassination plot, but her dignity suggests a nobility of spirit, quite unlike the brutal, deranged criminality of the conspirators in other period suspense pieces. In fact, the real villains in the film are not the conspirators themselves but the state, the media, and the public who are so hungry for vengeance that they will do whatever it takes to see someone—anyone—hang for Lincoln's murder.

In contrast to the diverse depictions of the Lincoln conspirators in these suspense narratives, representations of Lincoln are surprisingly uniform. He is benevolent, compassionate, honorable, sensible, good humored, and fatherly. The protagonists of the young-adult novels express respect and affection for Lincoln. One teen heroine says she "admired Mr. Lincoln beyond my weak ability to express."[35] He is the "beloved president," "a saint."[36] One young boy looks up to Lincoln because he had risen to the top "through hard work and determination."[37] In *President Lincoln's Spy*, the heroic captain admits that he has a generally low opinion of politicians, but he notes that Lincoln is an exception.

> Here was a different kind of politician; a man with ideas uncluttered by rhetoric, a man whose desire for office didn't reduce him to pandering to the lowest layer of the population. Lincoln's thinking was clear, and his powers of analysis rendered even the most complex problems into simple issues of right and wrong.[38]

In *Booth*, even Lincoln's assassin recognizes the "innate generosity of his character."[39] Although some narratives feature deranged conspirators railing against the president, it is clear that their extreme views are simply the products of their unbalanced minds or their pathological prejudices.

While these tales of suspense represent Lincoln in uniformly positive ways, he is not a fully fleshed-out character. There are almost no encounters between Lincoln and the main characters, and almost no coverage of Lincoln's words, thoughts, or actions. Rather, he is largely an abstraction, a symbol of goodness, patriotism, and authority, a symbol of the nation itself. In fact, in some of these narratives, Lincoln is barely there at all. We glimpse him only from a distance, or, as in *The Conspirator*, we see him only briefly before he is struck down by the assassin's bullet. Nonetheless, in these narratives, it is the *idea* of Lincoln that fuels the plot with tension and pathos. Most readers will know how the conspiracy actually ended, so there can be no suspense in the story's ending. Rather, the suspense comes from mounting threats to the MacGuffin president and the nation for which he stands.

LINCOLN IN CONTEMPORARY SUSPENSE: THE UNIMPEACHABLE PRESIDENT

In John's McKinsey's (2008) novel *The Lincoln Secret*, a journalist expresses his dismay when he is assigned a story investigating the possibility of President

Lincoln's illegitimate birth. "You want to attack the person who many consider to be the greatest president we have ever had by calling him a bastard?" he asks his editor. "You want to cast shadows on the 'Great Emancipator'?"[40] Like its cousin the period suspense narrative, the contemporary Lincoln suspense story often features the sixteenth president as a MacGuffin, the abstract object of concern. But in these contemporary settings, the MacGuffin president has a very distinct character. He is the embodiment of American history and American values. His name is synonymous with the noblest of human (and national) virtues. His image is thus unimpeachable. As the main characters of the stories encounter the full spectrum of modern corruption, vice, and violence, Lincoln's nobility shines all the brighter in contrast.

Among these contemporary suspense narratives, we will consider three novels, John McKinsey's (2008) *The Lincoln Secret*, quoted above; James Best's (2008) *The Shut Mouth Society*; and Brad Smith's (2005) *Busted Flush*, in addition to the 2007 action-adventure film *National Treasure: Book of Secrets*.[41] Although each story line is quite distinctive, there are striking similarities among these tales. Each of the novels centers on a salt-of-the-earth male protagonist with little knowledge of Lincoln. In the course of uncovering a Lincoln mystery, he meets a feisty and beautiful woman, and the two strike up a partnership to solve the mystery. The film offers a slight variation on this formula, featuring an expert historical treasure hunter as the protagonist, assisted by his (perhaps predictably) feisty and beautiful estranged girlfriend. In all of these narratives, the main characters are pitted against powerful and shadowy figures, good triumphs over ill, and the villains get their comeuppance.

The hero of *The Lincoln Secret* is Sean Johnson, a freelance journalist and an ex-Navy Seal special ops commando. He is handsome and charming with a winning smile, and he quickly gains the trust and confidence of everyone around him. He is highly skilled in hand-to-hand combat and in evading capture by the powerful organization that is stalking him, and he readily puts his life on the line to help others simply because "it's the right thing to do."[42] James Best's hero in *The Shut Mouth Society* is Greg Evarts, a down-to-earth police detective and, coincidentally, an ex-special-ops officer. He is a humble man of simple tastes with an old-fashioned sense of chivalry. He is also muscular, well armed, technologically savvy, and a fierce fighter. In *Busted Flush*, the hero is Dock Bass, a laconic, plainspoken carpenter. His large frame is as solid as the structures he painstakingly builds by hand. He lives simply and quietly; he cannot abide liars, cheats, or social climbers; and he is not afraid of getting bloodied in a fight for a good cause. One character jokes that he should have a white horse to ride as he saves the world.[43] Finally, the hero of *National Treasure* is Benjamin Franklin Gates, a swashbuckling scholar with a vast knowledge of even the most obscure historical facts. He is highly intelligent and daring, with the skills to break into the queen's private office in Buckingham Palace and briefly kidnap the president of the United States. Although his previous exploits have left him a wealthy man, he cares little for money. Rather, he is on a quest for historical truth and the defense of his family honor. All of these heroes possess extraordinary mental and physical prowess, remarkable courage, and a strong code of honor.

We find greater differences between the heroines of these suspense narratives. Kimberly Poole, in *The Lincoln Secret*, is a divorced mother and a small business owner. She is confident and attractive and proves to be cool and competent when facing the ruthless villains who are trying to silence her. By contrast to this middle-class, middle-American mother, Patricia Baldwin in *The Shut Mouth Society* comes from a moneyed family and has expensive tastes. A strikingly beautiful history professor at an elite West Coast university, she has made a high-profile career of debunking idealistic myths about Abraham Lincoln. She is obsessive about diet and fitness and has a low opinion of men. However, when murder shatters her well-ordered world, she opens up both emotionally and sexually and becomes a fearless fighter with an appetite for danger. In the end, she is part damsel in distress and part Rambo, and she realizes how wrong she has been to criticize Lincoln. Like Patricia Baldwin, Amy Morris in *Busted Flush* possesses expensive tastes and startling beauty. A celebrated television "personality," she longs to be taken seriously as a journalist and will resort to lies, bribery, and shameless flirtation to get her story. She is African American, but in her success she has lost almost all traces of her heritage. Her father barely recognizes her and says she's "looking decidedly . . . Caucasian these days."[44] Although she attempts to manipulate the hero at the behest of her boss, in the end she aids the protagonist in his quest for justice and historical truth. Finally, *National Treasure* features Abigail Chase, historian at the National Archives. A beautiful and highly skilled researcher, she met and fell in love with the hero during a previous escapade. Now she has grown weary of his obsessive historical quests, and the two have separated. She nonetheless trusts his instincts and his competence and joins him to uncover certain secrets related to Lincoln's assassination. Despite the differences between these heroines, each is characterized by beauty, impressive skills, and natural physical courage. All of these women are cool and resourceful in the face of extreme danger, and all are sexually available.

There are three marked similarities between the villains in contemporary Lincoln suspense narratives: they are typically secretive, spectacularly wealthy and powerful, and Southern in origin or sympathy. *The Lincoln Secret* features a Georgia state senator and his defense contractor brother who will stop at nothing to protect their family's Civil War secrets. In *The Shut Mouth Society*, there is the fabulously rich North Carolina businessman who is willing to betray his country in order to expand his empire and defend the honor of the South. In *Busted Flush*, a secretive millionaire collector employs Thaddeus St. John, an unscrupulous antiques dealer, and his brawny henchman, Stonewall Martin, in an attempt to defraud the hero. St. John, an aging gay man who wears makeup and favors mauve cashmere sweaters and silk scarves, passes himself off as a Southern gentleman and a Civil War historian. Stonewall Martin is a hulking thug with an unkempt beard, a buckskin coat, and a T-shirt proclaiming "The South Will Rise Again." Finally, *National Treasure: Book of Secrets* features the menacing Mitch Wilkinson, a ruthless dealer in Civil War artifacts. A rich Southern military man who is hungry for fame, he has both the skills and the resources to manipulate the hero into solving a potentially lucrative historical mystery.

As a MacGuffin character in contemporary suspense narratives, Abraham Lincoln is a constant source of tension. It is the promise of uncovering secrets related to the sixteenth president that draws all of the characters into the plot. And yet there is almost no exploration of Lincoln as a character. There is a strong assumption among virtually all of the characters in these narratives that Lincoln's greatness is not open to debate. He is simply "the Great Emancipator," "the great man," "the greatest President."[45] He is "a legend, a hero," almost "superhuman," the "most admired person in our history."[46] He "put an end to slavery," he "saved our country," and "under Lincoln we became one nation."[47] The lone dissenter from the cult of Lincoln, the skeptical history professor in *The Shut Mouth Society*, is proven utterly wrong in her criticisms of the sixteenth president. In the end she realizes that he was even greater than legend made him out to be. Even exposed to the harshest of modern scrutiny, the reputation of Abraham Lincoln emerges from the contemporary suspense narrative not only unscathed but also further enhanced.

LINCOLN IN ROMANCE NOVELS: THE PINUP PRESIDENT

"His big hands caught her arms, crushed her to him, as if she weighed nothing. His mouth was hot on her lips and his breath burned her cheek." Suddenly restraining himself, he pulled away from her, but she could "see the naked desire in his gray eyes."[48] Although the number of Lincoln romances is small, these narratives provide particularly vivid depictions of a living, breathing (sometimes panting) Abraham Lincoln. The two most prominent Lincoln romances are Barbara Hambly's (2006) *The Emancipator's Wife*, quoted above, and Irving Stone's (1954) *Love Is Eternal*. Other works, while not romance novels in the strictest sense, also provide glimpses of Lincoln's intimate relationships with women. For instance, Tony Wolk's (2004) *Abraham Lincoln: A Novel Life*, with its time-traveling Honest Abe, might best be classified as a work of science fiction, but at the heart of the narrative is Lincoln's brief but intense relationship with a twentieth-century woman. These romantic tales portray Lincoln as an extraordinary man who is nonetheless subject to ordinary human frailties and even animal passions. However, far from detracting from the image of the Great Emancipator, such narratives seem to suggest that Lincoln is all the more impressive for achieving such greatness despite being made of the same flawed raw material as the rest of us.

Typical of the romance genre more generally, the real protagonist in both *The Emancipator's Wife* and *Love Is Eternal* is a woman, Mary Todd Lincoln. Contrary to some biographers' unflattering representations of Mary, in these romantic tales, as a young woman, she is intelligent and independent and dreams of true love. She is beautiful, charming, and emotional, but also strong and resilient. Later in her life, she is shown to be a loving, devoted, and protective wife and mother and the beloved equal partner of Abraham Lincoln. After the death of two of her sons, the strains of war and public scrutiny, and a serious head injury in a carriage accident, she is plagued by blinding headaches and is often unable to control her emotions. But even as her behavior grows more erratic, she never loses the love of her adoring husband. Also typical of the genre are the steamy descriptions of the couple's passion. There is the heat of his body, "the naked hunger of his kiss," and "the hoarse gasp of his breath," while she half fears, half wishes that they would fall "coupling like animals in the hot darkness of the parlor."[49]

Lincoln himself is an exemplar of American manhood. Mary admires "the powerful muscles and the indestructible male strength of him." He is "almost like an oak tree" with his "incredibly virile trunk."[50] He is humble and self-critical, gentle and honorable, hardworking, courageous, and a natural leader of men. He despises slavery and signs the Emancipation Proclamation even though he believes it will cost him his life.[51] His character contrasts starkly with other men in the stories. For instance, while Lincoln is unconcerned with superficial matters of personal appearance, Stephen A. Douglas is described as "a dandified little dynamo," a "steam engine in britches," looking "natty" in his expensive suits. Mary finds him "slightly repellent."[52] And when the two men are asked whether they would ever consent to legally represent a slaveholder attempting to reclaim a fugitive slave in Illinois, Douglas says that it would be his professional duty to do so. Lincoln, on the other hand, answers no. "I would never raise my voice for slavery. . . . I consider it no part of my obligation as a lawyer to defend anyone who is attempting to bring slavery to a free land."[53] This Lincoln has a firm sense of right and wrong and will not sacrifice his principles for the sake of expediency.

The Lincoln of Tony Wolk's *Abraham Lincoln: A Novel Life* is likewise both principled and compassionate. When Lincoln falls asleep in 1865 and inexplicably awakes in 1955, he finds an immediate connection with Joan Matcham, a young widow who has lost both her husband and her child to a plane crash. The two are drawn together by their experiences of loss and loneliness, and Joan finds him "kind . . . gentle . . . quiet," "considerate . . . generous," a man totally at ease with himself, with "such a pure quality about him."[54] His spirits are buoyed by seeing evidence of racial and gender equality in mid-twentieth-century America. He says that he is a strong supporter of women's suffrage and would gladly welcome abolitionist Frederick Douglass into his house "any day of the week."[55] When he learns that he will die in 1865, he does not fear returning to that time. "We all have to die. . . . There is no cheating death," he observes, apparently untroubled at the thought of dying for "a good and vital cause."[56] In this narrative, Lincoln is a willing martyr, "the father of our country," "the Father of Fathers," but he is also a man of flesh and blood who finds comfort in the arms of a desirable woman.[57]

Twentieth- and twenty-first-century Lincoln romances celebrate not only the national ideals of compassion, honor, and self-sacrifice but also contemporary gender ideals. Here, Mary is (with the exception of her emotional instability later in life) the very model of modern American womanhood, smart and assertive, nurturing and charming, and as proficient in the realm of politics as in the domestic arts. As a young woman, she rebels against sexism and longs for "a man who will accept me as an equal."[58] For his part, Lincoln is the model of modern American masculinity, strong and tender, hardworking and well respected by his fellow men, virile and firmly heterosexual, and a man committed to women's equality. He is a man who, despite his weighty public responsibilities, still takes the time to change an infant's diaper, brush his wife's hair, and spend "long sweet nights of lovemaking and talk."[59] He is the modern woman's romantic ideal, her pinup president.

LINCOLN IN SCIENCE FICTION AND FANTASY: THE GREAT TRANSMOGRIFIER

Although Abraham Lincoln is certainly most often celebrated for his fight against the expansion of slavery, in science fiction and fantasy narratives we are more likely to find him battling vampires, werewolves, zombies, aliens, and even rapacious lunar property developers. In Lincoln, the creators of such narratives find a flexible hero, a general symbol of good whose specific characteristics can be bent to suit the needs of the plot. While Seth Grahame-Smith's (2010) *Abraham Lincoln: Vampire Hunter* is the highest profile of such tales, other recent offerings include the graphic novels *The New Adventures of Abraham Lincoln* (1998) and *Jesus Hates Zombies, Lincoln Hates Werewolves* (2009–2010), and prominent classics such as Philip K. Dick's (1972) *We Can Build You*, and *Star Trek:* "The Savage Curtain" (1969). The character of Lincoln changes dramatically from one period to the next, reflecting both the fantasies and the anxieties of the time.

Let us begin with a review of the social context in which the classics *Star Trek* (1969) and *We Can Build You* (1972) were produced. In the tumultuous 1960s and early 1970s, Americans witnessed the rise of the civil rights and modern feminist movements; the assassinations of John F. Kennedy, Robert F. Kennedy, and Dr. Martin Luther King Jr.; the escalation of the Cold War arms race and space race, culminating in the first human journeys into outer space; and the expansion of U.S. involvement in the Vietnam War. The same period saw the flowering of the hippie counterculture with its challenges to conventional social norms and its emphasis on pacifism, free love, nature, and the exploration of human consciousness and spirituality, often with the assistance of mind-altering drugs.

The original television series *Star Trek* (1966–1969) grew out of this period and often fairly explicitly referenced the concerns of the day. Among other pressing social issues of the time, the show addressed topics related to racial segregation, feminism, the Cold War, and the hippie movement. At first glance, the *Star Trek* episode "The Savage Curtain" (1969) is an exploration of human nature. Orbiting a new planet, the crew of the *Enterprise* is unexpectedly greeted by Abraham Lincoln. Although it is soon apparent to Captain Kirk that this is not the real Lincoln, the visitor bears an uncanny resemblance to the original, both in his appearance and in his character. He is brave, wise, humble, and forthright, and Kirk admits that the sixteenth president is his personal hero. When Kirk and science officer Spock beam down to the planet with Lincoln, an alien entity pits them in a battle to the death against a group of notorious galactic villains in order to better understand the concepts of good and evil. Kirk does not wish to fight, but with the lives of his crew hanging in the balance, he has no choice. With echoes of both the Civil War and the Vietnam War, Lincoln tells Kirk that although he deplores war, sometimes when war is thrust upon us, we must stand and fight. He reminds Kirk that he is a "backwoodsman" who can handle himself in a skirmish, and indeed he proves a competent comrade in arms.

In the end, Lincoln once again sacrifices himself for the greater good, Kirk and Spock prevail over the villains, and the alien learns the difference between good and evil. The audience is reminded of the futility of war but also of the nobility of self-sacrifice when war becomes inevitable. It was a message for all Americans at the time, no matter what their position on the contentious conflict in Vietnam.

Published just three years after "The Savage Curtain" aired, Philip K. Dick's *We Can Build You* likewise reflects the concerns of the age. The futuristic novel is set in an America where colonization of the moon is in its early stages, and the state closely monitors and medicates the population. In the quest for a moneymaking product, inventor Maury Rock and his daughter Pris invent a "simulacrum" (cyborg) that perfectly duplicates the appearance, thoughts, mannerisms, and character of Abraham Lincoln. Maury's partner, Louis Rosen, is appalled by the invention. The simulacrum is so convincingly human that Louis no longer knows what it means to be human.[60] Feeling his own humanity and sanity slipping away, Rosen develops an obsessive infatuation with the "cruel, cold and sterile thingthing" Pris, who has entered into a sordid alliance with an unscrupulous lunar property developer.[61] Rosen seeks the advice and assistance of the Abraham Lincoln simulacrum, which is kinder, more compassionate, and in some ways more human than Pris. This Lincoln is wise, calm, and good humored, a defender of "the proper values in life," a champion of love, an exemplar of fair play, and indeed rather "like Christ."[62] In the end, neither the Lincoln nor Rosen proves able to withstand the strains of a society increasingly dominated by technology, psychoactive drugs, and an intrusive state. Thus, Dick's novel mirrors some of the widespread anxieties and preoccupations of the early 1970s, and his synthetic Lincoln is, ironically, a reminder of a simpler, more natural way of life.

Two decades later, another Lincoln text reflected the issues of its day. In the late 1990s, the U.S. Congress was at an impasse. President Bill Clinton had been impeached, and his reputation was in tatters after the revelation of his affair with a White House intern. Speaker of the House Newt Gingrich led his party in a campaign to discredit and thwart the Democratic president, with the media gleefully feasting on both the public acrimony between the parties and the lurid details of the investigation into Clinton's sexual improprieties. It was in this climate that Scott McCloud published his graphic novel *The New Adventures of Abraham Lincoln* (1998). The plot features Byron Johnson, a twelve-year-old African-American schoolboy with a passion for American history. His teachers punish him for thinking critically about history, and his peers tease him for even caring about history until a brawny (and slightly green) Abraham Lincoln breaks through a brick wall to defend history. "That's right! I'm back!" he announces. "And this time I'm playing for keeps!"[63]

Lincoln then takes Byron on a magic carpet ride through history, but Byron begins to suspect that he is a fraud when he repeats common historical fallacies—that the Pilgrims came in peace and hosted a bountiful multicultural feast at the first Thanksgiving, that Native Americans welcomed the westward expansion of European settlers, that Benjamin Franklin was once president. Byron tries to warn the nation that the Lincoln imposter is plotting to take over the government, but Abe has already won over Washington by befriending a politician identified only as "Newt" and making jingoistic, sloganeering speeches. The public rallies behind this new Lincoln and calls for him to be installed as the forty-third president (supplanting Bill Clinton). Byron is relieved when the real Abraham Lincoln materializes to challenge the imposter, but the public prefers the imposter's demagoguery to the more complex and uncomfortable truths the real Lincoln offers them.

In a final showdown between the two Lincolns, we learn that the imposter is the tool of sinister extraterrestrials who are attempting to control the minds of Americans with devices shaped like the American flag. After the spirit of the real Lincoln animates the statue at the Lincoln Memorial and defeats the villains, he delivers a parting speech:

> My fellow Americans, I can't tell you what you want to hear. I don't know how to be your symbol. . . . It was *you* who built this temple. It was *you* who carved this body out of marble and set it upon a throne. . . . *Symbols*, America, can be useful tools. But beware of those who would have you used by them! . . . Otherwise, Dear Friends, there may yet come a day when a red, white and blue rectangle may be raised in importance high above the freedoms it once so humbly represented.[64]

In his "new adventures," Abraham Lincoln casts a harsh spotlight on the calculating national chauvinism and hollow rhetoric of contemporary politics, on media sensationalism, and on the willfully ignorant and gullible American public of the late 1990s.

Twenty-first-century resurrections of Lincoln in fantasy and science fiction often find him battling mythic creatures of darkness, including werewolves, zombies, vampires, and demons. The first decade of the century in America was defined, above all else, by the terrorist attacks of September 11, 2001. The attacks precipitated a fundamental shift in American society—a turn toward authoritarian policing practices, curtailed civil liberties, increased government secrecy, heightened state and media scaremongering, and a dramatic militarization of U.S. foreign policy. On top of these momentous developments, beginning in 2007–2008, the steepest economic downturn since the Great Depression dramatically increased unemployment, personal bankruptcy, and home foreclosures. The arcane banking and investment practices at the heart of the collapse were all but incomprehensible even to financial experts, leaving many ordinary Americans both stunned and confused at their losses. All of these events contributed to a climate of uncertainty, a sense of insecurity, and mounting fears of dangerous unseen forces.

It is perhaps not surprising, therefore, that authors working in this climate turned their imaginations to creatures who walk undetected among us, harboring evil intent and concealing their deadly powers. The phenomenally successful *Harry Potter* and *Twilight* series, among many others, center on potent hidden forces at work in our world that are beyond the control of ordinary humans.[65] *Abraham Lincoln: Vampire Hunter* (2010) and *Jesus Hates Zombies, Lincoln Hates Werewolves* (2009–2010) feature a muscular, steely nerved, axe-wielding Lincoln. In *Jesus Hates Zombies*, Jesus has returned to present-day Earth to fight a plague of zombies. Abraham Lincoln, inexplicably transported to the present from 1862 Washington, D.C., where he had been battling a werewolf, joins the resurrected Jesus, Freddy D (Frederick Douglass), and Mother T (Mother Theresa) in their fight against evil. Jesus, in this narrative, is the cocky, rebellious son of a jealous God who sends him back to Earth to teach him some humility. Lincoln is a noble, gore-splattered patriot. "The blood of freedom shall enrich the soil of this land that I so love!" he pronounces as he relieves a zombie of its head. In a final battle with a demon who seeks to destroy humanity, Lincoln implores his fellow crusaders, "If I should fail, do what you must to ensure that this land, and all the ideals it was built upon, remains."[66] Despite the iconoclasm of the work (God, for instance, is a dice-playing, Lean Pockets–eating, Hawaiian shirt–wearing "vindictive prick"[67]), the underlying message of the narrative is a conservative one: Jesus and Abraham Lincoln are enduring heroes; if we put our faith in them, they will deliver the nation and save humanity.

The narrative of *Abraham Lincoln: Vampire Hunter* is much subtler and more complex. (Spoiler alert: My analysis necessitates the discussion of certain plot elements here.) When young Abe discovers that his beloved mother has been killed by a vampire, he vows to hunt down and exterminate these evil creatures. But as he grows to manhood, he learns how deeply Southern vampires are implicated in the institution of slavery. Slavery provides the creatures with an ample supply of blood from a captive population with no means of resistance. Southern politicians, some in fear for their own lives, some in the thrall of the powerful creatures, do the political bidding of the vampire lobby. Lincoln realizes that he must enter politics in order to counter the growing influence of the undead.[68]

In this tale, we learn that vampires are responsible for many of the most disturbing and shameful episodes in American history. The disappearance of the first Roanoke settlers? Vampire predation. Frontier violence between Native Americans and European settlers? Engineered by vampires to cover up their own crimes against humanity. Massive outbreaks of diseases thought to be cholera, typhoid fever, or "milk sickness"? Actually plagues of vampirism. And the Civil War? It was not, in fact, a battle over slavery or states' rights or the preservation of the Union, but an attempt by vampires to seize control of the government, subjugate humans, and turn the nation into a kind of vampire Promised Land. It was, in short, a battle between good and evil. The unprecedented carnage of the war and countless humiliating Union losses on the battlefield are likewise readily explained by the presence of vampires in the Confederate ranks. President Lincoln recognized that with the vampire soldiers' superhuman strength, their contempt for human life, and their insatiable bloodlust, the Rebel army was almost unbeatable. Only out of military necessity did Lincoln then sign the Emancipation Proclamation in an attempt to starve the vampires into weakness by taking away their main source of sustenance, Southern slaves. Although the strategy led to the defeat of the vampire Confederacy, it ultimately cost Lincoln his life at the hands of the vengeful fiends.

Although *Abraham Lincoln: Vampire Hunter* is set, for the most part, in the mid-1800s, this Lincoln is a distinctly twenty-first-century hero. He pits himself against the hidden forces that threaten the nation from within (albeit vampires instead of terrorists or investment bankers). And he turns the vampire's own evil institution, slavery, against them. For a contemporary audience worn down by mortgage foreclosures, increasingly invasive security screenings, and color-coded terror alerts, the message is a comforting one: the forces conspiring against us may be powerful, but their comeuppance is inevitable. As Lincoln, with his well-known penchant for biblical allusions, might have observed, as ye sow, so shall ye reap.

AN OUTSIDER'S PERSPECTIVE ON LINCOLN: WHAT "TELLING FICTIONS" TELL US

As this chapter has demonstrated, Abraham Lincoln features in a vast array of fictional texts, and his portrayal changes considerably from one time period to the next. The real puzzle, from a social scientific perspective, is how to explain both the persistent presence of Lincoln as a fictional character and the dramatic transformations of that character over time. Three quite different theoretical perspectives shed light on representations of Lincoln in fiction: the first, psychoanalytical theory, focuses on the psychological needs of authors and audiences; the second, structural-functional theory, stresses the normative imperatives of society; and the third, the production of culture model, emphasizes the material processes that shape symbolic expression. Although some scholars fiercely defend their favored theoretical perspective and dismiss all others out of hand, arguably each of these social scientific models contributes to a fuller understanding of fictional constructions of Lincoln.

The Psychoanalytical Model

The insights of psychoanalytical theory are all too easily derided today as "psychobabble," the pretentious jargon employed by the self-obsessed "me generation" to justify its own foibles and deficiencies.[69] However, while classical psychoanalysis has been criticized (quite justly, I think) for its biases, assumptions, and omissions, it has nonetheless profoundly reshaped the way we think about ourselves and others, and it has much to offer the analysis of literary and artistic works.

Sigmund Freud, the founder of psychoanalysis, and his disciples bequeathed to us a new vocabulary of the inner life. It is now commonplace to hear people use concepts such as denial, displacement, sublimation, projection, and of course the unconscious to explain the workings of the mind. Building on Freud's revolutionary ideas about the unconscious, some social scientists have suggested that the tools of psychoanalysis can shed light not only on the deepest recesses of the individual psyche but also on the hidden desires, fears, and fantasies of a society as a whole. Leading social theorists including Erich Fromm, Herbert Marcuse, and Louis Althusser employed the principles of psychoanalytical theory to the study of social processes, particularly processes of political, economic, and ideological domination. Although there are substantial differences between these theorists, at the heart of their analyses is the conviction that if we want to understand what appear to be social pathologies—such as crime, racism, or violence—we need to understand how the individual unconscious both shapes and is shaped by the collective. Central to these discussions are the ways social institutions, such as the family, the mass media, and the state provide us with powerful messages that structure our thoughts and actions to the benefit of the most powerful and influential groups in society. Although we are often not even aware of our own indoctrination, these theorists argue, we are encouraged through implicit or sometimes explicit messages to repress our (natural) drives, accept the (false) desires imposed on us by those in power, and become obedient workers and eager consumers in a quest to satisfy the very appetites that have been created within us.

From this theoretical perspective, one way of exposing and resisting such manipulation is to examine the language and other symbols of a given group (an institution, an organization, even a nation) for the underlying messages that shape our understandings and experiences of the world. Works of literature and art, in particular, are ripe for such analysis because such works of imagination both flow from the creator's unconscious and engage the unconscious of the audience. We can bring such insights to bear on the use of Lincoln in fiction, television, and film. If we look carefully, reading against the grain for implicit messages, we can see denial, displacement, and desire at work through fictional representations of Lincoln.

Denial and displacement often work in tandem in Lincoln fiction. For instance, across a broad range of genres, authors deny historical complexity and lay the blame for our national traumas on a variety of straw-man villains. Lincoln, for the most part, is unambiguously and uncomplicatedly good, and his enemies—whether pathologically bigoted Southerners, fiendish madmen, or hordes of the undead—are evil. Supernatural characters such as vampires and zombies offer particularly clear-cut examples of denial and displacement. Such figures allow authors and audiences to deny some of the most disturbing aspects of the human experience—warfare, genocide, terrorism, and violence more generally, social and economic collapse, disease, and ultimately death itself—and project responsibility for them onto sinister phantasms. In his essays on understanding dreams, Freud asserted that we cannot take dream symbols (the people, places, objects, and events in our dreams) literally, because they often serve as proxies for issues that are too frightening or too threatening to confront directly. Arguably, fiction serves a similar purpose. Fantastical tales, in particular, allow us to glimpse our deepest fears, our shame, and our heart's desire in a well-disguised and therefore less discomfiting form.

Denial is at times quite conspicuous in Lincoln fiction, as evidenced by the wishful thinking and historical revisionism of some narratives. When a fictional Lincoln refuses to defend a slave owner in court (*Love Is Eternal*), or when he reminds readers that he was always a strong supporter of women's suffrage (*Abraham Lincoln: A Novel Life*) or that he had a close boyhood friendship with a local Indian who taught him profound lessons about man and nature (*Abe: A Novel*), the historical record is conveniently ignored. In one fictional work (*Second Sight*), even a monumental event in American history is rewritten, when—spoiler alert—the hero and heroine thwart the assassination attempt by John Wilkes Booth, and Lincoln lives on. "As you have seen," the book concludes, "even things that seem inevitable can be changed or prevented, often by people who may appear, at first glance, to be quite ordinary. . . . People like you."[70] The denial here is the denial of death itself, and the comforting message is that we can triumph even over the "inevitable."

Another form of denial in Lincoln fiction is found in its careful avoidance of homoerotic desire and its quite pronounced insistence upon Lincoln's heterosexuality. Particularly in romance novels and biographical fiction, Lincoln is a man with powerful sexual desires for women, and women find him equally desirable. By contrast, seldom in these fictional portrayals do we glimpse even emotional intimacy between Lincoln and the many men in his life. Moreover, the only gay character included in this sample of works, Thaddeus St. John (*Busted Flush*), is both ridiculous and contemptible. Campy, vain, pretentious, and an unrepentant swindler, he is constructed as the polar opposite of plain, honest, "straight" Abe. Such depictions across a wide variety of genres point to the long-standing culturally mandated repression of nonnormative sexual impulses in America.

Of course denial and displacement in Lincoln fiction also tell us something about desire—of both authors and audiences. In a sense, Lincoln fiction functions as national wish fulfillment. Through thrilling, fantastical, romantic, or even historically realistic fiction, we can glimpse our collective desires: our desire for a brawny, authoritative, yet loving father figure; our desire for gender and racial equality (at least in the abstract); our desire for social advancement, the American Dream; our desire for simple, black-and-white answers to complex issues; our desire for traditional gender and sexual roles, with beautiful, nurturing women following and being protected by their burly men; and our desire for the triumph of good over evil. In national wish fulfillment, class boundaries lose their sting, racial tensions evaporate, everyone is contented in their prescribed gender roles, and the American capitalist democracy is the pinnacle of human achievement, "the most perfect [system] that ever was."[71]

Perhaps most prominently, across all genres there is a palpable desire for a Christ figure, or even a god. The fictional Lincoln is "Christlike" (*We Can Build You*); he fights at the side of a resurrected Jesus (*Jesus Hates Zombies*); he is "superhuman" (*The Lincoln Secret*); he is "a saint" (*Love Is Eternal, An Acquaintance with Darkness*, and Gore Vidal's *Lincoln*).[72] He is a willing martyr (*Abraham Lincoln: A Novel Life* and *The Emancipator's Wife*); the "father of our country" and the "Father of Fathers" (*A Novel Life*).[73] His forgiveness knows no bounds. "If Pa had lived," his son Tad observes in *Love Is Eternal*, "he would have forgiven the man who shot him. Pa forgave everybody."[74] The fictional Lincoln is both giving and forgiving, willingly sacrificing himself for the sake of the nation, and offering absolution, of sorts, for our collective sins. Perhaps such forgiveness represents fulfillment of the deepest of our collective desires. In the realm of Lincoln fiction, slavery, warfare, genocide, and all manner of brutality and exploitation, all the transgressions of the "bad old days," are washed clean in the blood of the martyr president.

The Structural Functionalist Model

While the psychoanalytical model has considerable intuitive power, from a sociological perspective it does not give sufficient attention to the social function of fictional representations of Lincoln in American society today. We can draw insights on this point from structural functionalism, which can be traced back to the very beginnings of sociology as a discipline. Auguste Comte and Emile Durkheim, among other nineteenth-century thinkers, conceived of society as an organism that was only sustained through the smooth functioning of its constituent "organs," or social institutions. Therefore, according to this perspective, if we want to understand why any social phenomenon exists, we must ask how it functions to sustain society as a whole. While this theoretical perspective faded from prominence in the mid-twentieth century, its lasting influence is evident in sociological thought today.

Barry Schwartz, for instance, suggests that we can understand changing representations of Abraham Lincoln as the result of changing societal norms. He argues that in the 1960s, relatively idealized portrayals of Lincoln began to decline, with Lincoln gradually becoming a figure of fun, the butt of jokes, an all-purpose symbol of stodgy establishment ideals, and the object of what he characterizes as "benign ridicule."[75] Schwartz attributes this dramatic shift in fictional treatments of Lincoln to a number of interrelated factors. Certainly, as already noted, the tumultuous events of the 1960s (the civil rights movement, Watergate, and the Vietnam War, among others) led many people to question the legitimacy of long-standing power structures. At the same time, Schwartz explains, the midcentury "postmodern turn" in thought encouraged people to question authority and interrogate taken-for-granted "constructions" of reality. No idea, no institution, no hero was too sacred to challenge. As part of these changing currents of thought, our religious commitments lessened, and so did our willingness to see the nation's great men as the agents of divine will.[76] At the same time, as women, African Americans, and other minority groups began to make political and economic gains, Schwartz says, we became a less starkly divided nation, and therefore we no longer needed a sanctified figure, like Lincoln, to bind us together.[77]

Thus, the structural functionalist perspective suggests that from the time of his death through the mid-twentieth century, the exalted image of Abraham Lincoln served as a kind of glue that held a deeply fragmented nation together by reminding us of our shared norms and values. However, as previously marginalized groups began to achieve greater equality and more meaningful integration into the political and economic life of the nation, the need for unifying heroes diminished, and so did Lincoln's image. As Schwartz contends, "The very conditions that promote equal rights and make society more just and decent reduce Lincoln's stature by undermining tradition, authority and social boundaries."[78]

Collective Memory and the Production of Culture Model

While the psychoanalytical model explains fictional representations of Lincoln in terms of individual psychological needs, and the structural functionalist perspective explains such portrayals in terms of their function in society, we have yet to explain how desires, fears, and meanings associated with Abraham Lincoln spread from individual minds through societies (or nations) as a whole. For guidance on this question, we turn to research on collective memory and the production of culture.

The concept of "collective memory" grew out of the work of French sociologist Maurice Halbwachs, who asserted that memory resides not only in the minds of individuals but also in the very fabric of society.[79] Collective memory is embedded, he contended, in the language, images, material objects, and even bodily habits and mannerisms of a people. And, just like individual memories (which are inevitably reshaped when others share their own recollections with us), collective memory is constantly "supplemented" and "renovated" in light of new developments in the life of the group.[80] So, from this perspective, when we see shifting representations of Abraham Lincoln—whether in fiction or elsewhere—we are witnessing shifts in collective memory.

Just how such changes occur is another question. According to the "production of culture" model, although creative expressions—whether paintings, musical compositions, works of fiction, or even scientific theories—are often assumed to be the result of individual genius and inspiration, they are in fact profoundly shaped by mundane factors such as technology, copyright laws, corporate linkages, career reward structures, and market demands. Analyses of such factors have been used to explain the rise of everything from French impressionism and American adventure fiction to contemporary soap operas and rap music.[81]

Although space limitations necessitate only the most cursory foray into this broad field of inquiry, certain studies do bear directly on portrayals of Lincoln. Researchers have demonstrated, for instance, that where publishing output is controlled by a small number of firms, there is a high degree of standardization and stability in creative production because there is little motivation to take a risk on inventive texts. When the number of publishing firms increases, however, competition between them intensifies and opens up space for narrative innovation.[82] The same holds true for electronic media outlets. So some of the changes we have witnessed in the fictional portrayal of Lincoln may be due in part to increasing diversity and competition in the publishing, film, and television industries since the mid-twentieth century. Such competition no doubt encourages the use of a long-standing symbolic resource, Abraham Lincoln, in new and creative ways. Consider also recent technological changes—particularly the rise of digital culture, new niche marketing techniques, and the general acceleration of media flows—and it is hardly surprising that images of Lincoln have become so diverse. While traditionalists will regard such reinventions of Lincoln as evidence of the coarsening of American culture and the loss of respect for our national heroes, shifting fictional portrayals of Lincoln may have less to do with changed attitudes toward the sixteenth president than with changes in the processes of cultural production.

A Tale of Three Theories

Each of these theoretical models adds to our understanding of both why Abraham Lincoln is an enduring symbol in American fiction and why representations of him change dramatically over time. But one question remains to be answered: why do such representations matter? After all, these imaginative tales are not seriously asserting that the Civil War was caused by vampires or that Abraham Lincoln actually travels through time to battle zombies or extraterrestrials. Nonetheless, such inventive portrayals of Lincoln are worthy of careful analysis because of the capacity of fiction to both mirror and mold our collective memories and our perceptions of the here and now. It is no doubt comforting to conceal the anxieties and injustices of the past and present within the enchanting folds of fiction, but only critical examination of these narratives will help us come to terms with the traumas of history and the challenges we face today.

What Would Lincoln Do? The Sixteenth President in Twenty-First-Century Politics

$\mathcal{A}$few years ago, it became fashionable to wear bright plastic bracelets bearing the inscription *WWJD* ("What would Jesus do?"). Not only would the slogan remind you to live a godly life, it would also signal to others that you were a person of faith, a virtuous person, a person who was "right with the Lord." In the ideological and political landscape of twenty-first-century America, publicly calling God to your side can imbue your enterprise with respectability and solemnity. Calling on Lincoln serves much the same purpose. As David Donald has pointed out, almost from the moment of Lincoln's death, public figures have profited by "getting right with Lincoln."[1] The higher the stakes, it seems, the more likely they are to invoke the martyr president—the more likely they are to ask, in effect, "What would Lincoln do?"[2]

Of course, it was not always so. Abraham Lincoln was a polarizing figure in his time. Having come to office with less than 40 percent of the popular vote and against the fervent wishes of the South, the sixteenth president was portrayed in the political press as both angel and demon, both savior and tyrant (see figure 5.1). In the realm of American politics, there is nothing particularly unusual about such partisan representations. What is unusual is that, since Lincoln's assassination, he has been adopted as a de facto spokesperson by forces as diametrically opposed as agnostics and evangelists, socialists and corporate executives, the civil rights movement and the Ku Klux Klan. In today's political marketplace, both the Democratic and Republican parties capitalize on Lincoln's image, and his name is invoked in heated public debates over such issues as civil liberties, homosexuality, and abortion. Abraham Lincoln has become an icon of legitimacy. His name and image lend credibility, moral soundness, and a seemingly illustrious historical pedigree to radically conflicting causes. In this chapter, I examine the ways Lincoln is employed

Figure 5.1. Thomas Nast, "The President's Inaugural," *New York Illustrated News,* March 23, 1861. *Courtesy of Northern Illinois University Libraries*

in support of a remarkable range of political and ideological projects, and I consider what this means for the public sphere today.

IN LINCOLN WE TRUST: LINCOLN AND LEGITIMACY

A few short years after the Republican Party was founded, Abraham Lincoln became the first member of the fledgling party to take the White House. With such historical connections to the sanctified sixteenth president, it is hardly surprising that today's Republican Party often bills itself as the "Party of Lincoln" and claims Lincoln as a founding father. Since 1887, local party chapters have held fundraising and solidarity-building events known as "Lincoln dinners,"[3] or more recently "Lincoln-Reagan dinners," uniting Honest Abe with the patron saint of the neoconservative movement. Republican politicians and their supporters also frequently call on Lincoln in debates over public policy.

In the wake of the September 11, 2001, attacks on the United States, the Bush administration set about curtailing civil liberties in the name of "homeland security." Among the more controversial measures were the selective suspension of the writ of habeas corpus and the establishment of military tribunals to try suspected terrorists. While civil liberties groups decried such practices as unconstitutional, even totalitarian, the administration's supporters were quick to point out that President Lincoln had employed these same methods to combat the Southern rebellion that threatened to irrevocably fracture the nation. In a lecture for the Heritage Foundation, Rhode Island Supreme Court chief justice Frank Williams called Lincoln to the defense of the administration:

> During the American Civil War, Abraham Lincoln declared martial law and authorized [military tribunals] to try terrorists because military tribunals had the capacity to act quickly, to gather intelligence through interrogation, and to prevent confidential life-saving information from becoming public. . . . During Lincoln's presidency, he was criticized for taking what were considered "extra-constitutional measures." But in the end, the verdict of history is that Lincoln's use of power did not constitute abuse since every survey of historians ranks Lincoln as number one among the great presidents.[4]

In other words, Lincoln did it, so it must be okay.

Four years later, amid the hotly contested 2008 presidential race, Republican vice presidential candidate Sarah Palin likewise called Lincoln to her defense. At issue was her controversial comment that the 2003 U.S. invasion of Iraq was "a task from God." Asked whether she believed that the United States was fighting a "holy war," Palin explained that she had simply been paraphrasing President Lincoln.

> The reference there is a repeat of Abraham Lincoln's words when he said . . . never presume to know what God's will is, and I would never presume to know God's will or to speak God's words. But what Abraham Lincoln had said, and that's a repeat in my comments, was let us not pray that God is on our side in a war or any other time, but let us pray that we are on God's side. That's what that comment was all about.[5]

Of course Republicans by no means have a monopoly on Lincoln. In fact, during the 2008 presidential race, it was Democrats who most aggressively leveraged Lincoln's image. Even before Senator Barack Obama had officially entered the presidential race, parallels were being drawn with Lincoln's journey to the White House. Both men rose from humble origins to become Illinois lawyers. Both spent eight years in the Illinois legislature. Both served two years in Washington, D.C., before running for president. Both were outspoken in their opposition to wars in which the United States was engaged. In addition, some commentators saw the promising candidacy of an African American as the realization of Lincoln's vision of equal opportunity for all. The Obama campaign capitalized on such associations. In February 2007, Obama declared his candidacy on the steps of the Old State Capitol building in Springfield, Illinois, where Lincoln made his historic "house divided" speech. The candidate peppered his speech with allusions to Lincoln.

Throughout the lengthy campaign, Obama continued to quote Lincoln and adorn his speeches with recognizably Lincolnesque language. Political cartoons across the nation played up the connections between Obama and Lincoln in myriad ways: Lincoln, from his marble seat at the Lincoln Memorial, giving Obama a thumbs-up sign; Lincoln giving Obama a celebratory fist bump; and Obama trying on a stovepipe hat and asking his wife whether it was perhaps "too Lincolny" (see figure 5.2).[6] Internet commerce sites offered a full range of Lincoln-Obama merchandise, including buttons, T-shirts, hats, mugs, bumper stickers, and tote bags (see figure 5.3). And artists from New York to Los Angeles began producing double portraits of the men, sometimes even morphing them into a single figure to emphasize their unity of character and purpose. Oil was put to canvas, chalk to sidewalks, and at least one artist, Zilly Rosen, used 5,600 cupcakes to create a double portrait of Obama and Lincoln in an edible installation at the Smithsonian's American Art Museum.[7]

Little wonder, then, that on the eve of his election victory, Obama again echoed the man who had become his unofficial running mate. He thanked the "millions of Americans who volunteered, and organized, and proved that more

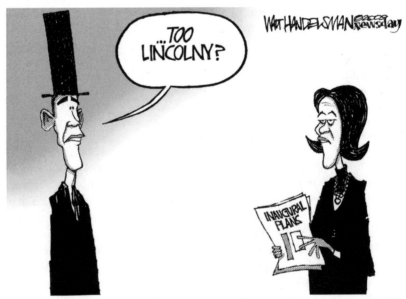

Figure 5.2. Obama invokes Lincoln (Walt Handelsman, January 15, 2009). *Tribune Media Services, Inc.*

**Figure 5.3. Lincoln endorses Obama on 2008 presiden-
tial campaign button.** *Photo by Matthew Behnke*

than two centuries later, a *government of the people, by the people, and for the
people has not perished from this Earth.*[8] In the buildup to Obama's inauguration,
with its Lincolnian theme of "A New Birth of Freedom," the president-elect
continued to cultivate his Lincoln connections. First, in a farewell letter to his
state, Obama employed the Lincoln quote perhaps most beloved by Illinoisans:
"To this place, and the kindness of these people, I owe everything." Then, the
Obama inaugural team announced that the president-elect would retrace part
of Lincoln's famed rail journey to Washington, D.C. and appear at a star-studded preinaugural concert on the steps of the Lincoln Memorial. And finally,
Obama chose to take his oath of office on the so-called Lincoln Bible, the one
Lincoln himself laid his hand upon at his first inauguration.

Throughout the 2008 presidential race and into his presidential term,
Obama capitalized on what has become one of America's most recognizable "brands," Abraham Lincoln, a brand strongly associated with honesty,
integrity, and courage. Obama sold his candidacy from the stage at Cooper
Union, New York, where Lincoln first rose to national attention in what
historian Harold Holzer has called "the most pivotal public appearance of his
career."[9] Obama began with a nod to the sixteenth president. "The last time
an Illinois politician made a speech here it was pretty good," he quipped.[10]
Obama returned to the same stage as president to sell a controversial financial
regulatory reform package in the midst of a national financial crisis in 2010.[11]

Again, it seems the higher the stakes, the more likely public figures are to invoke the spirit of Lincoln.

It is difficult to judge how effective such Lincoln appeals are, and whether Obama could have won as decisive a victory without the Great Emancipator by his side. What is clear, however, is that the pairing of Lincoln and Obama served not only Democratic political interests, but a range of economic interests as well: the manufacturers and retailers of Lincoln-Obama merchandise; the political artists whose works were purchased by media outlets, galleries, and manufacturers nationwide; and the publishers and broadcasters who sold feature stories on the parallels between the two men. It is likewise clear that Lincoln's name and image now serve as a kind of shorthand for "all-American" values. If some voters were uncomfortable with Obama's policies, or reluctant to vote for an African-American candidate, Lincoln, with his indisputably all-American credentials, may have served as a reassuring presence. Just as Lincoln is used to sell sleeping pills, financial services, and hotel rooms, the 2008 election demonstrates how effectively he can be used to sell political candidates and political agendas to the American public.

THE FIGHT FOR LINCOLN'S SOUL

In the course of the 2008 presidential race, Barack Obama's religious commitments were subjected to intense scrutiny. Although Obama spoke openly of his Christian faith and professed "praise and honor to God" on the campaign trail,[12] rumors abounded that he was a closeted Muslim, a kind of Manchurian candidate being maneuvered into a position of power by "Islamic terrorists." Obama added fuel to the fire just days after his inauguration when he told an interviewer from Al Arabiya News that he had Muslim relatives. The comment attracted the attention of anti-Obama commentators, some of whom, in their indignation, gave free rein to Islamophobic stereotypes. At issue was not just a single man's faith, but the Christian identity of the nation. Skirmishes over Obama's spirituality can be seen as a contest between those who sought to preserve the notion of America as a Christian nation and those who embraced a more inclusive national identity. The battle over Obama's faith was a battle to define the nation.

Likewise, Abraham Lincoln's faith has long been a matter of public debate. The Lincoln record overflows with apparent contradictions and inconsistencies. Raised in a Baptist household, Lincoln avidly studied the Bible, and both his private and public writings abound with biblical allusions and references to a divine being and God's will. However, as an adult, Lincoln did not take up membership in any church, and as a young man he reportedly expressed agreement with the freethinker doctrine, irreverently referred to Jesus as "a bastard," and even wrote a short "infidel" pamphlet that a concerned friend later destroyed.[13] Lincoln's professions of skepticism were strong enough for his former law partner to assert that "he died an unbeliever."[14]

No church, denomination, or philosophy, therefore, has an unassailable claim on the martyr president. At his funeral in Washington, D.C., Episcopalian, Methodist, Presbyterian, and Baptist clergy took turns at the pulpit.[15] But far from diminishing Lincoln's status in the eyes of the nation's faith factions, lack of certainty about his religious beliefs has made him an even more flexible icon for diverse and often antithetical religious and philosophical positions. Lincoln has been claimed through the years by Baptists, due to his upbringing; by Quakers, due to his Quaker forebear Samuel Lincoln; by Methodists, Presbyterians, and Episcopalians, due to his friendships with certain clergymen; by Unitarians, due to his apparently anti-Trinitarian beliefs; by spiritualists, due to reports that after the death of his son Willie, Lincoln participated in séances at the White House; and by deists due to his supposed rejection of orthodox Christianity.[16] Catholics have also adopted Lincoln as a moral exemplar and a champion of the downtrodden, with his image being featured in the stained-glass windows of at least one Catholic cathedral.[17] Even Jews have staked a claim on the sixteenth president, with one Rabbi asserting that Lincoln was "bone to our bone, flesh to our flesh," in other words, that he was Jewish by descent.[18]

Despite this rather "unseemly tussle for [Lincoln's] soul,"[19] in biographies, in classrooms, and at historical sites across the nation today, the complexities and uncertainties of Lincoln's spiritual beliefs tend to be forgotten. Instead, Lincoln is presented as a rather conventionally pious and generic Christian.

Prominent Lincoln tourism sites promote this idea. In an introductory video at Lincoln's Kentucky birthplace, for instance, a folksy voiceover declares, "He's probably the most religious president we ever had," while in the introductory gallery to the site, the Lincoln family Bible is prominently displayed along with Lincoln's assertion that "it is the best gift God has given to man." Likewise, the Abraham Lincoln Presidential Library and Museum never hints at Lincoln's well-documented doubts about Christian doctrine, although it features many of his more orthodox statements about the truth of the scriptures and the need for divine assistance. Similarly, at the nation's premier history museum, the Smithsonian National Museum of American History in Washington, D.C., Lincoln's pronouncement that "the judgments of the Lord are true and righteous altogether" is not only on display while his challenges to conventional Christianity are kept in storage, but the quote is repeated at least three times, so that even the most casual visitor will be left with an impression of Lincoln's orthodox piety.

In classrooms and lecture halls across the nation, Lincoln educators reinforce the image of Lincoln as a devout Christian. Lincoln impersonators, for instance, performing across Illinois for bicentennial celebrations, repeated these same Lincoln quotations about scripture and divine will, further attesting that Lincoln was always guided by the Holy Bible.[20] During the Lincoln bicentennial period, one adult education instructor at a community college in the Lincoln heartland examined Lincoln's spirituality in greater depth. "Lincoln hungered and thirsted for righteousness," he explained. Lincoln struggled with the idea of a personal savior, but he progressed from agnosticism to deism, to true faith that God exists. While Lincoln was not a "technical Christian," he knew the Bible better than most ministers today and longed to travel to the Holy Land to "walk where our Lord walked," the instructor asserted.[21]

Best-selling biographies have long promoted the notion of Lincoln's Christian piety. In the earliest biographies after his assassination, he was routinely characterized as a conventional Christian, and his administration was said to be "the finest exhibition of a Christian democracy the world has ever seen."[22] Lincoln's spirituality only became a matter of public contention with the 1872 publication of Ward H. Lamon's Lincoln biography, with its controversial assertions about Lincoln's lack of faith and casual heresies.[23] In the intervening years, it seems that Lincoln biographers have been obliged to examine Lincoln's spirituality from every possible angle. By 1957, eminent biographers J. G. Randall and R. N. Current had seen enough to conclude that, "since Lincoln's death, more words have been wasted on the question of his religion than on any other aspect of his life."[24] And yet Randall and Current themselves devoted the culminating chapter of their Lincoln biography to the martyr president's spirituality. They concluded not only that "Lincoln believed in God" but that he was "a man of more intense religiosity than any other president the United States has ever had."[25]

Certainly compared with a museum display case or classroom lectures, full-length biographies allow Lincoln scholars more space to examine the nuances of Lincoln's religious views, and many recent biographers do just that. And yet most biographers repeat the same standard quotations: Lincoln "never denied the truth of the Scriptures"; he urged his father to rely on "our great, and good, and merciful Maker"; he believed that "the will of God prevails" and that "the judgments of the Lord, are true and righteous altogether." Not surprisingly, then, even after more detailed consideration of the topic, most best-selling biographies ultimately return to the conventional image of Lincoln as a man with a deep and abiding faith in the Christian God.

Of course, the message in these biographies, classrooms, and tourist sites is not only that Lincoln was a faithful Christian. If we accept the premise that the stories we tell ourselves about Lincoln are really stories of who we think we are and who we want to be as a nation, then such strident assertions of his Christian faith are assertions that we are, and *should* be, a Christian nation. Tales of Lincoln's adherence to the Bible, his obedience to God's will, and his desire to walk with "our Lord" may or may not be true. It is not my place to evaluate the veracity of such claims. But it is certainly the case that the more strongly we stress the Christian faith of our national heroes, the more firmly we reinforce the notion that ours is a nation created by and for Christians. While Christians may embrace this idea, to non-Christians it means material and psychological marginalization. It means being expected to pledge allegiance to a nation under someone else's god; being asked to take oaths on someone else's holy book; being effectively excluded from consideration for certain elective office; and being defined as somehow Other, as not fully American. The prize in the battle for Lincoln's soul is the right to define the nation's identity.

EMANCIPATION PROCLAMATIONS: HOMOSEXUALITY AND ABORTION

Perhaps nowhere is Lincoln's current role as an icon of legitimacy clearer than in contemporary debates over such heated social issues as homosexuality and abortion. A closer examination of the ways Lincoln is employed in such public debates reveals the degree to which the Great Emancipator is used in struggles over identity and ideology.

"My Old Kentucky Homo": Constructing the Gay Lincoln[26]

In the build-up to the Lincoln bicentennial, new Lincoln titles crowded bookstore shelves. Two of the most controversial among them were Joshua Wolf Shenk's (2005) *Lincoln's Melancholy* and C. A. Tripp's (2005) *The Intimate World of Abraham Lincoln*. The content of the two books is quite different, with Shenk examining evidence that Lincoln suffered from depression and Tripp examining evidence that he was homosexual.[27] Yet it is useful to examine both books in greater detail here, because both employ Lincoln as a means to an end: both use him to advocate a shift in public attitudes.

The subtitle of *Lincoln's Melancholy* neatly captures its core argument: *How Depression Challenged a President and Fueled His Greatness*. Shenk suggests not only that Lincoln suffered from what today would be diagnosed as depression but also that his struggle with depression made him one of our nation's greatest leaders. Shenk puts depression in historical context, explaining that in Lincoln's day, "melancholy" was not seen as emasculating or as an indication of moral failure. Rather, "To be grave and sensitive—to feel acutely the agony and sweat of the human spirit—was admired, even glorified."[28] If Lincoln were running for office today, Shenk argues, his depressive tendencies would almost certainly count against him, but amid the romanticism of the early to mid-nineteenth century, his melancholy worked to his advantage. Not only did others likely perceive him as a man of great depth, but they were moved to support and protect him. In this way, Shenk contends, Lincoln's depression better allowed him to build up valuable networks of friends and political allies.

Perhaps more importantly, Shenk suggests, Lincoln's depression led him to develop the skills and fortitude he needed to lead the nation through its most dire crisis, the Civil War. It was in an attempt to master his depression that Lincoln applied himself so single-mindedly to the study of such things as grammar, logic, and law, disciplines that served him well in public life. Like many depressives, Shenk says, Lincoln became a workaholic and an overachiever as a way of coping with inner turmoil. Likewise, it was as an antidote to melancholy that Lincoln developed his famous wit and humor and in the process won many friends and admirers. It was also his intense inner suffering that led him to develop the empathy that fueled his abhorrence of slavery. And it was his years of facing down the darkness of depression that gave him the strength to face the national trauma of secession, rebellion, and bloody conflict.

So *Lincoln's Melancholy* makes three major assertions: first, that Lincoln was a depressive; and second, that his mood disorder was one source of his greatness, as it was, Shenk points out, for many of the period's most illustrious figures, Edgar Allen Poe, Emily Dickinson, Charles Darwin, Leo Tolstoy, and Queen Victoria among them. But the book's third and most overarching assertion is that we need to change current attitudes toward depression and current treatments for depression. If Lincoln were alive today, Shenk says, he would be treated with medications to alleviate his symptoms, but this would also dull his emotions and his creativity, rob him of his energy and drive, and deprive us of his genius. Shenk, a mental health activist who openly discusses his own struggle with depression, suggests that we need to destigmatize depression, to stop defining happiness as the only normal and healthy mental state, and to develop a greater appreciation of the ways that depression can spark genius. *Lincoln's Melancholy* is certainly a book about Lincoln himself, but it appears equally aimed at changing attitudes about mental illness.

Similarly, while C. A. Tripp's *The Intimate World of Abraham Lincoln* is a book about Lincoln's sexuality, it seems equally aimed at reshaping American attitudes toward homosexuality. Tripp, a sex researcher and gay rights activist, interprets the historical record in light of contemporary scholarship on sexuality and concludes that on Alfred Kinsey's six-point scale of sexual orientation, Lincoln was a five: "predominantly homosexual, but incidentally heterosexual."[29] Drawing on correspondence and recollections by Lincoln's associates, Tripp speculates about Lincoln's sexual relationships with a number of men.

Tripp places a heavy emphasis on evidence that Lincoln experienced precocious puberty. He asserts that Lincoln reached sexual maturity at the age of nine, as suggested by his rapid physical growth during that period. His early sexual maturity, Tripp concludes, would have led to same-sex erotic experimentation, establishing a lifelong pattern of homosexual contact. In addition, Tripp claims that Lincoln's early sexual maturity explains other defining features of his personality. His love of off-color jokes and bawdy stories grew out of his early and intense interest in sex. His independence of mind and his extraordinary drive to learn and push himself in new directions originated in his sense of difference from those around him. His heightened empathy, that quality most often assumed to have shaped his attitudes on slavery, was also likely the result of Lincoln feeling like an outsider. His skepticism about Christian doctrine developed because of biblical injunctions against such things as masturbation and homosexuality, which he experienced not with a sense of guilt, but with joy and pleasure. If the Bible was wrong on these points, he may have wondered, in what other ways was it wrong? Even Lincoln's famously stormy marriage can be explained by his sexual orientation, Tripp claims. Mary Lincoln did not suffer from a personality disorder, as some have suggested. Rather, she was a "highly sexed female" who knew she had no hope of keeping her husband in the marriage bed. Her frustration at having to share her husband with a series of gay lovers pushed her toward fits of jealousy and emotional instability.

Tripp concludes his book with the cautionary tale of World War II British code breaker Alan Turing. A brilliant mathematician and an early computer scientist, Turing was instrumental in decoding crucial Nazi ciphers, thus saving countless lives. He was only exposed as a homosexual, and prosecuted for his criminalized sexuality, after he helped to win the war. But Tripp asks us to consider what would have happened had he been barred from service due to his sexual orientation. How many more Allied soldiers would have died? How many more innocent civilians? He cites the more recent case of much-needed Arabic-speaking linguists being fired by the administration of George W. Bush for their sexual orientation, even as military tensions with the Arab-speaking world intensified. Tripp's larger message is clear. Any society that marginalizes, rejects, and punishes homosexuals risks losing visionaries, heroes, and geniuses like Lincoln.

Tripp does not claim to be the first to suggest that Lincoln was homosexual. He notes that a number of Lincoln biographers, including Ida Tarbell and Carl Sandburg, made at least oblique references to Lincoln's emotionally intense, and possibly physical, relationships with men. More explicit assertions of homosexuality would emerge in the 1970s in the writings of gay rights activist James Kepner,[30] with further coverage in the work of Charles Shively in 1989 and in stories that were carried by media outlets including the *New York Times*, the *Los Angeles Times*, and C-SPAN in the 1990s.[31] Then, in February 1999, author and gay rights activist Larry Kramer ignited a firestorm of controversy when he asserted that he had new proof that Lincoln was gay.[32] Although that proof ultimately failed to materialize, newspapers across the country picked up on the story.

When the *State Journal-Register* in Lincoln's Springfield, Illinois, ran the story on the front page of its Sunday edition, the newspaper faced a vitriolic backlash from the public. In a stream of protest letters, readers voiced their disgust and disapproval. Readers were "shocked," "appalled," and "saddened" at what they perceived as an attempt to "shame" and "smear the reputation" of their favored son. One reader suggested that the story was an "effort by the gay community to push their agenda towards a general societal acceptance of homosexuality . . . [and] to subtly plant the seed in the general public's mind that if 'Old Abe' was gay, it surely must be normal human behavior." Others dismissed the story as "trash" and "a bit of nonsense," while one reader warned that such stories could harm the local economy, as dependent as it was on Lincoln tourism.[33] The public outcry was so pronounced that the paper was forced to issue an apology for its coverage of the story.[34]

I have no interest in weighing in on the debate over Lincoln's sexuality. Unless new and extraordinarily candid historical documents come to light, it is unlikely the issue will ever be resolved beyond all doubt. Rather, I am interested in understanding why the sex life of a man more than a hundred years in his grave should provoke such dramatic responses. Again, I must return to one of the main contentions of this book: that the stories we tell ourselves about Lincoln are stories about who we are as a nation and who we want to be. To accept that Abraham Lincoln was gay, a depressive, or perhaps an atheist is to acknowledge the existence of these groups in American society and grant them some measure of legitimacy in the national narrative. Such a change would challenge both long-standing national self-conceptions and the privilege of dominant majorities.

"If Abortion Is Not Wrong, Nothing Is Wrong": Constructing the Pro-Life Lincoln

In early twenty-first-century America, few issues are more divisive than abortion. Abortion has become a decisive factor not only in elections, political appointments, and domestic and foreign policy decisions but also in boardroom deliberations, as growing numbers of corporations face boycotts for giving charitable donations to reproductive health organizations.[35] It should come as no surprise, then, that Lincoln features in the American debate over abortion. Again, the higher the stakes, the more likely it is that his spirit will be invoked.

It is the opponents of abortion who most forcefully employ the Lincoln gambit. Those calling on Lincoln include everyone from eminent political scientists, legal scholars, clerics, and politicians to activists so radical and confrontational that they are marginalized even by other opponents of abortion. While the style of discourse varies with the context and the interlocutors, the core argument is relatively consistent: Lincoln's stance on slavery can and should be applied to the case of abortion. Abortion opponents point out that even though the *Dred Scott* decision defined blacks as property rather than persons, Lincoln insisted on recognizing slaves and free blacks as people. In his response to Stephen Douglas in 1854, Lincoln asserted that few if any defenders of slavery would argue that "there is no difference between hogs and slaves." They acknowledge through their words and actions, he said, that "there is humanity in the negro." And, he continued, "If the negro is a man, then my ancient faith teaches me that 'all men are created equal,' and that there can be no moral right in connection with one man's making a slave of another. . . . Slavery is founded in the selfishness of man's nature, opposition to it in his love of justice." Ten years later in a letter to A. G. Hodges, Lincoln stated his position succinctly: "I am naturally anti-slavery. If slavery is not wrong, nothing is wrong."

Some opponents of abortion claim that abortion is the new slavery and fetuses the new slaves.[36] They argue that just as the *Dred Scott* ruling denied the humanity of blacks, *Roe v. Wade* denies the humanity of fetuses. Just as Lincoln suggested that no rational and honest man could deny that blacks were people, opponents of abortion argue that no one who sees an image of a fetus in utero or views the grisly photographs of aborted fetuses commonly displayed by antiabortion protesters could deny that fetuses are human beings. Just as defenders of slavery selfishly denied basic human rights to blacks, women who terminate pregnancies selfishly deny fetuses the single greatest human right, the right to life itself. And just as defenders of slavery argued that the federal government should not interfere with the right of each state or territory to determine its own policies on slavery (the "popular sovereignty" position), abortion rights advocates argue that the state should not impinge on a woman's right to choose abortion.

Lincoln is commonly pressed into service by abortion opponents who suggest that we can find moral clarity on this heated issue by simply substituting the concept of abortion for that of slavery in many of the Great Emancipator's pronouncements. Doing so, we find Lincoln asserting that abortion is like a cancer that cannot be allowed to spread. Abortion is "the eternal struggle between these two principles—right and wrong." Fetuses are entitled to the basic rights enshrined in the Declaration of Independence. And, quite simply, if abortion is not wrong, nothing is wrong.[37] Ronald Reagan, framing his case against abortion, similarly invoked the martyr Republican. "Abraham Lincoln recognized that we could not survive as a free land when some men could decide that others were not fit to be free and should therefore be slaves," he wrote. "Likewise, we cannot survive as a free nation when some men decide that others are not fit to live and should be abandoned to abortion or infanticide."[38]

Not surprisingly, Lincoln has also been invoked in attacks against Barack Obama's position on abortion. "Barack Obama claims the legacy of Abraham Lincoln," one Illinois letter to the editor begins. But "Lincoln opposed, and gave his life in opposition to, the great legal evil of his day, slavery. Obama, conversely, embraces and vows to expand the great legal evil of our day, abortion."[39] "President Obama has chosen the opposite side of Lincoln, the side of oppression and injustice" to the unborn, asserts another. "I challenge President Obama to step up and become a man who is really like Abraham Lincoln, as he so obviously wants to be."[40]

Obama's stance on abortion rights came under intense scrutiny when the president was invited to be the 2009 commencement speaker at the University of Notre Dame. In the lead-up to the commencement, media outlets across the nation gave extensive coverage to protests over the appearance of a prochoice president at a Catholic institution. In the course of Obama's speech, which was interrupted several times by antiabortion hecklers, he urged those assembled to engage in civil dialogue on even the most challenging issues facing the world today, including abortion. Even as opponents of abortion invoked Lincoln to criticize Obama's stance on the issue, Obama himself invoked the Great Emancipator in his concluding remarks. Just as Lincoln in his first inaugural address called for calm and concerted efforts to preserve the "more perfect union" envisioned by the framers of the Constitution, Obama asserted that if we can only treat each other with respect and compassion, "America will continue on its precious journey toward that more perfect union."

The use of Lincoln in fiery battles over abortion gives us further evidence that this nineteenth-century politician continues to be a powerful presence in the public sphere of twenty-first-century America. His name serves as shorthand for moral rectitude, and no matter how controversial the cause he champions, his image is unimpeachable. The abortion debate also aptly demonstrates the now rather commonplace practice of putting words into Lincoln's mouth, making him take positions he never took, making him endorse causes he never supported, making him back or denounce laws that did not exist in his lifetime. Of course the danger is that doing so further distorts our understanding of Lincoln. As Lincoln becomes all things to all people and all causes, he is in danger of being reduced to an empty symbol.

WHITEWASHING LINCOLN?
THE GREAT EMANCIPATOR IN RACIAL POLITICS

As W. E. B. Du Bois observed, "We love to think of the Great as flawless. . . . [N]o sooner does a great man die we begin to whitewash him."[41] Just as Lincoln is employed in other contemporary political and ideological battles, he has long featured prominently in debates over race and racism in America. Twenty-first-century scholars remain divided on how to read Lincoln's record on race. Was he a committed but closeted abolitionist, an unrepentant racist, or somewhere in between?

There are those who suggest that he was very much a man of his racist times. As the historical record attests, he was an open fan of blackface minstrel shows and "darky" jokes. He defended a slaveholder attempting to reclaim his fugitive slaves. He had a long record of supporting "colonization," the removal of blacks to subsidized colonies outside the United States. He publicly declared that he had "no purpose to introduce political and social equality between the white and the black races" and that there existed a "physical difference between the two [races]" that would "probably forever forbid their living together upon the footing of perfect equality."[42] He further pledged in his first inaugural address that he had neither the right nor the inclination to interfere with the institution of slavery where it already existed. He forcefully resisted calls to abolish slavery and to allow blacks to serve in Union uniform. And when Union general John C. Frémont issued orders granting limited emancipation of slaves in Missouri as a wartime measure, Lincoln countermanded the order.

Others suggest that by the standards of his age Lincoln was uncommonly progressive in matters of race. Although he once defended a slaveholder, he also defended fugitive slaves and free blacks. Although he told racist jokes, he was also the first president to invite black leaders to the White House. Although he was critical of radical abolitionists, he also stated, without room for ambiguity, that slavery was a moral wrong to which he was opposed. And although he did not advocate full equality of the races, he consistently asserted that blacks were entitled to the fruits of their own labor. Furthermore, those who see Lincoln as an enlightened emancipator suggest that when he spoke of a natural and inevitable divide between the races, he likely did so primarily to appeal to a racist electorate. After all, he could only affect change if he got elected. Likewise, they suggest, it is probable that Lincoln resisted emancipation and the enlistment of black troops not because he was a racist, but because these were politically and militarily risky policies that needed to be carefully timed.

I leave it to others to debate the strength of these two very different visions of Abraham Lincoln, confident only in the assertion that it is a debate that will not be easily settled to everyone's satisfaction. For again what we see is that the debate over Lincoln's character is really a debate over the national character, and, as such, our understandings of Lincoln's racial politics change as racial dynamics change. This is evident from even a brief review of the way Lincoln's views on race have been presented over the century and a half since his death.

In perhaps the earliest full biography of the president after his assassination, *The Life of Abraham Lincoln* (1866), biographer Josiah Holland was careful to distance Lincoln from the cause of abolitionism. Although Lincoln believed slavery was wrong, Holland asserted, Lincoln also insisted that slaves must be considered property, rather than persons, under the Constitution. Those who suggested otherwise, Holland said, "inflict a wrong upon his memory."[43] When Holland was writing his account of Lincoln's life, the wounds of war were still painfully fresh, the Thirteenth Amendment had just been passed, and deep-seated and widespread mistrust of abolitionist radicals still hung in the air. In such a context, no doubt, it would have been seen as an insult to suggest that Lincoln was an abolitionist at heart. Little wonder, then, that Holland takes pains to establish Lincoln's dispassionate and pragmatic view of slavery.

While most early biographers and eulogizers were careful to preserve and further elevate Lincoln's reputation, a decade after his death some notes of criticism crept into Lincoln commemoration. At the 1876 dedication of the *Freedmen's Monument* in Washington, D.C., famed black abolitionist Frederick Douglass reminded those assembled that Lincoln had long protected slavery, promoted colonization, and denied black men the right to serve in the Union army. Lincoln was "pre-eminently the white man's President, entirely devoted to the welfare of white men," he asserted. And yet Douglass commended blacks for honoring Lincoln's memory. Not only had Lincoln contributed to emancipation, but by honoring him, blacks demonstrated their patriotism and nobility of spirit to the rest of the nation. "In doing honor to the memory of our friend and liberator, we have been doing highest honors to ourselves and those who come after us," he said. "We have been fastening ourselves to a name and fame imperishable and immortal."[44] Douglass, it would seem, was keenly aware that in the ongoing struggle for racial justice, the martyred president could be as valuable an ally as the living Lincoln ever was.

Douglass was not alone in this knowledge. By the turn of the century, Lincoln's name and image were being freely employed by groups opposed to black advancement. In 1905, North Carolinian Thomas Dixon published *The Clansman: An Historical Romance of the Ku Klux Klan*, which characterized Lincoln as a "friend of the South." In 1915, D. W. Griffith brought the novel to the screen in *The Birth of a Nation*, the biggest-budget and highest-grossing film of its day. Griffith showed the South in the wake of Lincoln's assassination descending into chaos and debauchery as blacks and Northern Republicans seized the reins of power and terrorized white Southern innocents. It was only the Klan that restored order by defending the Aryan race and reuniting Southern and Northern whites in a fulfillment of Lincoln's dream of reconciliation. The film portrayed blacks as ignorant, lascivious, violent, and irrational, representations that sparked protests across much of the nation and led to a ban on the film in a number of major cities.

Leading the campaign against the film was the newly formed National Association for the Advancement of Colored People (NAACP), which invoked Lincoln for its own antiracist purposes. The group had been formed after the infamous 1908 race riots in Lincoln's adult hometown, Springfield, Illinois. In retaliation for alleged black crimes, white mobs raged through the streets, targeting blacks and their white supporters. At the end of a bloody weekend, seven people were dead, and sixty-four homes and businesses lay in ruins.[45] Responding to these and other similar outrages, a group of reformers announced the official founding of what would become the NAACP on the centennial of Lincoln's birth, February 12, 1909. "The celebration of the Centennial of the birth of Abraham Lincoln . . . will fail to justify itself if it takes no note of and makes no recognition of the colored men and women for whom the great Emancipator labored to assure freedom," they wrote. "Abraham Lincoln began the emancipation of the Negro American. The National Association for the Advancement of Colored People proposes to complete it."[46]

Among the founders of the civil rights group was W. E. B. Du Bois, who would become the editor of the NAACP's journal, *The Crisis*. It was in the pages of that publication in 1922 that Du Bois controversially portrayed Lincoln as a man of contradictions, "cruel, merciful; peace-loving, a fighter; despising Negroes and letting them fight and vote; protecting slavery and freeing slaves."[47] Even after his comments provoked a public outcry, Du Bois reiterated his point that blind hero worship of even so great a man as Lincoln diminishes both the man himself and those who idolize him. While Du Bois praised Lincoln for being "big enough to be inconsistent," he urged blacks to redirect their passion from hero worship to the active struggle for the betterment of the race.[48]

Lincoln's name and image would feature prominently in the civil rights movement to come. When the Daughters of the American Revolution barred African-American singer Marian Anderson from performing at Constitution Hall in 1939, First Lady Eleanor Roosevelt resigned from the organization in protest and helped reschedule Anderson's concert for Easter Sunday on the steps of the Lincoln Memorial. Anderson returned to the Lincoln Memorial to sing at the historic March on Washington in 1963 when Martin Luther King Jr. delivered his "I have a dream" speech. King's opening words had a decidedly Lincolnian ring. "Five score years ago," he said, Lincoln signed a proclamation that brought "a joyous daybreak to end the long night" of slavery. But, he continued, African Americans still were not free. They remained shackled by discrimination, segregation, and racism. On what King called "this hallowed spot," the shrine to the Great Emancipator, he exhorted the nation to ensure liberty and justice for people of all colors and creeds.

Not all civil rights leaders embraced Lincoln as a symbol of freedom and equality, however. Just months after the march on Washington, Malcolm X characterized the event as a government-orchestrated farce designed to corral blacks "at the feet of another dead President, Abraham Lincoln."[49] Then, amid growing public recognition of the institutionalized nature of racism, historian Lerone Bennett published his controversial 1968 article, "Was Abe Lincoln a White Supremacist?"[50] Lincoln neither emancipated the slaves nor believed in equality between blacks and whites, Bennett asserted. Rather, Lincoln was a confirmed white supremacist who wanted to racially cleanse America by purchasing slaves from their masters and then deporting them to far-flung colonies. The article ignited heated debate within the academy, a debate that has continued into the twenty-first century.

In 2007, Bennett published a full-length examination of Lincoln's position on race and slavery, *Forced into Glory: Abraham Lincoln's White Dream.* Building on the core argument made in his 1968 article, Bennett asserts that Lincoln's words and actions show him to have been an unrepentant racist who did everything in his power to preserve the institution of slavery until he was forced, out of military necessity, to issue a toothless Emancipation Proclamation. It is crucial to strip the layers of myth and misinformation from Lincoln's record, he says, because African Americans are still enslaved by discrimination. As long as the nation believes that Lincoln is the great white father who set blacks free, we will be blinded to both the ways that blacks liberated themselves from slavery and the ways that blacks remain in bondage to institutionalized racism today. "If the Lincoln myths were the harmless fantasies of children at play, it would be possible to ignore them," he says. "But when the myths of children become adult daydreams and when the daydreams are used to hide historical reality and obscure deep social problems, it becomes a social duty to confront them."[51]

While Bennett has been fairly criticized for his selective use of historical evidence—citing only the evidence that proves his thesis while ignoring cases that undercut his claims—we must in all fairness acknowledge that this is precisely what many mainstream historians have done in their insistence that Lincoln was a proponent of black equality. Even Doris Kearns Goodwin, best-selling author of *Team of Rivals: The Political Genius of Abraham Lincoln*, overstates (some might say distorts) Lincoln's record on race when she asserts that "armies of scholars, meticulously investigating every aspect of his life, have failed to find a single act of racial bigotry on his part."[52] Of course the validity of this claim hinges on the definition of *bigotry* and whether using racial epithets, telling racist jokes, maintaining substandard pay and conditions for black Union troops, and advocating black deportation would count as bigotry in Lincoln's time. In the 2008 television documentary film *Looking for Lincoln*, Goodwin acknowledges that Lincoln's record on race is complex, but then she urges us to consider that "he was so far ahead of where anybody else would've been at that time."[53] Of course, this assertion ignores the many staunch abolitionists of the period—men and women, blacks and whites— many of whom despised Lincoln for what they perceived as his hostility to the cause of racial equality.

While many twenty-first-century scholars, including David Blight, George M. Fredrickson, Henry Louis Gates Jr., James Oliver Horton, and Lois Horton,[54] stress the complexities of Lincoln's racial politics, for one segment of the American public today Lincoln's views on race are clear-cut and indisputable. Groups such as the Knights Party of the Ku Klux Klan embrace Lincoln as a white supremacist forbearer. This arm of the KKK attacks the notion of Lincoln the Great Emancipator and quotes his pronouncements that he in no way favored social or political equality for blacks. "Lincoln believed in separation of the races," they assert. "He believed it was God's intention for the sons and daughters of Europe to be united in one great country under God. And . . . we must unite, not according to geographical location, but according to our race and faith. . . . As Lincoln would have wanted . . . our race must move on and reunite," they argue. "The future of our children is at stake."[55]

The future of our children, the future of racial and ethnic hierarchies, the future of liberty, of democracy, of the presidency, of civil liberties, of fetuses, of sexual morality, of mental health, of our very souls—in twenty-first-century America, when the stakes are high, people turn to Lincoln for his blessing or his absolution. As David Donald has observed, "Perhaps the secret of Lincoln's continuing vogue is his essential ambiguity. He can be cited on all sides of all questions."[56]

Such enduring popularity may have its costs, however. As Lincoln is invoked in support of a vast range of often antithetical positions, arguably we risk losing sight of the historical record. As we bend Lincoln to our modern purposes, the man as he was may be less important than the brand he has become. And as his words and actions are warped for the sake of expediency, his actual contributions to the nation, and whatever insights he might yet offer to the nation, are regrettably obscured. So, ironically, our enthusiastic embrace of Lincoln and our appropriation of him threaten to undermine our understanding of the man and hamper our ability to learn from him.

AN OUTSIDER'S PERSPECTIVE ON LINCOLN: MANUFACTURING HISTORICAL REPUTATIONS

In 1988, Herman and Chomsky's groundbreaking book *Manufacturing Consent* documented the ways that powerful entities, including the state, the mass media, and industry, work together to shape public opinion.[57] The propaganda model they developed suggested that, in modern liberal democracies like the United States, the mass media do not, in fact, act as a "fourth estate," monitoring and critically scrutinizing powerful elites, but rather the media generally mirror and protect the interests of those elites. It comes down to capital, the authors argue. Media organizations are for-profit entities, and they compete with each other for audience share. There is pressure to "scoop" other media organizations by presenting the first, the most novel, or the most sensational coverage of the issues of the day. In order to do this, the authors say, media organizations must rely heavily on "official" state and industry sources, a practice that, whether intentionally or not, ends up giving voice to elite views and stifling dissenting views.

This propaganda model has its roots in Marx's understandings of ideology and Adorno and Horkheimer's (Frankfurt School) critiques of the "culture industry."[58] While each of these perspectives has been criticized, often justifiably, for taking a top-down approach that sees conspiring elites exercising almost total control over the passive and naive masses, what *Manufacturing Consent* and its antecedents offer is keen insight into the ways popular opinion is shaped by material interests. Today, scholars in cultural studies and critical discourse analysis, among others, routinely scrutinize the ways that discourses both reflect and sustain (and occasionally even challenge) power relations.[59]

I am not adopting a propaganda or Frankfurt School model here. I am not suggesting that there is a Lincoln cabal manipulating public perceptions and public discourse about the sixteenth president. Indeed, the great variety of representations of Lincoln suggests that Lincoln's image is being constantly renegotiated by competing factions. And yet even with this great diversity of perspectives on Lincoln, there is almost universal consensus on this point: he is worthy of our attention. Herman and Chomsky assert that the media are constrained by the bounds of "thinkable thought" as it is established by elites.[60] Something similar can be said about depictions of Lincoln. Scholars and politicians might characterize him as liberal or conservative, gay or straight, as a devoted Christian or an agnostic, but almost without exception they agree on his greatness. Only the most committed Lincoln detractors (and white supremacists) transgress the boundaries of "thinkable thought" to portray Lincoln as craven, petty, or deeply bigoted, but even they reconfirm his significance in American history, American identity, and the nation's political, ideological, and material relations today.

What we must ask, then, is how the bounds of "thinkable thought" about Lincoln are defined. Whose views of Lincoln are considered more authoritative, and how do those perspectives come to shape public discourse? For insights into such questions, I turn to the work of sociologist Gary Alan Fine.[61] Fine explores the politics of historical reputation, specifically the ways that certain traits and narratives get fixed to historical figures. Historical reputations are not simply natural outgrowths of an individual's actions, he asserts. Rather, reputations must be built and sustained over time by "reputational entrepreneurs," players who have some interest in shaping our collective memory of historical figures.[62]

Of course, as we have seen in this chapter, different groups are invested in different constructions of Abraham Lincoln. As Fine demonstrates, however, those groups with greater resources, greater visibility, and greater institutional backing have greater influence over historical reputations. "Institutionally sanctioned knowledge" is viewed as the most authoritative.[63] Such seemingly authoritative views of Lincoln flow, in part, from the kind of mainstream biographies analyzed in chapter 3. Biographies that sell the most copies, those that garner glowing reviews and book awards, almost without exception reconfirm Lincoln's greatness. Let us examine just a small subset of these, the winners of the Lincoln Prize, perhaps the most prestigious award given for scholarship on Lincoln and his era.

In recent acceptance speeches, winners of the Lincoln Prize have characterized Abraham Lincoln as a "monumental figure," a "decisive figure," "the great American Man," and "our most admired president."[64] Among the most common themes in the speeches of these "gatekeepers of memory"[65] are Lincoln's hatred of slavery, his skill as a leader and politician, his intelligence, his eloquence, and his character—particularly his humility, his patience, his empathy, and his moral convictions. The question, of course, is to what extent the views of leading Lincoln biographers shape public perceptions of him.

Certainly biographies can inform the understandings of those who actually read them, but they may have broader influence as well. Consider Doris Kearns Goodwin's Lincoln Prize–winning *Team of Rivals*. The book received coverage in the *New York Times*, the *Los Angeles Times*, *USA Today*, the *Washington Post*, the *Boston Globe*, the *St. Louis Dispatch*, and *Time* magazine, as well as on National Public Radio and CBS News, among many other media outlets. The book was widely cited, and Goodwin herself was widely quoted, during the 2008 presidential race and in the early days of the Obama administration. The Abraham Lincoln Presidential Library and Museum later opened an exhibit entitled *Team of Rivals: Lincoln's Cabinet at the Crossroads of War*, with video commentary by the author to coincide with the sesquicentennials of Lincoln's presidential election and the beginning of the Civil War.[66] And Steven Spielberg announced that he would direct a Lincoln biopic based on the book.[67] Through all these channels and more, Goodwin's conclusions about Lincoln have now made their way into popular understandings of the sixteenth president. They have helped define "thinkable thought" about Lincoln.

It is not my intention to challenge widespread consensus about Lincoln's greatness or his significance to the nation that created him. Nor do I wish to imply that Lincoln's "reputational entrepreneurs" cynically manipulate his reputation for personal gain. As Fine points out, those who promote a particular vision of history may perceive that vision as both accurate and consonant with communal interests.[68] Nonetheless, the broader point is that when our understandings of Lincoln, and history more generally, are limited by hegemonic discourses—discourses that circulate so widely that most of us consider them simply natural, neutral, and commonsensical—both critical thinking and the democratic process suffer. If we rely on truisms and overgeneralizations, we will not develop accurate and complex understandings of history. If we cannot understand our past, we will have a more limited capacity to make informed decisions about our present and our future.

· 6 ·

A Is for Abe: Teaching Lincoln

*A*mong the most frequently repeated anecdotes from Abraham Lincoln's childhood years goes something like this. As a child, Lincoln loved books and would read everything "he could lay his hands on."[1] Because his family was poor, Lincoln often walked long distances to borrow books from acquaintances, including the well-off farmer Josiah Crawford. One stormy night, Lincoln set a book borrowed from Crawford on a shelf in the modest Lincoln cabin. In the morning, young Abe discovered that the book had been damaged by rainwater seeping through the cabin walls. Being an honest boy, Lincoln reported the damage to Crawford and offered to work off the cost of the book, two (some say three) hard days' labor in the cornfield.

The book was Parson Weems's *Life of George Washington*.[2] With chapter titles like "His Benevolence," "His Industry," and "His Patriotism," and its fabricated events (most famously the story of young George cutting down a cherry tree and admitting the offense to his father), the book seems more concerned with moral education than with historical accuracy. As the lanky boy Lincoln pored over the pages of this didactic biography, little could he have imagined that one day his own life story would make its way into the hearts and minds of schoolchildren throughout America and even beyond.

Today, Lincoln is employed in classrooms across the nation to teach subjects ranging from history and civics to literacy, math, the visual arts, and "character development" (moral education rebranded for the twenty-first century). This chapter examines Lincoln's presence in contemporary American education. What themes do teachers emphasize when presenting Lincoln? What themes feature prominently in children's books on Lincoln? How are Lincoln and his contemporaries represented in today's high school history textbooks? And what themes or issues are conspicuously absent from Lincoln education today? In answering such questions, we gain insight into both the aims and the broader social effects of these lessons in Lincoln.

LESSONS IN LINCOLN

During the 2008–2010 Lincoln bicentennial period, I attended public lectures, teacher workshops, and other educational events throughout the Lincoln heartland, observing and participating in the activities and arranging to interview many of the educators who were in attendance. The teachers I interviewed came from ten states and worked predominantly in elementary, junior high, and high schools.[3] Not surprisingly, most reported using Lincoln in their classrooms to teach about American history and the political process. However, a significant number also used Lincoln to build on students' literacy skills. For instance, in the lower grades, teachers emphasized Lincoln's love of reading, poetry, and storytelling, while in the upper grades, students were asked to engage in more complex tasks, such as analyzing Lincoln's rhetoric.

When asked what they most want their students to learn about Lincoln, it was clear that teachers placed less emphasis on Lincoln's actions and more emphasis on his personal characteristics (see figure 6.1). The majority of teachers interviewed voiced deep respect for Lincoln's determination, his work ethic, and his willingness to stick to his moral convictions. Likewise, in their classrooms, they stressed Lincoln's lifelong love of learning, his perseverance in the face of adversity, and his impressive rise from poverty and obscurity to influence and enduring fame. Many teachers specifically spoke of Lincoln as an

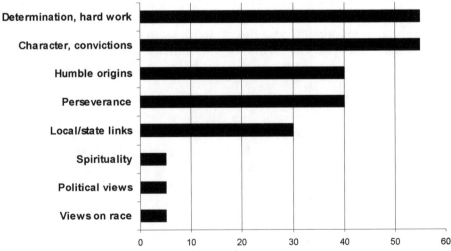

Figure 6.1. Lincoln Themes Emphasized by Teachers

exemplar of the "American Dream" of upward mobility. "He made a life from very humble beginnings that had a powerful impact on our country and the world," one teacher noted. "I'd like every child to feel that they, too, could do that." Teachers also emphasized Lincoln's fair and levelheaded leadership, his honesty, and his humor, and they encouraged their students to feel proud of any concrete links their state had with the sixteenth president.

So while Parson Weems's *Life of George Washington*, with its didactic emphasis on the great man's benevolence, patriotism, and industry, may strike contemporary readers as a quaint anachronism, interviews with Lincoln educators suggest that Lincoln is used in much the same way in classrooms today. He is presented as a moral exemplar: he is hardworking, studious, principled, good humored, and of course honest. He is the model student, the model citizen, the model worker, and the model politician and statesman. He teaches students what they can and should be.

Not surprisingly, the Lincoln curriculum materials employed in classrooms across the nation reinforce such lessons. American schoolteachers today can avail themselves of countless prepared lesson plans and course materials published online and in hard copy by such organizations as the National Archives, the Smithsonian Institution, the National Endowment for the Humanities, the National Park Service, state and national teachers' organizations, and commercial publishers. Projects range from elementary students building model log cabins out of pretzel sticks to high schoolers comparing the public speaking styles of Abraham Lincoln, Martin Luther King Jr., and John F. Kennedy. While the content of the Lincoln curriculum naturally varies by grade level, the underlying themes remain consistent with those illustrated in a Lincoln bicentennial edition of *Time for Kids*.[4]

Time for Kids, a biweekly periodical used in elementary school classrooms throughout the nation, presents current events to children in a glossy news-magazine format. Teachers can utilize lesson ideas and worksheets designed specifically for the content of each edition. The Lincoln bicentennial coverage focused on five major themes: Lincoln's impoverished childhood, his love of books, his fight to preserve the Union, his freeing of the slaves, and his extraordinary rise from humble beginnings to greatness. As prominent Lincoln scholar Harold Holzer asserted in the issue, Lincoln "showed that any young person in this country can rise to the highest opportunities." A comprehension quiz accompanying the issue tested children not only on the chronology of Lincoln's life but also on the article's main points: that Lincoln came from a poor family, that he was a "hard worker," and that he freed the slaves.

Lincoln scholars undoubtedly cringe at such an oversimplification of Lincoln's life and works. Indeed, many curriculum materials for the early grades end with Lincoln's election to the presidency in 1860, perhaps to avoid having to deal with the difficult topics of war, slavery, and assassination. One teacher at a Lincoln workshop advised her colleagues to sidestep any topics that would disturb or frighten young children. Judging by curriculum materials and teacher comments, by middle school students are learning to grapple with the more mature topics of slavery and the Civil War. And by high school, at least some educators are challenging mythic conceptions of Lincoln and his time. Some students may be surprised to learn that Lincoln was not an abolitionist; that the Civil War was not, from its start, explicitly a war to free the slaves; that the Emancipation Proclamation itself freed very few slaves; and that Lincoln was not generally an advocate of social and political equality for blacks.

However, there are some indications that even in advanced high school courses, educators are cautious about being too critical of the American hero their colleagues have spent years building up. In upper-level curriculum materials developed by the U.S. National Archives, for instance, students are informed that "the Lincoln administration wrestled with the idea of authorizing the recruitment of black troops."[5] Such wording obscures the fact that Lincoln *himself* was a staunch opponent of black enlistment and only relented out of military necessity. The National Archives lesson goes on to explain that "when Gen. John C. Frémont . . . in Missouri and Gen. David Hunter . . . in South Carolina issued proclamations that emancipated slaves in their military regions and permitted them to enlist, their superiors sternly revoked their orders." Again, the use of vague wording obscures the fact that it was Lincoln himself who countermanded these orders.

Of course, few teachers blindly adhere to prepared lesson plans and curriculum materials. They adjust lessons to suit their students' abilities, the schedules and resources of their schools, and even the local political climate. If conditions are right, high school teachers may choose to introduce a more critical perspective on Abraham Lincoln. The question is whether, after perhaps nine years of rehearsing the mythic Lincoln, students are able to move to a more complex, more critically informed understanding of the sixteenth president.

As a point of clarification, I am not suggesting that all teachers across the nation present Lincoln in the same way. Indeed, in my interviews and participant observation, I was constantly impressed by the creativity and innovation today's teachers bring to their Lincoln lessons. It is also crucial to note that the vast majority (95 percent) of the teachers I interviewed were white. Although there were significant African-American populations in most of the cities I visited for Lincoln educational events, the audience was overwhelmingly white. At the twelve venues where I was able to gather attendance figures, for instance, only 10 out of approximately 1,170 audience members were people of color. The slate of speakers was similarly homogeneous: 95 percent of the featured speakers were white, the vast majority of them being white men.[6] This left me with a numerically limited pool of nonwhite educators to interview. More research is needed, therefore, to investigate whether lessons in Lincoln vary with the ethnoracial identity of teachers.

PICTURING ABE: LINCOLN IN CHILDREN'S PICTURE BOOKS

Abraham Lincoln has been a staple of children's publishing since shortly after his death. Typical of early Lincoln biographies aimed at the youth of America, Horatio Alger's *The Backwoods Boy, or the Boyhood and Manhood of Abraham Lincoln* emphasizes Lincoln's humble beginnings, his virtuous character, his work ethic, and his incredible rise from a dirt-floor log cabin to the helm of the nation.[7] Like Parson Weems's *Life of George Washington*, the book brings a great historical figure to life with invented dialog and historically dubious anecdotes. Like Weems, Alger seems more concerned with moral instruction than with historical accuracy.

More than a century later, America's young people can choose between standard Lincoln biographies and photobiographies, Abraham Lincoln alphabet and counting books, and books on Lincoln's virtues, his love of books and animals, his family life, his funeral train, his hat, and even his whiskers.[8] Lincoln biographies for children are so plentiful, in fact, that at my local library the bookshelf symbol for all juvenile biographies—whether of Pocahontas, Susan B. Anthony, Jackie Robinson, or Kurt Cobain—is a Lincoln silhouette. Despite the vast number of titles and the diverse range of topics they cover, children's books on the sixteenth president largely repeat the clichés of the folk-hero Lincoln: his log-cabin birth and childhood poverty, his work ethic and honesty, his humor, physical vitality, and love of learning, and his unwavering conviction that slavery was wrong (see figure 6.2).[9]

While some children's books do not refer to the Emancipation Proclamation by name, the majority of children's books note Lincoln's role in freeing the slaves. Among Lincoln scholars, the intent and the effects of the Emancipation Proclamation are matters of ongoing debate. Critics have

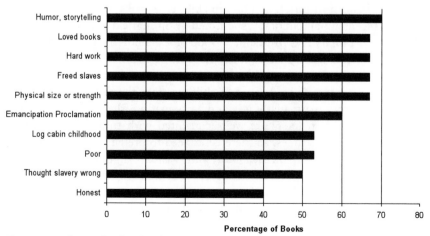

Figure 6.2. Themes in Lincoln Picture Books

pointed out that Lincoln only granted freedom to those slaves he was unable to free (those in the Rebel South), while keeping slaves in the border states and occupied South firmly in bondage. At most, such scholars point out, the Emancipation Proclamation liberated only a tiny fraction of the nation's slaves.

Many children's books, especially those targeted to young children, ignore such complexities with passages such as the following:

> Lincoln thought slavery was wrong. In 1863, he signed a paper called the Emancipation Proclamation (e-MAN-sih-pay-shun PROCK-luh-may-shun). This freed all of the slaves.[10]

Some children's books cleverly sidestep the nuances of the issue by noting that Lincoln "*freed slaves*" (technically true), or freed all slaves *in Rebel territory*, or signed the paper that "was a milestone *on the road to* the final end of slavery."[11] One book carefully avoids saying that Lincoln freed all slaves but includes a cartoon illustration of a black man with broken chains standing next to Lincoln who is holding a paper that reads, "Emancipation Proclamation: All Slaves shall be free."[12] In this way, the book preserves the image of the Great Emancipator while not blatantly misrepresenting historical fact.

A few books provide a broader context for the Emancipation Proclamation, exploring Lincoln's strategic reasons for issuing it: namely, concerns about European powers siding with the Confederacy, fears of defection by the border states, and dwindling numbers of Northern army recruits.[13] One book even addresses negative reactions to the Proclamation, noting that many abolitionists thought it did not go far enough, many Northerners did not want to allow black soldiers into the Union army, and Southern Confederates simply did not recognize Lincoln's authority on the matter.[14] However, such detailed discussions of the issue are in the minority.

The issue of historical accuracy in children's books is a thorny one. At a Lincoln bicentennial roundtable sponsored by Springfield's Abraham Lincoln Presidential Library and Museum, a group of six children's authors discussed the challenges of writing Lincoln for the juvenile market.[15] The panel members agreed that writing for children was more difficult than writing for adults. There is an impulse to try to protect children from the disturbing details of the Lincoln story, particularly war and assassination, they noted. But some argued that children today are well acquainted with these things through television and video games, so there is no need to pretend such things never happened. "Kids pick up on dishonesty and evasiveness," one author asserted. "You can't lie to them." The writers agreed that children wanted and deserved honesty in accounts of Lincoln's life, and one panelist urged aspiring authors to remember that "writing for children is writing for ourselves."[16]

This last comment raises an important question: if writing for children is writing for ourselves, then to what degree are Lincoln children's books a reflection of adult authors' desires—the desire for a national hero, the desire for a triumphant Everyman, the desire to believe in the promise of the American Dream, and the desire to instill in the next generation the traditional virtues of honesty, humility, and the Protestant work ethic?

It would seem that such considerations often trump the desire for historical accuracy and complexity in American classrooms. Among the Lincoln books most frequently recommended in the educator workshops I attended were Winters and Carpenter's (2003) *Abe Lincoln: The Boy Who Loved Books* and Raymond Bial's (1998) *Where Lincoln Walked*. While *The Boy Who Loved Books* is a colorfully illustrated picture book tracing Lincoln's life from childhood to his presidential election, *Where Lincoln Walked* is, in effect, a photo essay with glossy images of significant Lincoln sites: his Kentucky birthplace, the fields of Indiana, the Sangamon River, and his Springfield law office, among others.

It is worthwhile asking what makes these volumes so appealing to Lincoln educators. Certainly Bial's book brings history alive through its evocative images. The use of color photographs rather than black-and-white or sepia images gives Lincoln an immediacy and contemporary relevance sometimes lacking in historical accounts. Indeed, in Bial's attempt to create a living Lincoln, he bends certain historical facts. His captions indicate that readers are seeing, among other things, the actual Kentucky cabin where Lincoln was born, the actual Indiana cabin where he spent most of his childhood, and the actual New Salem store he ran with William Berry. All of these structures are, in fact, latter-day recreations of the originals. He also repeats certain anecdotes now considered rather dubious by many historians, such as his tragic love affair with Ann Rutledge, and chooses to ignore a great deal of evidence in his assertion that, "By all accounts, [Abe and Mary] had a loving, happy marriage" during their Springfield years.[17] Clearly, it is not historical accuracy and complexity that draw teachers to the book.

Through vivid illustrations and lyrical text, *Abe Lincoln: The Boy Who Loved Books* also brings Lincoln to life. Unlike some biographies that dwell on Lincoln's many hardships, perhaps aimed at making his triumphs seem all the greater, the author and illustrator work together to make the young Lincoln a blessed and bright-eyed optimist. His childhood family is happy and loving, and their home is modest but comfortable. No scenes of grim, barefoot poverty here. Even the bearskin rug at the family hearth sports a smile on its snout. Young Lincoln is eager and physically robust, with compassion for all living creatures and dreams of greater things. Above all else, it is a love of learning that drives him and ultimately leads him to the highest office in the land. The narrative is a simple one, but perhaps all the more powerful for its simplicity. Primary school teachers can employ Lincoln to teach young children about the value of determination, hard work, and education, while not having to address more discomfiting issues such as poverty, racial injustice, warfare, and political violence.

Both in children's books and in the nation's classrooms, Lincoln is, above all else, a moral exemplar. While some teachers may introduce a more nuanced perspective on the sixteenth president, most of the juvenile biographies available to them celebrate Lincoln as the kind of folk hero Parson Weems would heartily endorse.

NODS TO DIVERSITY:
THE LINCOLN ERA IN HIGH SCHOOL TEXTBOOKS

It is hardly surprising that teachers discuss Lincoln and the Civil War era in more detail and more complexity as children get older. As noted above, by middle school and high school, many teachers are introducing their students to more "mature" themes related to race, war, and assassination. Additionally, in recent decades history education has begun to consider the experiences of ordinary people rather than focusing exclusively on rulers, generals, and wealthy industrialists. Thus secondary school history textbooks now routinely include the stories of women, African Americans, and other minorities in their discussion of the Lincoln era.

Barry Schwartz dates this change to the mid-twentieth century when the civil rights movement, the women's movement, and the "postmodern turn" in thought, among other developments, sparked widespread rebellion against authority and tradition.[18] Drawing on longitudinal survey data, he suggests that the perceived greatness of all American presidents, including Lincoln, began to decline during this period. He asserts that today Americans have little appetite for the veneration of "great men." Multiculturalism and feminism have so successfully reinforced the notion of pluralistic equality, he says, that we are now reluctant to acknowledge the true greatness of historical figures. Instead, we find our "heroes" in the more superficial realms of pop music, sports, or Hollywood celebrities, and we are more likely to celebrate "victimhood" than greatness.

Schwartz is critical of what he perceives as undue attention currently being given to minor players in history at the expense of great historical figures such as Lincoln. He singles out attempts by the U.S. Mint to introduce the Susan B. Anthony and Sacagawea one dollar coins as alternatives to the one dollar bill featuring George Washington, whom he characterizes as "the man who did most to found and form the nation itself."[19] He suggests that Lincoln may be the next great man to be pushed aside to make way for a more diverse cast of heroes and heroines. Our current emphasis on diversity, he says, "casts doubt on all political legacies, promotes the belief that all social distinctions are arbitrary, that any one viewpoint and heritage can no longer be considered more relevant than another, regardless of its historical importance. . . . To admire all ethnic, racial, and national heroes equally is to esteem none."[20]

In examining what he perceives as the declining prominence of great men in the national narrative, Schwartz quotes conservative columnist Peggy Noonan. "Who is at fault?" she asks. To Noonan the answer is clear:

> The politically correct nitwit teaching the seventh-grade history class who decides the impressionable young minds before him need to be informed, and their first serious history lesson, that the Founders were hypocrites, the Bill of Rights nothing new and imperfect in any case, that the Indians were victims of genocide, that Lincoln was a clinically depressed homosexual who compensated for the storms within by creating storms without.[21]

Schwartz furthermore suggests that school textbooks today reflect this same tendency, by overemphasizing women, African Americans, and other minority groups at the expense of great white men, or, as he puts it, by "commemorating too many people for too few achievements."[22]

A systematic survey of school textbooks reveals something quite different, however. I analyzed a sample of recent secondary school history textbooks for representations of white men compared with white women and ethnic minority men and women.[23] My primary objective was to measure the amount of coverage afforded to white men versus other groups. It was clear from the outset that most textbooks today do make a concerted effort to include at least some details on the lives of women and ethnic minorities in the Civil War era. Civil War nurses such as Clara Barton and Dorothea Dix, the black abolitionist Frederick Douglass, and the Fifty-Fourth Massachusetts Regiment of free black soldiers are consistently mentioned in the texts. The overall trend in the textbooks, however, is to emphasize the white politicians and white fighting men of the era.

As figure 6.3 demonstrates, white men accounted for the vast majority (83 percent) of individuals named in the Civil War sections of the textbooks analyzed. Only 12 percent of those mentioned by name were white women; a mere 5 percent were nonwhite men; and nonwhite women accounted for just under 1 percent of named individuals. An analysis of images in the texts yields similar results. Of all the individuals pictured in the Civil War chapters in the sample, the overwhelming majority (75 percent) were white men; white women and nonwhite men accounted for between 9 and 11 percent; and nonwhite women accounted for less than 1 percent of images.

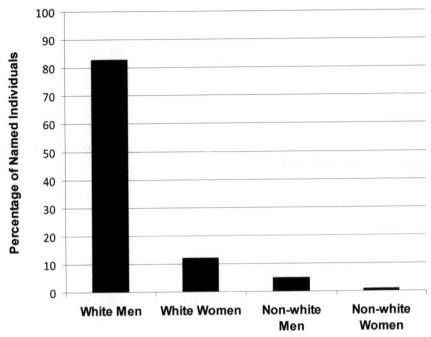

Figure 6.3. Named Individuals in Secondary School History Textbooks, by Gender and Race

This trend is even clearer when we narrow the pool to individuals who were identified by name in the images. White men accounted for 77 percent of such images.[24] Moreover, half of the texts featured three men—Abraham Lincoln, Robert E. Lee, and Ulysses S. Grant—in multiple portraits, while no woman or ethnic minority was pictured more than once in any of the volumes analyzed. Of course it is possible that fewer women and African Americans were pictured, in part, because fewer images of them exist. But that factor alone does not account for the dramatic disparity. Consider, for example, one text that included a small section on the important role of war-time reporters. Along with information on Civil War era reporting was an image of a contemporary war correspondent reporting from Iraq.[25] Despite the prominent presence of female correspondents in the media today, the reporter chosen for inclusion was a white man.

Numerical analysis simply does not support the assertion that women and ethnic minorities are crowding out white men in our nation's history curricula today. Without a longitudinal analysis it is not possible to determine whether, and to what degree, textbook coverage of Abraham Lincoln has changed over time. However, the "critical thinking" questions included in the sample of textbooks suggest that Lincoln is still portrayed in strongly positive terms. Let us consider three such questions. (1) "What qualities do you think made Lincoln an effective leader? Which of these qualities did Andrew Johnson lack?" (2) "Today Abraham Lincoln is considered one of our greatest presidents. [Evaluate the evidence.]" And (3) "Why was Lincoln's assassination 'one of the greatest tragedies of all American history'?"[26] The implications in these questions are clear: Lincoln was an exemplary president, perhaps our greatest president, and other leaders of the period pale in comparison to him. While secondary school textbooks certainly provide more details about the Civil War era than books aimed at younger children, and introduce a variety of perspectives on the period, there is little evidence that Lincoln's image suffers in the process.

As a final illustration of Lincoln's continued prominence in school texts, in the current sample, more images of Lincoln are included than images of any other historical figure of the period. In fact, four out of ten of the textbooks feature Lincoln on their covers, suggesting that he remains not only the face of the Civil War era but also of American history, and the American nation, as a whole.

SILENCE IS GOLDEN:
WHAT LESSONS IN LINCOLN LEAVE OUT

In any analysis of the ways Lincoln is represented and deployed, the absences and silences are just as revealing as the recurring themes. The details that educators and authors choose to leave out of their accounts of Lincoln's life suggest that some issues are seen as too difficult, too inconsequential, or too threatening to contemplate. Chief among such issues is race.

In the sample of children's biographies examined, few books explicitly address the issue of racial inequality. Lincoln's moral opposition to slavery is frequently included, but for the most part race is not mentioned. While the books teach children that slavery existed, curiously, they often fail to mention that people were enslaved based on their African descent. Often, illustrations of forlorn and shackled dark-skinned slaves provide children the only hint that slavery was a system based on race. Likewise, few books provide even a cursory description of the experience of slavery. Many children's books note only that slaves had to work hard, that they sometimes wore heavy chains, or that they were bought and sold at auctions. But scrupulously evasive passages provide almost no indication of the deprivations, violence, and sheer inhumanity of the system. Instead, for the most part, the books present slavery as an abstract evil that afflicted nameless, faceless unfortunates for no apparent reason.

Only two books in the sample include any named black characters. Brenner and Cook's (1994) *Abe Lincoln's Hat* briefly notes that Lincoln provided legal defense for Nance, a black woman who was "treated badly" by the man for whom she worked.[27] Giovanni and Collier's (2008) *Lincoln and Douglass: An American Friendship* provides much more extensive coverage of a black character, famed abolitionist Frederick Douglass.[28] The volume is quite unique among children's Lincoln books in that it affords equal narrative and pictorial space to Lincoln and another great historical figure. It draws strong parallels between the two men's lives and views. While the book does not include any of Douglass's well-documented criticisms of Lincoln, it does serve as a reminder of the widespread absence of African-American voices and perspectives in children's Lincoln biographies today.

Native Americans are likewise almost totally absent from Lincoln children's books. Several texts note briefly that Lincoln served in the Black Hawk War, and others include the story that Lincoln's grandfather was killed by Indians. One author emphasizes the significance of that event: Lincoln's own father, a child at the time, had almost been killed in the attack as well, so if the Indians had been successful, "Abe would have never been born."[29] So, despite Lincoln's well-established record on Indian policy (most notably his authorization of both the largest collective pardon and the largest mass execution in U.S. history in the Sioux uprising of 1862), in the majority of children's books about Lincoln, Native Americans are either represented as menacing frontier marauders or are simply erased from history.

Just as Lincoln books for children tend to sidestep the issue of race, many Lincoln educators urge caution in broaching the issue in the classroom. At one educator workshop, an advocate of using Lincoln to teach about race nonetheless warned her fellow teachers that doing so often makes both white and black students uncomfortable. White students often feel they are being unfairly cast as villains, she said, while black students often feel embarrassed about being positioned as victims. Another educator noted that if teachers are going to deal with race in their Lincoln lessons, they need to make sure that they have enough time and students who are mature enough to deal with the issue in all its complexity. If not, she suggests that teachers, at least at the elementary level, just skip the topic. As she succinctly put it, "Don't open that can of worms."

In interviews, Lincoln educators likewise report that other topics are seldom addressed in their classrooms. Educators were asked whether they discuss or plan to discuss in their classrooms Lincoln's depressive tendencies or his sexual orientation (see figure 6.4). On the issue of depression, the teachers were split down the middle. Many teachers, particularly in the early grades, said they avoided the topic because children were too young to understand it. By contrast, others suggested that it was important to address

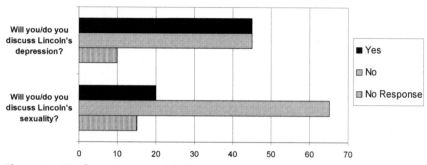

Figure 6.4. Teachers: Controversial Themes

the issue because it teaches children that even someone with a serious illness or disability can succeed if they work hard enough. They also stressed the desire to "humanize" Lincoln, to make him into a flesh-and-blood man with problems just like everyone else. As one teacher noted, "It is important for students to see that Lincoln did not use [his illness] as an excuse for his failure and that he kept on going and never gave up." This part of the Lincoln story "gives hope to us all," observed another.

Opinions were stronger on the issue of Lincoln's sexual orientation. The majority of teachers said they would not discuss it in class. Many noted that this decision had nothing to do with their own views on homosexuality, but rather that the historical evidence on the issue was very flimsy, that their students were too immature to deal with the issue, or that parents and administrators would be upset if they raised the matter in class. Some teachers commented that Lincoln's sexuality simply did not matter, that it was not "relevant to what I want students to understand about him."

Those teachers who reported discussing or being willing to discuss the topic often noted that they do so primarily to dispel misconceptions about Lincoln's alleged homosexuality. "One of the main reasons I discuss the homosexual question is to discuss the errors we make when we make 2008 assumptions on facts reported in the 1860s," explained one educator. Others said they are willing to discuss the issue in order to better demonstrate to students that individuals can succeed despite their "personal problems" and the "mistakes" they make along the way. Of course, the strong implication in such observations is that homosexuality is a problem, a weakness, or a flaw.

There are several ways to interpret the silences in Lincoln education. Some silences on issues such as Lincoln's alleged homosexuality may be primarily due to the incomplete historical record. Educators may be understandably reluctant to teach on issues that are not supported by copious historical scholarship. Likewise, teachers may wish to avoid topics on which historians have not yet reached consensus, such as Lincoln's views on race. As Gary Alan Fine observes, "When history is too contested by rivalrous parties, schools and other institutions simply ignore it."[30] No doubt educators' decisions are also shaped by concerns over distressing their students and angering parents and administrators. But, just as importantly, silences in the Lincoln curriculum can also serve as a kind of social barometer. Based on what is being said (and not said) in the nation's classrooms, it appears that depression is becoming destigmatized. It can therefore be discussed more openly in schools without the fear of disturbing students, parents, or higher-ups. By contrast, despite some claims that Barack Obama's election signals an end to racism in America, race is clearly still an issue regarded by many as too difficult, or too dangerous, to openly address. And, perhaps most dramatically, although gays and lesbians have become more visible in America over the last decade, teachers' reluctance to address the possibility that Lincoln was gay suggests that homosexuality is still highly stigmatized today.

AN OUTSIDER'S PERSPECTIVE ON LINCOLN: THE LINCOLNIZATION OF AMERICAN CHILDREN

Whether through classroom lessons or children's books, American children today are exposed to a relatively cohesive, and largely celebratory, narrative of Lincoln's life and works. If we agree that lessons in Lincoln are used in part to inculcate certain virtues and habits in the next generation, then we could say that such lessons are intended to Lincolnize the young. As Fine notes, schools teach children "a national narrative larded with 'facts' that they should be able to understand and that provide lessons necessary for citizenship. . . . The real goal of a history lesson is not to have students 'learn about the past,' but to enable them to shape the present."[31]

From the perspective of critical theory, creating a nation of Lincoln wannabes best serves the interests of dominant groups. We can draw insights from the work of Louis Althusser. Althusser suggests that relations of dominance are supported by two primary mechanisms, repressive state apparatuses (RSAs) and ideological state apparatuses (ISAs).[32] RSAs include such armed enforcers as the military and the police, which states can mobilize to coerce the masses into complying with the rules that maintain the social order. While RSAs can be an effective way of keeping dominant groups in power, particularly in the most heavy-handed of totalitarian states, such tactics inevitably breed resentment and often resistance to authority.

Far more effective, Althusser suggests, are ISAs, institutions that are not directly controlled by the state, but which nonetheless serve the interests of the state and the groups who, for all practical purposes, control the state: in capitalist nations these are the owners of the means of production—those who own the factories, the corporations, and the bulk of the resources. ISAs including the media, religious organizations, and the education system, among others, help maintain relations of dominance by cultivating in the masses the norms and values that serve the interests of dominant groups. For instance, the notions that anyone can rise to the top of society through hard work, that we all can achieve ideal beauty by consuming the right products, or that those who suffer misery and want in this life will be rewarded in the afterlife, are ideas that are instilled in Americans from an early age through our schools, our magazine advertisements, and our houses of worship. They teach us to be dedicated workers, enthusiastic consumers, and docile subjects, never rebelling against those in power. ISAs are so effective at shaping our thoughts and actions, Althusser suggests, because we do not even realize that we are being indoctrinated. Rather, we simply come to accept such notions as natural and commonsensical.

Althusser has been justly critiqued for being too deterministic. Yet his perspective on the role of schools in the reproduction of inequalities remains highly relevant today. A large body of scholarly work, particularly in the sociology of education, documents the many ways that schools instruct students in the "hidden curriculum," latent messages about such things as race, class, and gender. Pierre Bourdieu, for instance, discusses the ways that schools reproduce relations of dominance by privileging ruling-class culture.[33] Bowles and Gintis describe the ways that schools train the nation's children to conform to authority and social hierarchy.[34] Cookson and Persell analyze the ways that elite boarding schools help privileged students develop the values, skills, and social networks that prepare them to assume their roles in the ruling elite.[35] Sadker and Sadker discuss the subtle and not-so-subtle ways that gender messages in schools help reproduce patriarchal social relations.[36] And Jonathan Kozol reveals the many ways that the U.S. education system teaches poor and ethnoracial minority students to accept a place as second-class citizens.[37]

This is not to suggest that there is some active conspiracy to maintain long-standing social hierarchies. In fact, some studies have convincingly demonstrated that teachers themselves may be quite unaware that they are reinforcing particular ideological paradigms.[38] Moreover, as Paul Willis asserted in his classic study of the British school system, the reproduction of relations of dominance is not merely a top-down process. Schools do not simply manipulate passive children into their designated positions. Rather, in his study of working-class boys, Willis found that the rigid ruling-class values of the British school system often provoked defiant responses that led working-class boys to reject school. Ironically, the boys' failure in school virtually assured that they would remain in low-pay, working-class jobs. Willis's work serves as a somber reminder that while teachers and administrators may not be consciously trying to keep students in their predetermined social positions, the education system may be structured in ways that create such outcomes.

Such scholarship sheds light on Lincoln education today. From this critical perspective, by Lincolnizing the young, lessons in Lincoln help create studious pupils, loyal citizens, and, ultimately, eager workers. If taken to heart, the tantalizing image of the American Dream, emphasized in so many Lincoln children's books and curriculum materials, may inspire young people to labor tirelessly in pursuit of dramatic upward mobility. Of course, this may or may not pay off for young people when they join the workforce. After all, even working extraordinarily hard at a minimum-wage, low-skill job without the prospect of promotion is unlikely to lead from rags to riches. But having an eager, compliant workforce will *always* benefit the business owners and stockholders by increasing productivity and profit. And having a diligent, obedient citizenry will always serve the interests of the state.

Finally, regardless of the intentions of teachers and children's authors, their lessons in Lincoln may teach children more than historical facts and positive messages about character, morality, hard work, and equality. The stories we tell our children about Abraham Lincoln may (unintentionally) help perpetuate stigmatizing silences and damaging misconceptions about such issues as homosexuality, patriarchy, and racism.

• 7 •

Lincoln under Glass: The Great
Emancipator in American Museums

_$\mathscr{P}$_opular understandings of Abraham Lincoln's life and works are profoundly shaped by the many cultural forms already discussed in this volume: children's books and schoolroom lessons, political rhetoric, best-selling biographies, tourist sites, advertising, and Lincoln kitsch, among others. However, it is museums that are regarded by the public as the most reliable and most objective source of information about the past.[1] With their displays of authentic artifacts and their staging of historical scenes, museums serve as "time machines" that propel us into convincing productions of the past.[2]

In a work devoted to examining perceptions and representations of Lincoln, it is crucial to analyze the ways the sixteenth president is presented in the nation's museums. From the smallest local historical societies with their shoestring budgets and dusty dioramas to the high-tech installations and glossy guidebooks of prestigious national museums, museum exhibits both reflect and reproduce popular ideas about Lincoln. Occasionally they even challenge popular assumptions and urge visitors to see beyond Lincoln the myth to Lincoln the man. What is more, Lincoln exhibits teach us not only about the martyr president himself but also about our national self-conceptions. Theologian G. B. F. Hallock reminded Americans in his 1919 reflection on the birthdays of Presidents Washington and Lincoln that "Washington taught the world to know us. Lincoln taught us to know ourselves."[3] Memorializing Lincoln is a way of honoring and celebrating our own past. Preserving Lincoln's memory under glass is a way of cherishing a shared vision of who we are, where we came from, and where we are going.

113

ON CURATORS AND CURIOSITIES

Before examining the common themes in Lincoln museum exhibits, we would do well to take a moment to consider the many factors that shape curatorial decisions. Modern museums have their roots in the "cabinets of curiosities" that reached the height of their popularity among European elites in the seventeenth century.[4] Those with sufficient wealth and inclination amassed considerable collections of plant and animal specimens and cultural artifacts from around the world. Displayed in elaborate cabinets or rooms, these curiosities were primarily valued for their novelty. Such collections could enhance the collector's reputation, for only the richest and most powerful could acquire the rarest treasures of the natural and ethnological world. Unlike modern museums, these curiosity cabinets were seldom systematically organized by era, geographic region, or taxonomy and were not open for public viewing. By the nineteenth century, however, many of these collections were being consolidated into what would become public museums, where items were studied, cataloged, carefully preserved, and organized for public display. One explicit aim of the modern museum movement was to educate and enlighten the masses. In more subtle ways, modern museums often served to bolster regional or national pride and to legitimate particular points of view.[5]

Museums in the twenty-first century still struggle with the legacy of the curiosity cabinet. Visitors yearn for rare and "authentic" artifacts and stand hushed and seemingly transfixed by such "relics" as Lincoln's hat, his suit, or his pocket watch. As one guide at the Lincoln Home National Historic Site noted, he could give visitors detailed explanations of Lincoln's complex views on slavery or race, but all they really want to know is whether the objects on display are "real"; that is, whether they were actually owned and used by the Lincolns. Museums today also face new challenges. With the proliferation of mass-mediated forms of entertainment and such immersive attractions as theme parks and megamalls, museums today have to work hard to attract and engage visitors. Those museums with the resources to do so have replaced static display cases and printed placards with multimedia installations and hands-on, interactive displays. Curators today must also carefully consider the issue of historical perspective. Because many visitors are now more keenly aware of the ways that less powerful groups have been marginalized and misrepresented in historical narratives, museum professionals must take care to be as inclusive as possible in their exhibits.

In addition to these twenty-first-century challenges, curators today often find themselves embroiled in disputes with academic historians, boards of directors, and exhibit sponsors. A curator who creates an "accessible" Lincoln exhibit may be accused by professional historians of dumbing down or distorting historical fact. Curators who want to explore edgier issues[6] such as Lincoln's views on race may be thwarted by museum boards or commercial sponsors who do not want to attract controversy. The Abraham Lincoln Presidential Library and Museum (ALPLM) in Springfield, Illinois, provides an apt case study of the kinds of material considerations that shape curatorial choices.

Even before the $115 million ALPLM opened its doors in 2005, scholars were divided on its merits. At issue was the museum's combination of "scholarship and showmanship" in exhibits created by ex-Disney designer Bob Rogers and his BRC Imagination Arts.[7] With lifelike latex Lincoln figures, storytelling ghosts, smoke machines, and mock "Campaign 1860" television coverage by Tim Russert, some historians criticized the museum for Disneyfying the martyr president. John Y. Simon, historian at Southern Illinois University in Carbondale, dubbed the enterprise "Six Flags over Lincoln."[8] In response to the controversy, Springfield's local *State Journal Register* ran an editorial cartoon featuring a proposed new display for the museum: "a life-sized figure of a pompous scholarly naysayer, complete with egg-shaped head [and] turned-up nose." "Wow!" one onlooker in the cartoon exclaims. "They really captured the snootiness."[9]

Defenders of the museum praised its innovative design as a way of drawing technologically savvy young people into the study of Lincoln, and history more generally. And state and local leaders praised the ALPLM as an attraction that could bring tourists to the region with open pocketbooks.[10] Curators faced the daunting task of creating a compelling, detailed, and accurate historical narrative that would appeal to the tourist market. Tourism consultants urged museum staff to approach issues such as slavery very carefully so as not to distress visitors. For similar reasons, firearms, tobacco products, Confederate flags, and the N-word were quite consciously left out of museum exhibits, despite their prevalence in Civil War–era America.[11] After all, happy tourists are more likely than distressed ones to linger in the museum gift shop browsing for souvenirs to help them remember their experience. Happy tourists are more likely to become members and return visitors and are more likely to encourage family and friends to visit. An upbeat Lincoln story is, simply put, good for business.

In addition to the commercial considerations that necessarily shape curatorial decisions, curators at all museums are constrained by the limits of both their collections and the historical record. The reality is that for most of America's history, white men have dominated public life, and the records and artifacts of their lives have been considered most worthy of preservation. So it is that museums now hold the diaries and private letters, the boots and eyeglasses, the beds and even the dentures of the nation's wealthiest and most prominent white men, while comparatively few such artifacts survive from the lives of women, ethnoracial minorities, and the working class. So even if curators want to create detailed and engaging displays on, say, free Northern blacks during the Civil War, they may lack the records and the artifacts to do so.[12]

With such constraints firmly in mind, it is not my intent to take curators to task for their presentation of Lincoln. (Indeed, I am an enthusiastic patron of Lincoln museums.) Rather, my aim is to examine the ways that museum representations of the sixteenth president reflect, reinforce, or challenge certain assumptions both about Lincoln and about the nation that produced him.

EXHIBITING LINCOLN

In creating Lincoln exhibits, museum professionals rely in large part on the biographers who have come before them. While they may turn to archives and private collections for materials to flesh out their portrait of the martyr president, seldom is "new" material uncovered about perhaps the most exhaustively researched man in American history. It should come as no surprise, then, that Lincoln museum exhibits tend to closely mirror the themes found in Lincoln biographies (see figure 7.1).

Systematically coding the content of the nation's premier Lincoln museum, the ALPLM, for the themes identified in an analysis of twenty best-selling Lincoln biographies[13] reveals remarkably similar representations: an emphasis on Lincoln's humor, his godliness, his achievement of the American Dream of upward mobility, his depression, his physical strength and stature, and his honesty. The majority of the fourteen Lincoln museums I analyzed also explicitly noted that Lincoln was strongly (or "naturally") antislavery, that he firmly believed that slavery was wrong, and that he freed the slaves. On this latter topic, most museums are careful to point out the limited scope of the Emancipation Proclamation. Lincoln himself did not abolish slavery, they remind visitors, but he paved the way for comprehensive and permanent abolition.

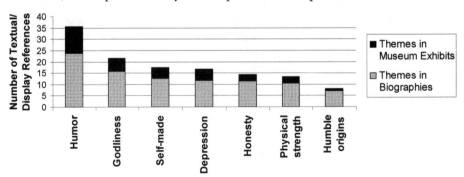

Figure 7.1. Themes in Biographies and Lincoln Exhibits

Also not surprisingly, Lincoln museums seldom include incidents and quotations that portray Lincoln in a negative light. His legal defense of a slave owner, his authorship of a heretical "infidel pamphlet," and his assertions that he did not support political and social equality for blacks or that blacks and whites had essential differences that would forever prevent them from coexisting on an equal footing, get little exposure in the nation's Lincoln museums. Even those exhibits with a slightly edgier approach, like the traveling exhibit *Forever Free: Abraham Lincoln's Journey to Emancipation,* note that Lincoln's views on race were shaped by the times in which he lived. Lincoln "embodied the contradictions" of Civil War–era attitudes to race, we are told, but he still unequivocally "hated slavery" and was eventually "transformed into the Great Emancipator."[14]

Indeed, many museums appear to be quite protective of Lincoln's reputation. At the Smithsonian National Museum of American History (SNMAH) in Washington, D.C., for instance, Lincoln's ornate gold pocket watch is on display, but an interpretive plaque assures visitors that Lincoln "was not outwardly vain." Although the exhibit notes that Lincoln's biggest legal client was Illinois Central Railroad, it then notes that "he was just as likely to oppose railroads in the courtroom as represent them." And although the display acknowledges that the Emancipation Proclamation did not free slaves in all areas, it adds that "it was widely understood that Union victory would mean the end of slavery." Meanwhile, across town in the exhibit galleries of Lincoln's Cottage, one historian's observation that some of Lincoln's statements on race were "notorious to say the least" is counterbalanced by Frederick Douglass's assertion that Lincoln "was the first great man that I talked with in the United States freely, who in no single instance reminded me of the difference between himself and myself, of the difference of color."

Although the basic themes of Lincoln exhibits are strikingly similar to those in mainstream biographies, many museums make additional claims on Lincoln, suggesting that he in a sense "belongs" to a certain locality because it made him what he was. The Abraham Lincoln birthplace in Kentucky reminds visitors that this is where he took his first steps, and that when he left Kentucky he took memories, determination, and "the very strength of the people with him." The Lincoln Boyhood National Memorial claims that Lincoln lived in the area longer than he lived anywhere else,[15] and that it was in Indiana that he developed his personality and ideals. Lincoln's New Salem asserts that "whatever it was that changed Lincoln, it started right here. . . . He had come to New Salem as directionless as a piece of driftwood. Six years later, he left as a lawyer and a statesman." And the Lincoln home in Springfield, Illinois, reminds visitors that "it was here that he raised his family, developed his beliefs about freedom and equality, and attained the highest public office in the country." A quote from Lincoln's farewell speech to Springfield features prominently in the exhibits: "To this place, and the kindness of these people, I owe everything."

Such claims serve to remind visitors of the historical significance of the regions and sites they are visiting. Just as importantly, however, such assertions about Lincoln are assertions of local pride, a way for struggling cities and regions to claim a place for themselves in national narratives. "If there hadn't been a David Davis, there may not have been an Abraham Lincoln," visitors are told at Clover Lawn, the mansion of Lincoln supporter David Davis in Bloomington, Illinois. Or "Without Freeport, there would be no Lincoln."[16] We can hold our heads high because we produced our nation's greatest leader. Our native son became Father Abraham.

WHAT LIES BENEATH:
UNIFYING THEMES IN LINCOLN EXHIBITS

Lincoln museums and exhibits present the public with myriad concrete details of Lincoln's life: the dates, traits, events, and quotations for which he is best remembered. In addition, however, certain unifying themes often knit together the varied strands of the Lincoln narrative. Two such themes run through most of the Lincoln museums and exhibits examined here. The first positions Lincoln as an exemplar of the American Dream; the second positions him as the standard bearer, or even the founding father, of the modern civil rights movement. Two Lincoln exhibits best illustrate the ways that such themes are employed in museums across the country: the ALPLM's traveling exhibit *Abraham Lincoln: Self-Made in America*, and the educational gallery on the ground floor of the Lincoln Memorial.

Abraham Lincoln: Self-Made in America was a cooperative effort by the ALPLM in Springfield, the National Endowment for the Humanities, and the Illinois Bureau of Tourism, among others. The fifty-three-foot-long double-wide trailer served as a "mobile museum" that took the narrative of Lincoln's life to more than forty locations throughout the nation during the two-year Lincoln bicentennial period.[17] As the name of the exhibit suggests, its overarching theme was Lincoln's achievement of the American Dream. Lincoln "embodied a new emphasis on personal initiative, risk-taking, and ambition," visitors were informed. "[H]is own talents and ambitions combined with hard work and a dedication to self-improvement to produce a unique specimen—the self-made man." Lincoln's own words were used to remind us of a crucial component of upward mobility: "Work, work, work is the main thing," he advised an ambitious young man.[18]

The exhibit featured a display on Lincoln's genealogy, at least through the paternal line, from Mordecai Lincoln Sr. (born 1657) through to the Great Emancipator himself. Significantly, beside the name of each of Lincoln's forefathers was a figure for the number of miles he migrated during his lifetime. With each generation, the distance increased, suggesting that Lincoln came from a long line of men who were determined to seek out new opportunities for advancement, wherever such opportunities might take them. Also on exhibit were two silver half-dollar coins to illustrate the story of the first full dollar Lincoln earned in a single day, the dollar that prompted him to dream larger dreams, as the narrative goes. "The world seemed wider and fairer before me," Lincoln reportedly recollected.

Lest anyone miss the overarching theme of the exhibit, a video at the exit reminds visitors that "Lincoln's life inspires us, even helps define us as a people and a nation . . . [and] shows us how far one can travel when fueled by determination, perseverance and a finely tuned moral compass." In other words, if we follow Lincoln's example, work hard and live a life of virtue, we too can achieve the American Dream. While not all Lincoln museums elaborate on this theme so fully, it nevertheless features in most Lincoln exhibits to some degree. As the introductory gallery of the Lincoln birthplace site in Kentucky succinctly puts it, "The story of Abraham Lincoln is the story of the American Dream—the ability to rise from simple beginnings to one's highest potential."

According to the nation's museums, the story of Abraham Lincoln is also the story of racial egalitarianism. In fact, many Lincoln exhibits draw quite a direct line between the Great Emancipator's words and actions and the modern civil rights movement. This is most clearly exemplified by the educational galleries of the Lincoln Memorial in Washington, D.C. Certainly the memorial itself has had an important place in contemporary racial politics. When African-American soprano Marian Anderson sang on the steps of the Lincoln Memorial in 1939, when Martin Luther King Jr. delivered his "I have a dream" speech there in 1963, when Nation of Islam leader Louis Farrakhan led the Million Man March that stretched from the U.S. Capitol to the Lincoln Memorial in 1995, and when Barack Obama marked the eve of his inauguration with a star-studded concert at the martyr president's shrine, Lincoln's name and image became indelibly linked to the cause of racial equality.

The Lincoln Memorial galleries reinforce the image of Lincoln as a champion of civil rights. Not surprisingly, his statements about innate differences between blacks and whites and the impossibility of racial equality have no place in the exhibits there. Instead, a dramatic introductory video intersperses many of Lincoln's best-known quotations with images and words from the civil rights era. "As I would not be a slave, nor would I be a master," an actor reads in a booming, heroic voice. (In fact, most museums recite Lincoln's words in similarly deep, refined, resonant voices, although the historical record suggests his voice was "shrill, squeaking, piping, unpleasant."[19]) The quote is followed by footage of the March on Washington and layered with Martin Luther King Jr. proclaiming, "Free at last, free at last." The video continues, showing images of protest marches—for women's rights, gay rights, labor rights—then antiwar vigils and visits to the Lincoln Memorial by heads of state, Olympic athletes, and music and film stars. Among other prominent faces, we see Eleanor Roosevelt, Coretta Scott King, and the Reverend Billy Graham. But among the many historic figures featured in the film, two men are shown repeatedly: Abraham Lincoln himself and Martin Luther King Jr. This trend is repeated in a display of photos in the video alcove where representations of King and the March on Washington actually outnumber pictures of Lincoln himself.

In addition to affording such a prominent place to the modern civil rights movement, the gallery of the Lincoln Memorial also includes many Lincoln quotations that position Lincoln as an advocate of black equality. "Allow all the governed an equal voice in the government, and that, and only that, is self-government," Lincoln is quoted as saying in his Peoria speech of 1854. Visitors are left with the impression that well before Lincoln attained the presidency, he was advocating not only emancipation but black suffrage. What the exhibit does not include, however, is the very next line of the Peoria speech: "Let it not be said I am contending for the establishment of political and social equality between the whites and blacks. I have already said the contrary."[20]

With a striking emphasis on Martin Luther King Jr. and the modern civil rights movement, the galleries of the Lincoln Memorial present Lincoln as a champion of not only liberty but also equality for blacks. Many Lincoln exhibits across the nation make similar assertions: Lincoln helped usher in an "interracial democracy,"[21] Lincoln declared equality an "inalienable right" for *all* people,[22] Lincoln "dreamed of making 'the race of life' open to *all* Americans,"[23] Lincoln insisted that "*all* men are created equal,"[24] and Lincoln was dedicated to "a new birth of freedom" that would include African Americans.[25] In constructing this overarching narrative of Lincoln as Great Emancipator and civil rights leader, copious evidence of Lincoln's views on colonization, miscegenation, and innate racial differences is conspicuously absent. Such evidence would not only threaten the flawless veneer of the mythic Lincoln but also undermine cherished conceptions of the nation itself as a model of racial equality.

SAINT ABE: THE VENERATION OF LINCOLN

In addition to educating the public about Lincoln's life and works, many Lincoln museums are structured in ways that promote the veneration of the martyr president. For instance, four National Park Service sites dedicated to Lincoln (the birthplace, boyhood home, Lincoln home, and Lincoln Memorial) include museum-style introductory galleries, but they also position themselves as "shrines" or "temples" to the great man. The architecture of the sites reinforces the sanctity of Lincoln's memory. The Lincoln birthplace and the Lincoln Memorial are modeled on ancient Greek temples dedicated to the gods and goddesses. Their gleaming white stone, Doric columns, and steep ascents announce to visitors that they are entering sacred space (see figure 7.2). In fact, anyone who has visited the Lincoln Memorial has undoubtedly witnessed the crowds of people gathered at Lincoln's marble feet. Visitors' arms are raised high above them not in supplication but in an attempt to capture the great man's image in the perfect snapshot, a kind of twenty-first-century act of worship.

Similarly, signage at the Lincoln home in Springfield reminds visitors that they are attending a "shrine" for "those seeking a personal connection to Lincoln's home, life, and legacy." And the boyhood home memorial in Indiana builds sacred elements into its spaces. At the heart of the memorial

Figure 7.2. The Lincoln Memorial, a sacred shrine to Lincoln. *Photo Courtesy of the Author*

is a cruciform site incorporating a soaring American flag at one end; a long, narrow allée; and the museum galleries and "cloisters" at the other end (see figure 7.3). The structures and the dramatic landscaping were designed to provide a "portal" to the hallowed ground beyond: the cemetery where Lincoln's mother was buried and the soil on which the Lincoln cabin once stood.[26] Both the gravesite and the cabin site are now protected by barriers that prevent visitors from venturing too close to the sacred.

Lincoln museums, galleries, and historic sites likewise utilize music, lighting, and other sensory experiences to promote veneration of the martyr president. During an introductory video in the galleries of the Lincoln birthplace in Kentucky, a hymn swells to crescendo with the message that "he" is always guiding us. But whether this refers to God, Jesus, or Father Abraham himself is left, perhaps intentionally, unclear. Another introductory video, this one at Lincoln's New Salem, speaks of Lincoln's mysterious transformation in the short-lived village. "It's like something happened here that can't be quite explained. Something happened to Abraham Lincoln," the narrator explains as otherworldly flutes play in the background. At the SNMAH, those who visit *Abraham Lincoln: An Extraordinary Life* are invited to rest their hands for a moment on casts of Lincoln's own hands, allowing for a more personal connection with this larger-than-life figure. And at the ALPLM, visitors are led through a dimly lit funeral gallery in which a replica of Lincoln's coffin lies in state beneath an ornate catafalque. Black crepe, white lilies, and solemn music serve as palpable reminders of the nation's grief. The gallery marks the completion

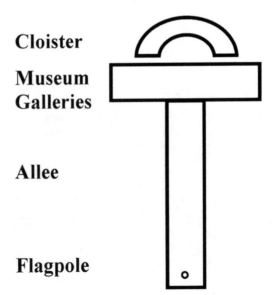

Cloister

Museum Galleries

Allee

Flagpole

Figure 7.3. The Cruciform Lincoln Boyhood National Memorial

of Lincoln's transformation, from backwoods boy to prairie lawyer, statesman, and finally national martyr and national demigod.

The veneration of Lincoln is certainly nothing new. Almost from the moment of his shooting on Good Friday of 1865, the rush toward deification began. In memorial sermons heard across the nation on the "Black Easter" following the assassination, at the White House funeral, along the route of the twelve-day cross-country burial procession, and in newspapers, speeches, and artistic tributes from coast to coast, comparisons were drawn with Christ: God had sent Lincoln to deliver us and then called him back home; Lincoln had given his life that the nation might live. Barry Schwartz observes that although Lincoln was by no means universally esteemed before his death, such "ritual acts of national affirmation and national communion . . . elevated Lincoln to a new and higher plane."[27] In fact, Schwartz argues that Lincoln was not mourned so lavishly "because he was a unifying symbol; rather he became a unifying symbol because he was mourned" with such extravagance.[28]

This powerful legacy of veneration accounts in part for the atmosphere of hushed reverence in the nation's Lincoln "shrines," its museums. They have become the reliquaries of the new millennium.

CONSUMING LINCOLN

Clearly, many museums and historic sites across the nation contribute to the sanctification of Abraham Lincoln. But to what degree do visitors themselves participate in the veneration? In one sense, visiting the "temples" and "shrines" devoted to Lincoln constitutes an act of worship.[29] Although not worship of Lincoln as a divine being, it is worship of the ideals that Lincoln now exemplifies: integrity, determination, self-sacrifice, equal opportunity, and the American Dream, among others. While visitors may arrive at Lincoln sites with a whole range of motivations and desires, they all tend to abide by the same posted and unspoken rules of decorum. Music, lighting, and "Quiet Please" signs encourage hushed reverence as visitors take in the artifacts and the atmosphere of the sacred spaces. Children and adults alike express delight and wonder at authentic Lincoln relics, his coat, his shawl, his inkwell. They marvel at holding the same handrail he touched and treading the same floorboards he paced, almost as if they were in the presence of the great man himself.

This veneration has its limits, however. The sanctification of Lincoln appears to be most earnestly embraced by white Americans. Attendance figures at five prominent national Lincoln exhibits reveal that during the course of my observations the vast majority of visitors—91 percent—were white (see figure 7.4).[30] When comparing this figure to the most recent U.S. Census figures, which indicate that whites account for approximately 72 percent of

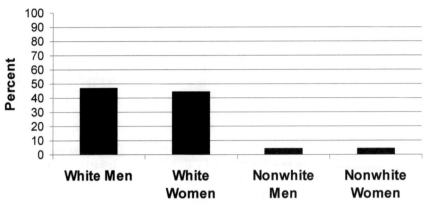

Figure 7.4.   Visitors to Select Lincoln Museums by Race and Gender

the American population, it is clear that visitors to Lincoln museums are disproportionately white.[31] These figures are consistent with national opinion surveys. On surveys since 1956, white Americans have always voiced a more favorable opinion of Lincoln than African Americans. In fact, in every year except one, a solid majority of whites rated Lincoln as our greatest president, while African Americans have consistently ranked him below John F. Kennedy and sometimes Franklin D. Roosevelt.[32]

For insights into what makes whites such eager consumers of Lincoln, we must look to the content of museum exhibits. Despite Lincoln's prominent role in the debate over slavery, few museums openly discuss race, and still fewer include the names and perspectives of African Americans. As mentioned earlier, this may be due in part to gaps in the historical record. However, even the well-documented lives of figures such as Frederick Douglass, Sojourner Truth, and Mary Lincoln's African-American seamstress Elizabeth Keckley typically receive little or no coverage in the nation's Lincoln exhibits. Likewise, even with Lincoln's service in the Indian wars and his important presidential decisions on Indian affairs, Native Americans are almost completely absent from Lincoln exhibits.

The ALPLM exemplifies patterns at the nation's Lincoln museums. In a systematic analysis of the content of the museum's exhibits, 92 percent of named individuals were white (see figure 7.5).[33]

And even when people of color are identified by name, visitors are given few, if any, details about their lives, experiences, or views. Take the displays on Lincoln's White House years. Lifelike figures of black abolitionists Frederick Douglass and Sojourner Truth stand at the entrance to the gallery, apparently preparing to enter the White House as guests. Just inside the re-created White House, black seamstress Elizabeth Keckley makes adjustments

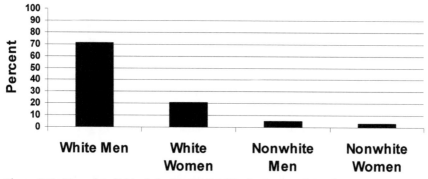

Figure 7.5. Named Individuals in ALPLM Exhibits by Race and Gender

to Mary Lincoln's gown. While all three African-American figures are identified by name, visitors to the gallery are given little explanation of how they fit into the Lincoln story. There is no hint of Douglass's very public criticisms of Lincoln, no mention of Sojourner Truth's struggle to change Lincoln's ban on black soldiers in the Union army, no reference to Keckley's explosive memoir that permanently estranged her from Mary Lincoln.[34] Rather, the depictions appear designed primarily to suggest that Lincoln presided over a harmoniously multicultural household, thereby reinforcing the notion that he advocated full political and social equality for blacks.

With so little coverage afforded to people of color, it is little wonder that nonwhites are less eager consumers of Lincoln. In fact, there is evidence that when Lincoln exhibits give greater voice to minority historical figures, people of color are more likely to visit. Compare, for instance, the visitor figures for the Lincoln exhibits at four Washington, D.C., museums: the Smithsonian National Museum of American History, the National Portrait Gallery, the Ford's Theatre Museum, and the Lincoln Memorial Educational Center (see figure 7.6).[35]

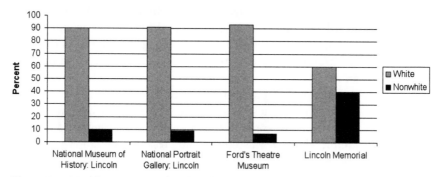

Figure 7.6. Washington, D.C., Lincoln Exhibit Visitors

The markedly greater proportion of nonwhite visitors to the educational galleries of the Lincoln Memorial is at least partly explained by the extensive coverage given not only to Lincoln and his all-white cast of politicians, administrators, and generals but also to significant African-American figures, including Dr. Martin Luther King Jr., Dr. Robert Moton, Marian Anderson, Coretta Scott King, Jesse Jackson, and Harry Belafonte, among others. Coverage is also given to other typically underrepresented groups, including Asians, Native Americans, gays and lesbians, and the poor. It is not surprising that more diverse museum representations draw a more diverse audience. But acknowledging this fact forces us to consider whether the overwhelming whiteness of most Lincoln exhibits discourages minority groups from fully participating in an important public affirmation of Americanness—the worship of the nation through the public veneration of Abraham Lincoln.

AN OUTSIDER'S PERSPECTIVE ON LINCOLN: PROFITING FROM THE PAST

While it is tempting to view history as a catalog of objective facts, with its secrets simply waiting to be uncovered in dusty archives and attics, most scholars now recognize that the past is a cultural construction that is continuously reshaped by historians, filmmakers, curators, and politicians, among many others. It is crucial to acknowledge this fact because, to quote George Orwell in his dystopian novel *Nineteen Eighty-Four*, "Who controls the past controls the future: who controls the present controls the past."[36]

Let us start with Orwell's second proposition here, that those presently in power control our interpretations of the past. The ways we represent Lincoln today clearly reflect current hierarchies of power. There is little doubt that if African Americans were the economically and politically dominant majority in American society today, or if the American South had become strikingly more affluent and more powerful than the North, we would be telling very different stories about Lincoln. We would be working from the same Lincoln documents, but we would interpret Lincoln's words and actions very differently than we do now. Our current interpretations of Lincoln reflect the perspectives of the dominant groups in our society today.

Recent scholarship on museums suggests that exhibits worldwide tend to reflect and protect the interests of the most powerful groups in any given society—the groups who have the resources to preserve their stories and heirlooms for future generations, the groups whose stories are considered worthy of preservation, and the groups who make large donations to museums and serve as museum trustees.[37] So it is hardly surprising that representations of ethnic Japanese far outnumber representations of Japan's minority populations in its national museums;[38] that the perspectives of Han Chinese dominate even in the "ethnic" sections of China's museums and cultural theme parks;[39] that stories of well-heeled aristocrats outnumber those of peasants and laborers at British historic sites;[40] and that representations of white, Christian, heterosexual, ruling-class men are more common in American museums than representations of women, ethnoracial minorities, gays and lesbians, or the working class.[41] Museum representations reflect both past and present power relations.

In Lincoln exhibits, this means that the voices of women and ethnoracial minorities are seldom included. In some museums, in fact, the absence of these groups is so pronounced that visitors would be forgiven for thinking that Civil War–era America was populated entirely by white men: generals, politicians, bureaucrats, journalists, and soldiers. These men not only made war, it seems; they made the nation itself. They fought over its destiny, baptized it in blood, and bequeathed to its history the tales of manly valor, honor, and fortitude that still sustain us. By contrast, women, African Americans, and Native Americans, if they are mentioned at all, are typically positioned as passive, marginal, or even troublesome players in these dramatic events.[42]

This brings us to Orwell's other proposition, "Who controls the past controls the future." Constructions of history matter because they not only mirror past and present power hierarchies, they contribute to ongoing social inequalities. That is, the more we are told through our museums, history books, and broader material culture that women and ethnoracial minorities played little role in our nation's formative events, the harder it is for us to imagine them in positions of national leadership, and the harder it is for us to accept and support them in public office, in executive positions, or in other prominent public roles. The ways we imagine our nation's past has real material effects on our nation's present and future.

A critical perspective on historical representations also suggests that museums often serve to transmit ideologies that benefit dominant groups. From this perspective, the unifying themes examined above (Lincoln as an exemplar of the American Dream and as a champion of racial equality) serve the interests of whites and the ruling class. By celebrating the sixteenth president's dramatic rise from log cabin to White House, museums help inspire the masses to follow his example. Lincoln is frequently quoted as saying, "I happen temporarily to occupy this big White House. I am a living witness that any one of your children may look to come here."[43] The unambiguous message is that no matter how humble their circumstances, all Americans have an equal opportunity to rise to the top. All it requires is determination and hard work.

While this message is comforting, it ignores widespread patterns of institutionalized discrimination and the legacies of oppression that still disadvantage certain segments of the population, making it highly unlikely that they will experience dramatic upward mobility no matter how hard they might labor. In reality, few Americans go from rags to riches, and the American Dream remains, for most, just that—a dream. But that dream will encourage the masses to be diligent workers and eager consumers, and this is good for the factory owners, CEOs, and stockholders. As productivity and consumption increase, so do their profits. As their profits increase, so does their power. No matter what the intentions, when museums position Lincoln as a poster child for the American Dream, they quite clearly serve the interests of the ruling class.

Likewise, representing Lincoln as a champion of racial equality, even the founding father of the modern civil rights movement, not only distorts his record on race but also serves the interests of the white majority. Amid representations of Lincoln as the Great Emancipator, blacks' own contributions to the cause of freedom are obscured. Many of the museums and exhibits analyzed here include written accounts or drawings of Lincoln's visit to Richmond after it fell to the Union army. Blacks line the streets, kneeling down before Lincoln and hailing him as "Father Abraham." (In some renderings of the scene, the crowds even hail him as "Massa' Linkum."⁴⁴) In such representations, whites are benevolent liberators, and blacks are beholden to whites for *giving* them their freedom. Little wonder that whites are the most avid consumers of Lincoln exhibits: such narratives of benevolence celebrate white virtue and offer absolution, of sorts, for the white nation's sin of slavery.

Positioning Lincoln as the bearer of racial equality furthermore serves to obscure ongoing inequalities in America. In overplaying Lincoln's commitment to social and political equality for blacks, museums leave visitors with the impression that racism and racial inequality are historical artifacts, located firmly in the past. Our nation used to be plagued by racism, the exhibits seem to say, but Lincoln freed us from that burden. Such messages serve to reinforce the notion that any gaps we now see between whites and ethnoracial minorities in terms of such things as wealth, health, educational attainment, political representation, and incarceration rates must be due to certain pathologies within minority groups. If racism is a thing of the past, then minority groups themselves are to blame for falling behind, and whites should be lauded for their greater success.

I am not suggesting some kind of "museo-conspiracy" in which museum officials consciously attempt to indoctrinate the masses with ideas that privilege whites or men or the ruling class.⁴⁵ It is actually far more likely that the views of curators and museum boards have been so profoundly shaped by a century and a half of celebratory Lincoln biographies by largely white male scholars that such views seem simply beyond questioning.[46] In such a context, there is little room for minority views and voices, and scarcely a way of challenging the mythic Lincoln without risking charges of heresy or historical revisionism. It is hardly surprising, then, that the same rather limited set of quotations and anecdotes, images, and supporting characters are on display in the nation's Lincoln museums. Modes of presentation may vary, but the underlying messages are strikingly consistent.

Frederick Douglass once observed that "any man can say things that are true of Abraham Lincoln, but no man can say anything that is new of Abraham Lincoln."[47] His observation might well be applied to Lincoln museums today: they seldom present new information about Lincoln but rather present old information in new (and often interesting) ways. So, if we are unlikely to discover anything new about the sixteenth president in the nation's Lincoln museums, why do we continue to visit them?[48] Critical theorists suggest that in periods of rapid social change, such as our current era, people look to history and "tradition" for reassurance. As historian David Lowenthal puts it, "Beleaguered by loss and change, we keep our bearings only by clinging to remnants of stability."[49] The commonly accepted historical "facts" of Lincoln's life are now sufficiently ossified that he provides just the stability we yearn for. The ground may shift beneath our feet, but Lincoln holds steady, seemingly frozen in time, an unchanging marker to guide us as we navigate the changing terrain of the twenty-first century.

The late twentieth and early twenty-first centuries brought a rapid acceleration of globalization, the increasing interconnectedness of people and institutions worldwide in the economic, political, and cultural realms.[50] Some theorists suggest that as the world becomes more globalized and hybridized, both individual and national identities are becoming destabilized.[51] As individuals move from place to place, their identities are no longer firmly grounded in the locations and social networks that defined previous generations. As national boundaries become more permeable through such things as international commerce and tourism, transnational politics, and global social movements, nations themselves struggle to identify unique national traits. In this context, it is perhaps not surprising that we continue to visit Lincoln museums. He is quintessentially, unambiguously, and authentically American. In Lincoln, at least, our national identity is secure.

Of course, accelerated globalization has been possible largely due to advances in communication and computing technologies, which allow individuals, corporations, and other institutions to maintain a virtual presence around the globe. However, some theorists assert that as we intensify our use of such technologies—from television and the Internet to teleconferencing, virtual networking, and instant messaging—the very nature of human experience is being altered. As everything and everyone becomes mediatized, they argue, we start to see ourselves, others, and the world around us through real or imagined media lenses. Everything becomes a facsimile of something else, and we are left in a world without authenticity, without concrete reality.[52] In this context, theorists say, we come to long for original and authentic experiences. And Lincoln museums seem to provide this. After all, there we can view the actual desk Lincoln wrote on, the clock he watched, and the papers he labored over. Visitors may be drawn to Lincoln exhibits by the promise of such authenticity in an increasingly simulated world.

Ironically, a close reading of museum exhibits often reveals that what appears to be authentic and original may itself be a reproduction. At the SN-MAH, visitors to *Abraham Lincoln: An Extraordinary Life* marvel at Lincoln's circuit-court desk. Safely ensconced in a glass case, it is described by the museum as the "Lincoln desk," the desk "where Lincoln worked," and "the very desk Lincoln used." Only visitors who read to the end of the lengthy description will discover that, with the exception of one decorative rail, the desk is not original. Such cases seem to confirm theorists' contentions that in a mass-mediatized world of simulations it becomes more difficult to distinguish between originals and facsimiles. In such a world, we in fact come to accept these facsimiles as authentic originals.

If we accept that globalization and mass mediatization contribute to the continued popularity of Lincoln exhibits, we must also consider the influence of another hallmark of the current era, secularization. As the influence of organized religion has waned over the past half century in the West, people have sought out alternative forms of worship. This has led to the increasing popularity of such things as meditation, yoga, and back-to-nature retreats, designed not only to heighten self-awareness but also to provide practitioners an experience of something "real," elemental, and often larger than themselves. Likewise, theorists suggest that the veneration of our nation's past, and of key figures such as Lincoln, serves as a kind of "secular religion."[53] From this perspective, Lincoln museums are places to worship not a divine entity but rather "American ideals" or the "American spirit," however each person may choose to define them. In a sense, then, Lincoln museums provide an opportunity to contemplate our connection to something larger than ourselves, to a national community of believers.

Of course, it is difficult to quantify the motivations of museumgoers. They may be seeking authenticity, an affirmation of identity, or a sense of belonging and larger purpose, but they may simply desire distraction or novelty. After all, museums are tourist sites, and as John Urry has convincingly argued, novelty is a key touristic value.[54] What is clear, however, is that underpinning museum representations are material relations. Museums are economic entities. Even nonprofit institutions are constrained by commercial concerns—operating budgets, visitor numbers, and funding contracts, at the very least. Most museums are also partially reliant on gift-shop sales and therefore strive to assemble an inventory of feel-good souvenirs to bolster the bottom line. And many institutions enter into sponsorship agreements, as mentioned earlier. Often the first thing visitors to Lincoln exhibits see is a sponsorship plaque. In institutions across the nation, donors such as AT&T, Exelon, Ford Motor Company, the History Channel, and state and local tourism councils remind us of their contributions to the preservation of Lincoln's memory. As long as museums avoid controversy, sponsors garner positive publicity. While such financial arrangements economically sustain museums, they also constrain them. Commercial considerations are a source of conservative pressure for the nation's Lincoln museums. Curators must balance the drive for historical accuracy and complexity with the economic necessity of keeping both sponsors and visitors happy.

Historian David Lowenthal has observed that "the past is a foreign country whose features are shaped by today's predilections."[55] He asserts that we interpret (or construct) the past in ways that make us feel better about the present. We might glory in past successes while conveniently ignoring past defeats, we might focus on individual and collective virtues but overlook systemic injustices, or we might gaze back nostalgically to times that now seem simpler or nobler in order to comfort ourselves in periods of rapid social change. Lowenthal warns, however, that the more we romanticize, idealize, and commodify the past, the less we are able to learn from it. We would do well to remember that the higher we build Lincoln's pedestal, the harder it will be to hear him.

· *8* ·

Selling Lincoln:
Who Do We Think We Are?

*T*he chapters of this volume have examined not only the ways Americans think about and portray Abraham Lincoln, but the ways they "sell" Lincoln for a wide range of ideological, pedagogical, political, and commercial purposes. This nineteenth-century leader indisputably remains a living part of twenty-first-century American social life. In this final chapter, I examine what contemporary constructions of Lincoln and his intimates and associates reveal about national self-conceptions. I consider the ways that stories of Lincoln carry implicit, and sometimes explicit, messages about what it means to be an American. In other words, I ask what our constructions of Lincoln can tell us about who we think we are.

Since Lincoln's death, Americans have constructed him as an idealized reflection of ourselves—our beliefs, our agendas, and our distinctive characteristics. What is more, in the process of idealizing Lincoln, we have also constructed a number of foils to his greatness, what we might call anti-Lincolns. If Lincoln exemplifies all that is good and admirable about the nation, these individuals exemplify the traits and actions that we as a society seek to avoid, the traits and actions that we see as un-Lincoln-like, and ultimately un-American. Just as our stories about Lincoln can tell us who we think we are, constructions of the anti-Lincolns tell us who we do not want to be.

THE ANTI-LINCOLNS

The "Little Giant": Stephen A. Douglas

In accounts of Lincoln's prepresidential career, one foil is frequently singled out: Stephen A. Douglas (see figure 8.1). As attorneys, both Lincoln and

Figure 8.1. Stephen A. Douglas. *Courtesy of the Abraham Lincoln Presidential Library and Museum*

Douglas worked the Illinois courts and were later elected to the Illinois House of Representatives. Both served in the U.S. Congress, Douglas in the Senate and Lincoln in the House. Both strongly supported state spending on "internal improvements," largely the transportation infrastructure that both men considered crucial to economic development, and both had close ties to the rail industry. Both men moved in the same Springfield social circles, both reportedly courted Mary Todd, and both married into wealthy, slaveholding families. Despite such similarities, the two men are commonly portrayed today as polar opposites.

Politically, Douglas was a Democrat, and Lincoln was a Whig turned Republican. Douglas was a staunch supporter of the Mexican War, while Lincoln denounced it as "unnecessarily and unconstitutionally commenced."

Douglas defended the right of new states and territories to allow slavery, while Lincoln fiercely opposed any expansion of slavery. The men were also strikingly different in appearance. Douglas was short and stout, with dashing waistcoats and a well-tended mane of hair, his small stature and forceful personality earning him the sobriquet "the Little Giant." Lincoln, by contrast, was tall, lanky, and perpetually rumpled.

Beyond such objective differences, stories about Lincoln and Douglas today frequently emphasize the character of the two men. Douglas is usually portrayed as flamboyant, bombastic, and hard drinking, a cocksure politician bankrolled by powerful corporate interests. Lincoln, by contrast, is portrayed as humble and plainspoken, moderate in tastes and habits, and a man of the people. Representations of the two men at the Freeport, Illinois, celebration of the Lincoln-Douglas debates sesquicentennial exemplify widespread perceptions of these men today.

Take, for instance, the exhibit *Confronting Democracy's Boundaries: The Lincoln-Douglas Debates*, created by the Abraham Lincoln Presidential Library and Museum and displayed in the Freeport Public Library during the debate sesquicentennial celebration. The display offered visitors explanations of the larger political and social issues shaping the great debates. The emphasis was on presenting objective facts. Lincoln was not blatantly deified, nor was Douglas pilloried, and yet in subtle ways the exhibit portrayed Lincoln as morally superior to Douglas. The exhibit noted, for instance, that Douglas was seen by many in his own party as a "traitor" because he undermined the authority of Democratic president James Buchanan. It noted that Douglas spent lavishly on his senatorial campaign, outspending Lincoln by fifty to one. It noted that Douglas believed that the notion that "all men are created equal" applied only to white men, and that Lincoln saw Douglas's "popular sovereignty" argument as part of a "national conspiracy to extinguish Northern moral sensibilities and facilitate the spread of slavery." Lincoln, by contrast, was represented through select quotations, facts, and images as a humble Everyman who was committed to equality for all people, who believed that slavery was an indisputable moral wrong, and who won the hearts and minds of the Illinois electorate. A display panel headed "Government by the People: Democratizing Senatorial Elections" explained that although Lincoln won the popular vote in Illinois, Douglas was declared the winner because at that time senators were elected not by the people but by state legislators, a process that gave well-connected candidates like Douglas an advantage. The contest between Lincoln and Douglas (and its less than perfectly democratic outcome), it noted, helped move the nation toward more just electoral reforms.

Permanent displays in Freeport's newly renovated Debate Square further emphasized the differences between Lincoln and Douglas. One interpretive sign noted that although Douglas never owned slaves himself, he certainly used racial bigotry for political gain. He attempted to "stir up racial division" in Freeport, the display asserted, but he was unable to do so. By contrast, the panels noted that while some ridiculed Lincoln, he was ever willing "to sacrifice his own political ambition" to help defeat slavery.

Finally, the main focus of the Freeport debate sesquicentennial celebration was the so-called Debate Reunion, with actors playing the roles of Lincoln and Douglas. Before the two men spoke, Lincoln was introduced as a "champion of the common man," "the savior of our Union," and our "greatest American president." Stephen Douglas, by contrast, was consistently addressed as "Senator" or "Judge" Douglas, a reminder of his elite, political-power-broker status. Each man's scripted statements also helped define his character. Lincoln noted, for instance, that while Douglas traveled through the state in a luxurious private railcar, Lincoln himself chose to travel on riverboats, wagons, and public trains along with "the common man." Douglas, by contrast, admitted that over the course of the campaign, his health suffered due to his heavy drinking. Lincoln noted that he strongly believed that all men are created equal (a statement greeted with enthusiastic applause), that slavery was against natural law (more applause), and that all men should be granted citizenship and full rights (again applause). Douglas, by contrast, noted that he was tired of playing "second fiddle" to Lincoln (laughter). He complained that Illinoisans have "Lincoln-this and Lincoln-that" (more laughter), that Lincoln is on their money and their license plates, and that they can even buy Lincoln bobble heads (hearty laughter). Douglas described himself as a "skilled orator," a Unionist and a patriot, but described Lincoln as the "most revered man in our nation's history," and one who "reminds us of a higher moral calling."

As such portrayals suggest, Stephen A. Douglas is by no means demonized today, and indeed is often praised for his patriotism and defense of democratic principles. However, he is certainly positioned as an anti-Lincoln. We are told that while Lincoln was a man of humility and moderation, Douglas was a man of pride and excess; that while Lincoln acted out of a higher moral sense, Douglas was motivated by political and financial considerations; that while Lincoln was a political underdog, Douglas was a well-connected insider; and that while Douglas may have been better known and more celebrated in his prime, it is Lincoln who has earned the enduring respect and adoration of the American people.

The "Young Napoleon": George B. McClellan

The second of the prominent anti-Lincolns is General George B. McClellan, whom Lincoln appointed general in chief of the Union army in 1861 (see fig-

Figure 8.2. George B. McClellan. *Courtesy of the Abraham Lincoln Presidential Library and Museum*

ure 8.2). McClellan, a young, handsome West Point graduate from a distin-
guished Philadelphia family, cut a dashing figure in his Union blues. While
many historians note the early public enthusiasm for McClellan's command,
accounts typically give more attention to the general's failures, embarrass-
ments, and improprieties. Lincoln's patience, loyalty, and equanimity appear
all the more impressive set against the imperious Young Napoleon.

Let us return briefly to the best-selling Lincoln biographies analyzed
in chapter 3. Most of these biographies mention McClellan's privileged
background, his attractiveness, and his exaggerated sense of personal grandeur. Lincoln biographer Carl Sandburg observed that McClellan "looked
the part, with a well-modeled head, mustache and goatee, sat his saddle as
a trained Man on Horseback, issued commands with authority, [and] published proclamations modeled on Napoleon."[1] He was "handsome, with blue
eyes and reddish brown hair," David Donald noted. "He gave an impression
of strength and vigor."[2] A former officer and military scholar turned engineer
and railroad executive, he appeared to have all of the skills required for command of the Union army. "Official Washington swooned over him."[3]

However, most biographies note that from the beginning McClellan had inflated notions of his own importance. The general recorded all of his daily trials and rewards in letters to his wife, leaving historians a treasure trove of his uncensored thoughts. His own words are offered as windows to his character. "I seem to have become *the* power of the land," he wrote. He "could become Dictator or anything else," he speculated, if only he could overcome the incompetent meddling of Lincoln, whom he characterized as a "baboon," an "idiot," and a "gorilla." He was "driven by a mix of self-esteem and a Calvinist conviction of his preordained role as the nation's deliverer," Richard Carwardine suggests.[4]

But in a story almost tailor made for an American morality tale, McClellan, despite all his extravagant bluster, would not allow his army to take to the battlefield. Instead, biographers note that he organized and drilled his troops, staged "grand reviews and showy parades," hosted "sumptuous dinners" for Washington dignitaries, and enumerated endless excuses for not engaging the enemy.[5] William Herndon suggests that Lincoln likened his reluctant general to a puffed-up rooster, "great on dress parade, but not worth a d—n in a fight."[6] At the very least, Lincoln biographers include the president's eminently quotable observation that McClellan had a case of "the slows."

In addition to McClellan's "obstinacy and procrastination,"[7] most Lincoln biographers note his brazen contempt for his commander in chief. He was "rude" and "belligerent," Stephen Oates notes.[8] He "had no qualms about snubbing the president," Carwardine agrees.[9] In a frequently repeated anecdote, one evening McClellan returned home to learn that Lincoln was waiting for him in the parlor. Instead of receiving the president, the general simply went to bed without a word. Most Lincoln biographers note the president's temperate response to the snub: he told his fuming secretary that "it was better at this time not to be making points of etiquette and personal dignity."[10]

By contrast to Lincoln's self-effacing humility, Lincoln biographers note that McClellan was so vain and pampered that when he finally did take his army to the battlefield, he brought six wagonloads of personal belongings with him.[11] Most historians agree that he made disastrous military decisions, drastically miscalculating the size and location of rebel forces, building boats that proved too large to fit through the Chesapeake and Ohio Canal,[12] and being fooled not once but twice by the enemy's "Quaker guns," logs painted to look like cannons. Allen Guelzo suggests that McClellan simply "panicked" at the prospect of battle. As Guelzo imaginatively describes McClellan during the Peninsula campaign of 1862, "Clammy with fear at the prospect of defeat, the perfect general with the perfect managerial skills now began howling in self-pity and lashing out at everyone who had not made matters perfect for him."[13]

McClellan's tendency to blame others for his own failures is a frequent theme in the biographies. Whether he focused his accusations on his superior officers, the Republican Party, the empty-headed "geese" in the cabinet, or his commander in chief, as Doris Kearns Goodwin puts it, "At the first whiff of censure, McClellan shifted blame onto any other shoulder but his own."[14] Lincoln eventually relieved McClellan of his command, but the Young Napoleon rallied again to win the Democratic nomination in the 1864 presidential race. Despite being backed by "powerful forces," including industrialists, bankers, and the railroads,[15] and despite his confidence that he would win the soldier vote, both the military vote and the election went to Lincoln.

It is hardly surprising that McClellan is a prominent character in popular and scholarly Lincoln narratives. It seems evident from the historical record that McClellan was the source of great hope and even greater frustration for his commander in chief. However, the attention given to not only McClellan's job performance but also to his character serves a second purpose in Lincoln biographies. McClellan's failings make Lincoln's greatness shine all the brighter. McClellan's arrogance is contrasted with Lincoln's modesty, his wealth and privilege with Lincoln's humble background, his cowardice with Lincoln's bravery, and his disloyalty with Lincoln's steadfastness. While McClellan scoffs and sneers, Lincoln wants to "believe the best of everyone."[16] While McClellan blames others and makes excuses, Lincoln shoulders responsibilities and takes action. Kearns Goodwin asserts that when Lincoln made an error, he always owned up to it so others would not be blamed, and he even accepted criticism for things that were not his fault.[17] While McClellan failed despite all his advantages, Lincoln succeeded despite his many disadvantages.

"Old Mr. Greenbacks": Salmon P. Chase

A third anti-Lincoln found in the Lincoln narrative is Salmon P. Chase, Lincoln's secretary of the treasury (see figure 8.3). Unlike McClellan, Chase was not the child of privilege. When his father suddenly died, leaving behind a failed business and eleven children, the family was plunged into bankruptcy. But, like Lincoln, young Salmon Chase possessed the intellect and aspirations that propelled him toward self-improvement. He became a successful lawyer, the governor of Ohio, and a presidential contender in the race Abraham Lincoln would ultimately win. Lincoln biographers most often paint Chase as "priggish," "dour," "imperious," "sanctimonious," "confident of his intellectual superiority," and supremely, almost pathologically, ambitious.[18] Having lost the Republican presidential nomination to Lincoln, biographers suggest, Chase became even more fixated on attaining the presidency. Even as he served in

Figure 8.3. Salmon P. Chase. *Courtesy of the Abraham Lincoln Presidential Library and Museum*

Lincoln's cabinet, he was scheming to unseat the president, "eating a man's bread and stabbing him at the same time," as one of Lincoln's advisers put it.[19]

All of Chase's careful plans to replace Lincoln on the 1864 presidential ballot eventually backfired when a group of his supporters, lead by Kansas senator Samuel Pomeroy, produced a pamphlet roundly criticizing Lincoln and enumerating the many reasons he could not be reelected. As Republicans cursed his disloyalty, and Democrats savored it, a humiliated Chase pled innocence. The secretary claimed that he had no advance knowledge of the Pomeroy circular but had merely agreed to place his name in consideration for the race. Biographers suggest that Lincoln most likely saw through Chase's paper-thin lies but consciously decided to "shut his eyes to all these performances" because Chase was doing an invaluable service to the nation in his management of fiscal policy and his reform of the banking system.[20] But even after the Pomeroy affair, Chase continued to defy and undermine the president, and Lincoln was finally forced to accept his resignation, saying, "You and I have reached a point of mutual embarrassment in our official relation which it seems cannot be overcome, or longer sustained."[21]

Chase's fellow cabinet member Montgomery Blair commented that Chase "was the only human being that I believe Lincoln actually hated."[22] Yet, when Chief Justice Roger Taney died in 1864, Lincoln appointed Chase to the coveted position. Stunned colleagues said Lincoln told them he "would rather have swallowed a buckhorn chair than to have nominated Chase," but he did it for the good of the nation because Chase was simply the best man for the job.[23] Lincoln's secretary, John Nicolay, later observed that no one but Lincoln would have "the degree of magnanimity to thus forgive and exalt a rival who had so deeply and so unjustifiably intrigued against him. It is however only another most marked illustration of the greatness of the President."[24]

Lincoln and Chase were both men of humble origins, both self-made men, and both ambitious. But in our stories of the martyr president, Chase is positioned as Lincoln's antithesis. Yes, both men were ambitious, but while Lincoln is portrayed as a somewhat reluctant candidate—"The taste is in my mouth a little," he said of his run for office—Chase's "head was so full of Presidential maggots he would never be able to get them out."[25] While both men were intellectually gifted, Lincoln was ever the humble seeker of knowledge, while Chase grew arrogant and disdainful of his intellectual inferiors. While Lincoln found much-needed respite in humorous stories and jokes, Chase considered such things a waste of time and "seldom if ever laughed at himself."[26] While both men had good reason to feel pride at their accomplishments, it was Chase, "Old Mr. Greenbacks," whose vanity led him to place his own countenance on the one dollar bill.[27] And while Lincoln was famed for his honesty and loyalty, the scheming Chase was "embodied perfidy."[28] Perhaps above all, in our stories of Lincoln, Chase serves to illustrate the Great Emancipator's nobility of spirit. When political insiders were warning Lincoln against appointing Chase to the Supreme Court, Lincoln reportedly said, "I know meaner things about Governor Chase than any of those men can tell me . . . [but] I should despise myself if I allowed personal differences to affect my judgment of his fitness for the office."[29]

The Insufferable "Hellcat": Mary Todd Lincoln

The final anti-Lincoln we will consider here is the sixteenth president's wife, Mary Todd Lincoln (see figure 8.4). In appearance, the two could not have differed more: Mary was short, plump, and fashionable; Lincoln was gangly and chronically disheveled. Moreover, the two differed starkly in upbringing and temperament. Mary was the privileged, pampered, well-educated daughter of a Kentucky landowner, while Lincoln spent his childhood in rustic log cabins, largely without formal education or the finer material comforts of the age. Mary was hot tempered and status conscious, while Lincoln was tolerant

Figure 8.4. Mary Todd Lincoln. *Courtesy of the Abraham Lincoln Presidential Library and Museum*

and unassuming. Mary made enemies as easily as Lincoln made friends. While Mary had extravagant tastes and used deception to hide her reckless spending, Lincoln was the very picture of restraint and honesty. And while Mary had grown up in a slave-owning household and was largely untroubled by the institution of slavery, Lincoln viewed it as a moral abomination. Even Mary herself recognized their "opposite natures."[30]

Almost without exception, biographies of the Lincolns highlight such dramatic differences, and in most accounts Mary is portrayed as shrewish and unbalanced, a painful thorn in her sainted husband's side. As Mary Lincoln biographer Jean Baker has observed, Mrs. Lincoln "ranks among the most detested public women in American history."[31] Although some historians have begun to critically reassess such negative representations, the majority of twentieth-century Lincoln biographies still include accounts of Mary's "rages," "tantrums," deceit, and apparent selfishness.[32] Such unsympathetic depictions circulate so widely, in fact, that it is little wonder that best-selling Lincoln biographer Michael Burlingame describes Mary as "willful, impulsive, imprudent, superficial, vain, childlike, stingy, jealous, emotionally unstable, tactless, gossipy, malicious, materialistic, sharp-tongued, acquisitive, and indiscreet."[33]

It is of course possible that Mary earned her infamy and deserves the contempt of the nation. Perhaps the historical record is so rife with examples of her misdeeds that biographers have no choice but to represent her as her husband's ignominious foil. But a careful examination of the biographical accounts suggests that it is not so simple. The literature abounds with wildly contrasting interpretations of the historical record, seemingly based more on a priori assumptions about Mary's character than on alternative documentary evidence.

Most historians provide relatively complimentary descriptions of Mary in her youth. "She was a bright-eyed, buxom maiden . . . with glowing skin, abundant auburn hair, and shapely arms and shoulders which she displayed to the limit the fashion would allow."[34] She was "an alluring young belle with impeccable connections" and an impressive education; she was smart and outspoken, always "merry and smiling," with "precocious charm and a penchant for melodrama."[35] However, there is little agreement on the circumstances leading to the marriage of the charming Miss Todd to the awkward but promising Mr. Lincoln. No one disputes that the couple reached some sort of an "understanding" tantamount to engagement in 1840, broke up in January of 1841, and then reconciled and were married in a rather impromptu ceremony in November 1842. But there is a marked lack of consensus on the course of their rocky road to matrimony.

Mark Epstein, in *The Lincolns: Portrait of a Marriage*, suggests that Lincoln called off the engagement due primarily to concerns over the state of his finances, although he may have also initiated the break due to unfounded fears that he had contracted syphilis. According to Epstein, Lincoln was "lovelorn" and devastated by the split, but he kept himself busy to stay "a step ahead of his heartache."[36] Jean Baker, in *Mary Todd Lincoln: A Biography*, likewise offers that Lincoln may have backed out of the engagement because he doubted his ability to provide Mary with the luxuries to which she was accustomed. However, she also notes that Mary herself may have been reluctant to wed, which would have meant giving up her carefree life as a belle and submitting to a husband's authority. Baker concludes that they each had an equal hand in the breakup. "In view of the personalities of the principals, the romance would never have revived unless both had shared in its destruction."[37] Kearns Goodwin in *Team of Rivals* reminds readers, quite sensibly, that due to the dearth of documentary evidence, it is difficult to determine what actually happened in the course of the couple's courtship.[38]

Less charitable biographers paint a very different picture. Early biographers, including Lincoln associates William Stoddard and William Herndon, and more recent writers including Allen Guelzo and H. Donald Winkler, assert with great confidence that Lincoln broke off his engagement with Mary Todd because he realized he did not love her.[39] Some add imaginative details to this basic explanation. Stoddard suggests that Lincoln actually left Mary at the altar, precipitating their breakup.[40] Herndon, whose famed enmity with Mary must be taken into consideration, echoes this claim and adds that "the hideous thought came up like a nightmare" to Lincoln after the first aborted wedding—that he must yet wed Mary to fulfill his obligation.[41] Guelzo repeats this explanation and suggests that Lincoln had fallen in love with another woman but felt honor bound to go through with the wedding nonetheless. In support of his case he includes a quotation from a Lincoln acquaintance who claimed that the great man looked "as if he were going to the slaughter" on his way to the ceremony.[42] Winkler ups the ante. Not only was Lincoln unable to love Mary, but she "aggressively cornered him perhaps through unbridled passion," then demanded that he marry her. She was ambitious and power hungry, and she used "every tactic at her disposal" to snare him. "Did she lure him into bed," he asks, "thereby forcing his commitment?" The answer, to Winkler, is clear. Whatever form their indiscretion took, Lincoln "could not live down his guilty feelings. He gave up" and married her.[43]

Accounts of the Lincolns' domestic life are likewise varied. Ruth Painter Randall, in *Mary Lincoln: Biography of a Marriage*, describes the Lincolns' relationship as "an appealing love story."[44] Epstein likewise paints a romantic picture of the young couple as they "made love under the eaves in the soft fragrant air of June" and "discovered each other by candlelight and then by touch in the dark."[45] Their love was so intense, he explains, that Lincoln became "desperately homesick" when his work took him from Mary, so much so that she accompanied him to Washington, D.C., when he was elected to Congress, at a time when very few congressional wives made the trip.[46] Catherine Clinton, in the biography *Mrs. Lincoln*, claims that the couple's letters from this period show "just how much the couple cared for one another." They were "devoted to one another, and remained faithful to one another."[47] And Baker observes, "In general terms what he lacked she provided (and vice versa)," and their relationship "flourished in the excitement of this contrariety."[48]

However, even writers with the greatest sympathy for Mary acknowledge that her marriage could be volatile. Epstein admits, for instance, that "there are several picturesque anecdotes of Mary Lincoln's physical abuse of her husband during the Springfield years."[49] Many biographies include stories of her chasing Lincoln with a broomstick or a knife and striking him in the face with a piece of firewood. While not defending such alleged violence, some authors ask readers to consider the circumstances that may have sparked such outbursts. As Clinton points out, Abraham Lincoln was undoubtedly a difficult man to live with. He kept irregular hours, was absent for weeks or months at a time, paid little attention to domestic conventions, could be inattentive and distracted, and was prone to bouts of depression.[50] Baker asks us to remember that Mary, too, was a victim, "a victim battered by personal adversity and trapped by destructive conventions of Victorian domesticity."[51] Even C. A. Tripp, who asserts in *The Intimate World of Abraham Lincoln* that the martyr president was gay, pardons Mary. Her jealous eruptions were due to the fact that she could not sexually satisfy her husband and was forced to share him with a string of male lovers.[52]

Such exculpatory accounts are very much in the minority, however. Most Lincoln biographers portray Mary as an unmitigated harpy. Countless biographies repeat Herndon's characterization of the Lincoln marriage as "domestic hell." In three short pages, for instance, Guelzo refers to Lincoln's home life as "domestic hell," "domestic hell on earth," "an ice cave," and "burning, scorching hell."[53] In a variation on the theme, Winkler describes their home as "a suburb of Hades, where Mary served up steaming platefuls of invectives."[54] Winkler adds that Mary would force Lincoln to prepare breakfast, feed and dress the children, and clean the kitchen while she lounged in bed. Both Winkler and Burlingame repeat rumors of Mary's "alleged dalliances" and "unsavory" relationships with other men.[55]

Burlingame, in particular, draws a uniformly (some might say viciously) unflattering portrait of Mary. She was vain and selfish and threw childish "temper tantrums" when she did not get her way. She hounded and nagged and abused her husband, and she "meddled" excessively in official affairs. She was bigoted (especially against the "Wild Irish"), violent, jealous, and deceitful. She wore revealing and unbecoming fashions, attempted to dominate men through flirtation and manipulation, and was characterized by an "almost inhuman coldness."[56] Such scathing criticisms of Mary are, in fact, central to Burlingame's analysis of Lincoln's political life. He endorses the notion that "Lincoln's failure to create a sense of union between himself and Mary Todd . . . impelled him to try preserving the union of the states" and argues, more specifically, that a lifetime of dealing with a difficult and unhappy marriage helped him better manage the bloody trials of civil war.[57]

Opinions are likewise divided on the issue of Mary's maternal and wifely roles. According to Baker and Clinton, she was a devoted wife and dedicated mother who worked diligently to acquire the skills of cooking, housekeeping, and child rearing necessary for running a well-ordered nineteenth-century home. But according to Guelzo and Winkler, she was "ill-suited" to such work, and it proved "too much for her."[58] Baker asserts that "by every account

Mary Lincoln excelled as a mother"; she doted on her children and protected them at all times, even from her own temper.[59] Likewise, Clinton reports that Mary (and her husband) seldom had the heart to discipline the children.[60] Burlingame, by contrast, criticizes Mary for her "general ineptitude in her maternal role," and Guelzo asserts that after arriving in the Executive Mansion, she "became an even harsher disciplinarian" of the children.[61] Stoddard, Kearns Goodwin, and Clinton all note that Mary was able to lift Lincoln's spirits when he was overwhelmed by the enormity of events.[62] But according to Burlingame and Winkler, she offered him "little emotional satisfaction"; rather, she "vexed and harassed" her husband, leading him to avoid her as much as possible.[63]

Many biographers acknowledge that Mary contributed to her husband's political success. However, Mary supporters explain her contributions very differently from Mary detractors. Clinton asserts that Mary was "her husband's close adviser" in political matters.[64] Likewise, Baker suggests that "she consoled and encouraged and . . . advised" Lincoln, and that "Lincoln listened to his wife." Not only that, but Mary dressed him carefully and trained him in the "middle-class etiquette" he needed to be successful. She helped him strategize and served as a sounding board for his speeches.[65] Mary gave her husband the confidence he needed to put himself forward for high office, Epstein adds, because she was always so certain that he was destined for greatness. And Lincoln himself acknowledged Mary's contributions when he won the presidential election of 1860 and exclaimed, "Mary, *we* are elected!"[66]

Mary detractors have a very different interpretation of her influence on his career. She was obsessed with power and status, so she pushed him into the limelight. She made his home so miserable that he stayed away as much as possible, which led him to make many valuable social and political contacts.[67] Because she was such an intolerable companion, he sought refuge in "studious pursuits" that prepared him for public life.[68] And, perhaps above all, "The long years of dealing with his tempestuous wife helped prepare Lincoln for handling the difficult people he encountered as president. . . . The Lincoln's marriage was such a fountain of misery, yet from it flowed incalculable good for the nation."[69]

Although Burlingame has blasted biographers for what he calls "scholarly contortions to defend Mary Todd Lincoln," it is far more difficult to find complimentary depictions of her than to find her condemned.[70] In one account, she is even blamed for contributing to her husband's assassination in three different ways.[71] First, the argument goes, if she had not so alienated Ulysses and Julia Grant with her appalling rudeness, the general and his guard would have accompanied the Lincolns to Ford's Theatre that fateful night and provided better protection for the president. Second, the incompetent police guard who failed to protect Lincoln from the assassin's bullet only had his job because Mary had intervened to exempt him from military duty. And third, Lincoln only frequented the theatre in order to escape from the woes of his life, including the torment of his unhappy marriage. So not only was Mary an acid tongued, ungrateful, hysterical "Hellcat," as Lincoln's secretaries called her, but she helped get her sainted husband killed.

What the varied accounts of Mary Lincoln's life show beyond a doubt is that the same historical documents can be interpreted in vastly different ways. Why then is Mary so routinely demonized? As I said above, it may be that she truly deserves all the scorn that history has heaped upon her. But we must also consider that contemptuous representations of Mary serve another purpose in the Lincoln narrative. First, the worse Mary looks, the better her husband looks in contrast. Her temper better highlights his equanimity; her conceits illuminate his humility; her deceptions make his famed honesty appear even more exceptional. As Baker observes, "The maligned Mary guarantees her husband's nobility."[72]

Second, the "maligned Mary" adds pathos to our hero's story. She was his affliction, his burden, his "cross to bear," and he "bore it as Christ might have done, with supreme calmness and dignity."[73] During the war years, in particular, when—biographers tell us—he barely took the time to sleep or eat, when he was agonizing over every soldier's body being laid to rest, when his face was growing gaunt and haggard, Mary, according to her critics, only added to his misery. Her demands, her outrageous improprieties, and her histrionics were "almost more than Lincoln could endure."[74] And yet he did. He succeeded despite being saddled with such a liability. Giving his "last full measure of devotion," he saved the nation and ascended to national glory.

THE BARBER, THE SEAMSTRESS, AND THE ABOLITIONISTS: AFRICAN AMERICANS IN THE LINCOLN NARRATIVE

Prominent anti-Lincolns, such as those discussed above, reveal the traits we want Lincoln—and our nation—to have. We can also gain insight into national self-conceptions by examining minor characters in the Lincoln narrative. When historical accounts routinely downplay the presence of certain groups, the message is that these people did not really matter in the past and, by extension, do not really matter much today. We might examine any number of groups who are glaringly underrepresented in our stories of Lincoln—women, Native Americans, and recent immigrants, for instance. I focus here on the curious scarcity of African Americans in popular Lincoln discourses.

Given the significance of racial politics in Lincoln's life, it is remarkable that almost no African-American characters make regular appearances in our stories of Lincoln. There are, of course, plentiful references to the "negro problem," to the questionable humanity of blacks, black rights, black military service, and slavery. But such discussions position blacks as a monolithic class of people. Individual voices, individual stories, and the individual names of African Americans are seldom heard. Only four named African Americans make regular appearances in widely circulating Lincoln discourses: Frederick Douglass and Sojourner Truth, both high-profile abolitionists; Elizabeth Keckley, Mary Lincoln's Washington seamstress and confidante; and William de Fleurville, "Billy the Barber," Lincoln's client and friend in Springfield (see figure 8.5).[75]

A systematic content analysis of twenty Lincoln biographies reveals that while most of the volumes include at least one of these four individuals, the space devoted to their stories is very limited. This is not so surprising in the case of William de Fleurville. Lincoln frequented his Springfield barbershop, served as his attorney, and was on friendly terms with this up-and-coming Haitian immigrant, but such casual acquaintances rarely make it into the history books. However, the scant coverage given to Keckley, Douglass, and Truth is more remarkable. After all, Lincoln had a long and close relationship with Elizabeth Keckley, who visited the Executive Mansion almost daily, nursed the Lincolns' sick children, and consoled the First Couple after the death of their beloved son Willie. She even recorded the intimate details of her life with the Lincolns in a controversial memoir. Likewise, Lincoln's interactions with Frederick Douglass and Sojourner Truth are well documented, and both abolitionists left abundant written records of their thoughts and experiences, materials that might easily be incorporated into the Lincoln story. And yet these African Americans receive less attention than their white counterparts.

Take, for instance, Sojourner Truth and Harriet Beecher Stowe. Both were prominent female abolitionists, both met briefly with Lincoln, and both receive only brief coverage in the Lincoln biographies. Yet Beecher Stowe, the white abolitionist, receives more than three times the coverage afforded to Sojourner Truth (see figure 8.6).

Take, next, Frederick Douglass and Horace Greeley. Both were high-profile abolitionists, both met personally with Lincoln, and both publicly criticized Lincoln for his policies on slavery, emancipation, and the participation of blacks in the military. Yet Greeley is afforded almost three times the coverage given to Douglass. Finally, take Elizabeth Keckley and Lincoln's secretaries John Nicolay and John Hay. Although their duties differed, all three served in the Executive Mansion throughout Lincoln's tenure in office,

Figure 8.5. From top left: Frederick Douglass, Elizabeth Keckley, and Sojourner Truth.
Courtesy of the Abraham Lincoln Presidential Library and Museum

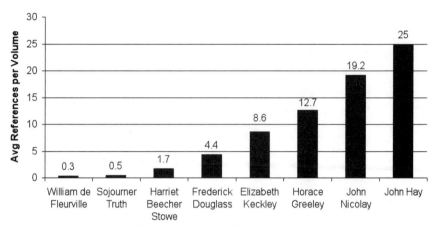

Figure 8.6. Figures Named in Lincoln Biographies[76]

and Keckley continued her intimate association with the Lincoln family long after the president was killed. Yet Nicolay and Hay receive dramatically more attention than Keckley in the biographies.

Of course, some of these discrepancies can be explained by the relative status of these individuals during their lifetimes. By virtue of their race, class, and public positions, the white figures named here were more prominent than their black counterparts. But in addition to the quantitative disparities in the coverage given to African-American and white characters in the Lincoln narrative, there are conspicuous qualitative differences in the representations. In Carl Sandburg's biography of Lincoln, for instance, John Hay and John Nicolay are introduced to the reader through lengthy descriptions of background, character, habits, and accomplishments. Nicolay was "a trusted, reliable, accurate, scrupulous young man, sober as a work horse, earnest as the multiplication table; he had freckles and reddish hair; a young Bavarian from [Pike County]." John Hay was

> a keen whimsical lad. . . . He had been class poet at Brown University, graduated, gone home to Warsaw, Illinois, then to Pike County, and later to Springfield to study law with his Uncle Milton, who had an office on the same floor as Lincoln and Herndon. He wrote notes in French to a sweetheart and had a handsome, careless elegance all the girls in Springfield liked.[77]

Elizabeth Keckley, by contrast, is described simply as "the comely mulatto woman" who demonstrated "rare loyalty and spirit of service" to Mary and won Mrs. Lincoln's "trust and confidence."[78] All of these representations are certainly complimentary. But while Hay and Nicolay are praised in great detail for their exceptional individual traits, Keckley's distinction lies in being an attractive and unusually trustworthy servant.

Some Lincoln biographies that include Keckley do not grant her even this distinction. Michael Burlingame draws liberally from Keckley's memoir (principally for evidence that Mary was overbearing and unbalanced, as discussed above). Yet he includes almost nothing about Keckley herself. Her memoir provides rich details of her extraordinary life—of earning her own freedom from slavery and becoming a prominent businesswoman in Washington, D.C., the much sought-after modiste to the capital's most prestigious families. Instead, he describes her briefly in a footnote as "faithful, sympathetic Elizabeth Keckley, formerly a slave in a good old Virginia family,"[79] the servant whom Mary treated as "a kind of surrogate mammy."[80] Thus, with a few carefully chosen words, this complex and quite significant woman in the Lincolns' lives is reduced to a tired Aunt Jemima stereotype.

We see other forms of omission in coverage of Frederick Douglass. Douglass was an outspoken critic of Lincoln—of his views on colonization, of his long refusal to declare universal emancipation, of his reluctance to allow blacks to serve in the Union army, and of his defense of unequal pay for the black soldiers who were eventually allowed to serve. He had derided Lincoln for "his inconsistencies, his pride of race and blood, his contempt for Negroes and his canting hypocrisy."[81] And, as noted earlier, Douglass even pushed the bounds of propriety by criticizing Lincoln after his death, calling him "preeminently the white man's President, entirely devoted to the welfare of white men."[82] Yet most Lincoln biographies use Frederick Douglass primarily to establish Lincoln's progressive views on race.

For instance, while relatively few biographies include Douglass's scathing criticisms of Lincoln, most include the fact that Lincoln received Douglass as an equal in the White House. A favorite quote of Lincoln biographers is Douglass's assertion that Lincoln was "the first great man that I talked with in the United States freely who in no single instance reminded me of the difference between himself and myself, or the difference of color."[83] Likewise, the most popular anecdote involving Douglass is the story of him attending the reception for Lincoln's second inauguration. "Here comes my friend, Mr. Douglass," the president reportedly exclaimed. "There is no man in the country whose opinion I value more than yours," Lincoln continued. He wanted to know what Douglass thought of his inaugural address. Lincoln biographers seem pleased to report that the abolitionist proclaimed it "a sacred effort."[84] Through such representational choices, biographers downplay Douglass's many valid criticisms of Lincoln and instead emphasize the Great Emancipator's seemingly race-blind magnanimity.

LESSONS FROM THE ANTI-LINCOLNS:
WHO DO WE (NOT) WANT TO BE?

By now it should be clear why our stories of Lincoln include both anti-Lincolns and at least a few minority characters—because these characters help prove the greatness of our martyr president. Stories of Stephen Douglas's pride and self-indulgence highlight Lincoln's modesty and near ascetic habits. Reminders about McClellan's privilege, his contempt for Lincoln, his braggadocio and cowardice, and his refusal to accept responsibility for his own actions (or inaction) only better demonstrate Lincoln's humble origins, the respect and courtesy he accorded even the lowly, his courageous determination, and his willingness to shoulder the blame even if it meant sacrificing himself to protect another. Tales of Chase's pomposity and self-serving betrayals bring to the fore Lincoln's genuine humility, loyalty, and self-sacrifice. Frequently repeated accounts of Mary's instability, her irrationality, her extravagance, and her deceit make her husband's steadfastness, his clarity of thought, his simplicity, and his honesty all the more striking by comparison.

In addition, Lincoln's treatment of these and other characters serves to remind us of his generosity of spirit. Despite Stephen A. Douglas's excoriating attacks on Lincoln during their senatorial election battle, Lincoln still welcomed him into the Executive Mansion and reportedly even had Douglas at his side at his first inaugural address. Despite McClellan's insubordination, his rudeness to his commander in chief, and his serious errors in judgment, Lincoln stood by his general long after members of Congress and members of his own cabinet were clamoring for McClellan's dismissal. Despite Chase's political treachery, Lincoln appointed him to the Supreme Court for the good of the nation. And despite Mary's outbursts, her volatility, her vanity, and the terrible political liability she was, Lincoln stood by her, compensated for her failings, and ever treated her with tender care. Moreover, stories of all these anti-Lincolns make the martyr president's achievements appear all the more impressive for having been hampered by such deeply flawed associates and intimates.

Stories of Lincoln's dealings with African Americans likewise serve to demonstrate his greatness, specifically his seemingly extraordinary commitment to racial equality. Yes, he may have enjoyed blackface minstrel shows, told "darky" jokes, and advocated the relocation of American blacks to outside the United States, but he litigated on behalf of "Billy the Barber," he entrusted Elizabeth Keckley with his sick children, he cordially received Sojourner Truth at the White House, and he addressed Frederick Douglass as "my friend." Stories of Lincoln's racially progressive actions are needed to counterbalance examples of his racially discriminatory comments, habits, and policies that appear with discomfiting regularity in the historical record.

AN OUTSIDER'S PERSPECTIVE ON LINCOLN: THE
SIXTEENTH PRESIDENT IN THE "IMAGINED COMMUNITY"

Nations are more than geopolitical bodies, more than collections of people and institutions within sovereign territories. Nations are discursive constructs. In other words, they are created and sustained in part through the "stories, images, landscapes, scenarios, historical events, national symbols and rituals which . . . give meaning to the nation."[85] To borrow Benedict Anderson's aphorism, nations are "imagined communities."[86] All nations tell themselves stories of national belonging, stories about the nation's origins, its struggles, its triumphs, its character, and its values, stories about where the nation has been and where it is going. These stories help us imagine the nation, help us feel a part of the nation, and therefore help unite us as a nation. We can call such stories discourses of national identity.

The scholarly literature on discourses of national identity suggests four general principles that concern us here.[87] First, discourses of national identity are not hard to find. They are all around us, in political speeches, national anthems, and public monuments, but also in a vast range of mundane cultural productions: printed T-shirts, television advertisements, postcards, sports pages, popular music and film, and folktales, to name just a few.[88] They serve as daily reminders that we belong to a national community with a shared history and shared cultural values and practices. Second, in any given nation, different groups imagine the nation differently, so there are always multiple and competing discourses of national identity, and those discourses change over time in response to social conditions. Third, discourses of national identity often carry implicit, or even explicit, messages about such things as gender, race, ethnicity, class, religion, and sexuality. And fourth, discourses of national identity reflect, reinforce, and occasionally challenge social hierarchies. That is, because our national stories convey messages about things such as gender, race, class, and so on, they reveal which groups (and which traits) are thought to be better, more important, or more significant. But such stories do not simply mirror attitudes; they also shape attitudes. They teach us to respect certain groups and certain traits, and to view others as less desirable.

We will return to these four aspects of national identity in a moment. First, however, let us turn to the place of Abraham Lincoln in our national imaginings. We can read our stories of Lincoln as discourses of national identity. They are idealized reflections of the nation. They tell us who we think we are, and who we want to be. We want to be honest, hardworking, humble, tolerant, good humored, ethical, spiritual, generous, self-sacrificing, determined, upwardly mobile, and successful. So these are the qualities we emphasize in our stories of Lincoln, whether in biographies, political speeches, novels and films, schoolrooms, museums, tourist sites, or product advertisements.

Just to clarify, I am not saying that Lincoln did not have these qualities. No doubt he did, to some degree. But he also had many other qualities that we choose to largely ignore. For instance, history gives us ample evidence of what might reasonably be considered Lincoln's racial bigotry. Granted, attending minstrel shows, telling racist jokes, and advocating the deportation of American blacks to subsidized colonies overseas were culturally acceptable in mainstream mid-nineteenth-century America. As we have seen, some Lincoln biographers claim that because bigotry was mainstream in Lincoln's day, Lincoln was not a bigot, and that it is unseemly to even raise that possibility. But this failure to come to terms with Lincoln's racial views strikes me as akin to arguing that because obesity is so common in America today, no one but the very largest among us should be considered overweight, and, furthermore, that doctors should avoid even inquiring about our weight. Clearly, just avoiding a troubling issue does not make it disappear.

We ignore Lincoln's less than exemplary traits because we do not want to see them in ourselves. Exposing qualities in Lincoln that are anything less than perfect would remind us that, as a nation, we too are less than perfect. The anti-Lincolns help us accomplish this collective denial. We love (to hate) the anti-Lincolns because not only does Lincoln look even greater by comparison to them, but so do we. Emphasizing the faults of these larger-than-life figures in the Lincoln narrative serves to comfort us with the confidence that we might be arrogant, but not as arrogant as McClellan; we might be excessive in our habits, but not as excessive as the hard-drinking Douglas or Mary with her compulsive shopping and emotional outbursts; we might be self-serving and status hungry, but not so much as Chase.

Likewise, representations of minority characters are no doubt gratifying for the white American majority. The underlying message of stories that position Lincoln as the Great Emancipator, a benevolent white father who liberated helpless blacks, is that whites were (and are) noble and powerful, and that blacks were (and are) powerless and dependent. There is almost no space in the Lincoln narrative for the voices, perspectives, and agency of blacks and other ethnoracial minorities. With implicit messages such as these, it is little wonder that whites are the most enthusiastic consumers of Lincoln. The Lincoln narrative offers affirmation of white nobility and absolution for racist sins of the past as well as for ongoing racial injustices. For if Lincoln gave the nation racial equality, then any racial disparities we see today in terms of such things as income, education, and political representation must be the fault of minorities themselves.

Now let us return to the four general characteristics of discourses of national identity discussed above to test how they apply to the Lincoln narrative. Principle one: discourses of national identity take many forms and are all around us. Throughout this volume, we have seen constructions of Lincoln not only in history books and classrooms, but in campaign rallies, gift shops, television shows, romance novels, product advertisements, and elsewhere. Lincoln has become an almost ubiquitous symbol of America at its best. In fact, he has become such a popular mascot of Americanness that he is now, like Ronald McDonald or Mickey Mouse, a bankable commodity, a "unique and ownable" asset, as one advertising executive put it.[89]

Principle two: in all nations, there are multiple and competing discourses of national identity, and they are constantly changing in response to shifting social conditions. Scholars such as Merrill Peterson and Barry Schwartz have painstakingly documented the ways that representations of Lincoln have changed over time as material, political, and cultural circumstances have changed.[90] We have also seen in this volume the ways that groups with diverse, often opposing, positions claim Lincoln as one of their own: the political left and the political right, prochoice politicians and antiabortion groups, the civil rights movement and white supremacists. Each portrays Lincoln, and by extension the nation, in their own image.

Principle three: discourses of national identity carry implicit, and sometimes explicit, messages about such things as gender, race, class, religion, and sexuality. We have seen through the course of this book that women are largely marginalized in the Lincoln narrative. Not only are most prominent Lincoln authorities men, but few named women appear in widely circulating stories of Lincoln. And when they do appear, they are either celebrated for being beatific mothers and virgins (think Nancy Lincoln and Ann Rutledge), or demonized as infernal shrews, like Mary. One underlying message here is that women were not really involved in the monumental historical events of Lincoln's age. They sat largely passive in their parlors as their men changed the world. A broader message is that conventional, passive femininity is the ideal, and women who step too far outside conservative gender roles will be punished for their transgression.

We have also seen that ethnoracial minorities, such as African Americans and Native Americans, receive little attention in the Lincoln narrative, despite the central role of racial politics in Lincoln's life and career. Such minorities are generally treated as monolithic and largely passive groups, managed and fought over by white men. These representations deny the individuality and agency of minorities and obscure their contributions to American history and to their own hard-won advancement. One larger underlying message is that our nation was built by and for white men, with minorities simply coming along for the ride.

In addition to messages about gender and race, we have seen ample evidence that our stories of Lincoln convey messages about class. The emphasis on Lincoln as a self-made man reveals our national fixation on the American Dream of upward mobility. On the one hand, such rags-to-riches tales provide hope and inspiration to the nation. On the other hand, however, the message that anyone can rise from poverty to power and everlasting fame ignores the many structural impediments to such dramatic upward mobility. Institutional discrimination, two-tiered educational and health-care systems, and deeply ingrained prejudices against the poor present substantial barriers to overcoming poverty, let alone rising to the top of American society. If Lincoln proves that anyone who works hard enough can get to the top, then the implication is that those at the bottom must not really be trying.

Finally, through the course of this book, we have seen that the stories we tell ourselves about Lincoln contain subtle messages about such things as religion and sexuality. As we have seen, in most widely circulating representations of Lincoln, his conventional Christianity and his heterosexuality are either forcefully asserted or simply assumed. Only when someone challenges such assumptions does the resulting backlash expose the degree to which the nation is invested in the notion of Lincoln's Christian faith and normative sexuality. If our national heroes must be straight and Christian, then the message is that nonheterosexuals and non-Christians cannot be our heroes, cannot be American exemplars.

Principle four: discourses of national identity reflect, reinforce, and sometimes challenge social hierarchies. Certainly the Lincoln narrative today reflects current social inequalities. Women earn less than men on average, hold markedly fewer top executive positions, and are dramatically underrepresented in elective office, especially at the national level. African Americans earn less on average than whites, are less likely to graduate from high school or college or own their own homes, and are much more likely to be incarcerated. Similar patterns of disadvantage are found in many other ethnoracial minority groups. And religious and sexual minorities face entrenched bigotry and both personal and institutional forms of discrimination—from stereotypical representations in the media to the desecration of mosques and synagogues, "gay bashing," and the denial of full civil and family rights. In other words, just as these groups are less powerful and less prominent in American society today, they are less visible in today's Lincoln narrative. Furthermore, we can see that as the balance of power in society changes, so does the Lincoln narrative. For instance, only when African Americans and women began to gain status and power in the twentieth century did we see more inclusion of these groups in the stories we tell ourselves about Lincoln. Indeed, the most encouraging aspect of my examination of Lincoln, Inc., is clear evidence of how much more inclusive the Lincoln narrative has become over time.

So the Lincoln narrative certainly reflects social inequalities, but, more than this, it can also help sustain such inequalities by making the dominance of certain groups, and the disadvantage of others, seem natural and normal. The more often we see only whites, Christians, and unambiguously "straight" men held up as national heroes, the more likely we are to look to them as exemplars. Likewise, the more often we are told that women, ethnoracial and sexual minorities, and the poor have contributed little to the nation, the harder it is for us to imagine such people in positions of power and authority, to hire them and promote them, and to accept them as our leaders and our heroes. It would be ridiculous to suggest that Lincoln himself is to blame for the social inequalities that are so evident in American society today, and overly simplistic to argue that the stories we tell ourselves about Lincoln are to blame. And that is not what I am saying. Rather, I am suggesting that the way we represent and use national heroes like Lincoln tells us something about the way we see both ourselves and our nation. Such perceptions shape the ways we treat others, for better or for worse.

CODA: IN DEFENSE OF LINCOLN, INC.

In my three-year foray into the world of *Lincoln, Inc.*, I have logged roughly eight thousand miles and spent countless hours exploring Lincoln museums, historic sites, monuments, and souvenir shops; watching Lincoln in film and television; and reading scores of Lincoln publications. It has been my great pleasure and privilege to learn more both about Lincoln and about the men and women who devote their lives to studying, teaching about, and promoting an understanding of our sixteenth president. Although this book sheds a critical light on the appropriation and starry-eyed veneration of Lincoln, I am not in general principle critical of scholars or history buffs who focus on Lincoln. After all, I have become one of them.

I wholeheartedly encourage readers to delve into the vast scholarship on Lincoln, to venture into the fascinating realm of Lincoln fiction and film, and to seek out Lincoln museums and historic sites. Armed with an awareness of the ways Lincoln is socially constructed, such an undertaking promises not only to teach us about Abraham Lincoln but also to teach us something about ourselves.

Notes

CHAPTER ONE

1. Merrill Peterson, *Lincoln in American Memory* (New York: Oxford University Press, 1994), 21.

2. For a full discussion of discourses of national identity, see Jackie Hogan, *Gender, Race and National Identity: Nations of Flesh and Blood* (New York: Routledge, 2009).

3. David H. Donald, *Lincoln* (New York: Simon & Schuster, 1995), 245; AL-PLM exhibit, 2008.

4. Donald, *Lincoln*, 252.

5. Gary L. Bunker, *From Rail-Splitter to Icon: Lincoln's Image in Illustrated Periodicals, 1860–1865* (Kent, OH: Kent State University Press, 2001).

6. Donald, *Lincoln*, 536–37.

7. Peterson, *Lincoln in American Memory*; Barry Schwartz, *Abraham Lincoln and the Forge of National Memory* (Chicago: University of Chicago Press, 2000); and Barry Schwartz, *Abraham Lincoln in the Post-Heroic Era: History and Memory in Late Twentieth-Century America* (Chicago: University of Chicago Press, 2008).

8. Schwartz, *Abraham Lincoln and the Forge of National Memory*, 35–37.

9. Walt Whitman, "Oh Captain! My Captain!" (1865); Julia Ward Howe, "Crown His Blood-Stained Pillow" (1865).

10. Peterson, *Lincoln in American Memory*, 131.

11. Schwartz, *Abraham Lincoln and the Forge of National Memory*, 267.

12. According to the U.S. Census, the median salary for full-time workers was $543 in 1909. Available at http://www2.census.gov/prod2/statcomp/documents/CT1970p1-05.pdf (accessed September 12, 2008).

13. Peterson, *Lincoln in American Memory*, 148.

14. CNN, "1864 Lincoln Letter Brings $3.4 Million." Available at http://edition.cnn.com/2008/US/04/03/lincoln.letter/ (accessed August 26, 2008).

15. In a discussion of Lincolniana, Andrew Ferguson notes that there is even a thriving market in Lincoln forgeries. Andrew Ferguson, *Land of Lincoln: Adventures in Abe's America* (New York: Atlantic Monthly Press, 2007).

16. According to the National Park Service, which maintains the site, the current gravestone, sculpted by J. S. Culver, was dedicated in 1902.

17. While estimates of the number of extant Lincoln books vary, I use the published estimate by the curator of the Abraham Lincoln Presidential Library in James Cornelius, "Abe's Day: What's New in the Annals of Lincolnology," *Newsweek*, February 12, 2008. Available at http://www.newsweek.com/id/110794 (accessed September 12, 2008).

18. Peterson, *Lincoln in American Memory*, 198.

19. Peterson, *Lincoln in American Memory*, 197.

20. Richard Carwardine, *Lincoln: A Life of Purpose and Power* (New York: Vintage, 2007), 33.

21. Donald, *Lincoln*, 599.

22. Schwartz, *Abraham Lincoln and the Forge of National Memory*; Schwartz, *Abraham Lincoln in the Post-Heroic Era*.

23. This position is most closely associated with the work of Jean Baudrillard, especially in his *Simulacra and Simulation*, trans. Sheila Glaser (Ann Arbor: University of Michigan Press, 1995), originally published as *Simulacra et Simulation* in 1981.

24. Peterson, *Lincoln in American Memory*.

25. Schwartz, *Abraham Lincoln and the Forge of National Memory*, 310.

CHAPTER TWO

1. Except when otherwise noted, I take all Lincoln quotations from *The Collected Works of Abraham Lincoln* compiled by the Abraham Lincoln Association, available at http://quod.lib.umich.edu/l/lincoln.

2. All items and prices are taken from Lincoln historic sites visited in 2008.

3. Available at http://www.railsplitter.com (accessed December 9, 2008).

4. Sergey Kadinsky and Christina Boyle, "On Abraham Lincoln's 200th Birthday, Handwritten Speech Breaks Auction Record at Christie's," *New York Daily News*, February 12, 2009, available at http://www.nydailynews.com/news/2009/02/12/2009-02-12_on_abraham_lincolns_200th_birthday_handw.html (accessed June 14, 2010).

5. Aaron Baar, "Lincoln Focuses on Its Name," *Adweek, Midwest Edition* 43, no. 30 (2002): 2.

6. The corporation was then known as the Lincoln National Life Insurance Company (Peterson, *Lincoln in American Memory*, 197).

7. Lincoln Financial Group, available at https://www.lfg.com/LincolnPageServer?LFGPage=/lfg/lfgclient/index.html (accessed January 31, 2011).

8. Baar, "Lincoln Focuses on Its Name," 2.

9. Marc Iskowitz, "Don't Blame DTC for Dismal Rozerem Sales," *Medical Marketing and Media*, June 15, 2007, available at http://www.mmm-online.com/Dont-blame-DTC-for-dismal-Rozerem-sales/article/24186/ (accessed December 9, 2008).

10. ALPLM, "Governor Blagojevich Announces That Abraham Lincoln Presidential Museum Has Welcomed Its 1 Millionth Visitor," January 6, 2007, available at http://www.alplm.org/news/jan06_07.html (accessed August 21, 2009); Tim Landis and Natalie Morris, "Tourism Booming, Museum Seems to Be Boosting All Attractions," *State Journal Register*, July 21, 2005, available at http://showcase.netins.net/web/creative/lincoln/news/boom.htm (accessed January 21, 2011).

11. Landis and Morris, "Tourism Booming"; Paul Povse, "Closure of Illinois Historic House Garners Protest; It's Just One of 14," *St. Louis Beacon*, September 15, 2008, available at http://www.stlbeacon.org/region/3194 (accessed January 21, 2011).

12. Quotations from *Looking for Lincoln*, pamphlet (Springfield, IL: Lincoln Heritage Coalition, 2005); and the *2008–2009 Heritage Corridor Visitor's Guide* (Joliet, IL: Heritage Corridor Convention and Visitor's Bureau).

13. Available at www.enjoyillinois.com (accessed July 23, 2008).

14. Stephen Douglas quoted in Donald, *Lincoln*, 218.

15. Personal communication with Freeport Visitor's Bureau staff.

16. Details from *The Stump, Publication of the Lincoln-Douglas Society* (Freeport, IL), no. 1 (Spring 2008).

17. Harriett Gustason, "Echoes of History," *Journal-Standard*, Debate Reunion Tour insert, August 17, 2008, 2.

18. Based on 2007 census and other data sources, available at http://www.city-data.com/city/Freeport-Illinois.html (accessed December 18, 2008).

19. Jane Lethlean, "*Untold Stories*: Multimedia Exhibit on Display," *Journal-Standard*, October 16, 2008.

20. In most social scientific literature of recent decades, *race* refers to certain physical markers (such as skin color) that a given society considers significant enough to distinguish one group of people from another, while *ethnicity* refers to cultural markers (such as language and religion) that are used to distinguish one group from another. In everyday usage, however, *race* and *ethnicity* are frequently conflated. To acknowledge this widespread coalescence of the concepts, throughout this volume I adopt the term *ethnoracial*, although I retain standard analytical terms, such as *racism*.

21. Edward M. Bruner, *Culture on Tour: Ethnographies of Travel* (Chicago: University of Chicago Press, 2005), 152–53.

22. James Loewen, *Lies across America: What Our Historic Sites Get Wrong* (New York: Touchstone, 1999).

23. For further discussion of the Lincoln birthplace cabin, see Loewen, *Lies across America*, 166–69; Ferguson, *Land of Lincoln*, 250–57; and Edward Steers Jr., *Lincoln Legends: Myths, Hoaxes and Confabulations Associated with Our Greatest President* (Lexington: University Press of Kentucky, 2007), 1–13.

24. Loewen, *Lies across America*, 168.

25. *Looking for Lincoln*, pamphlet (Springfield, IL: Lincoln Heritage Coalition, 2008).

26. In the midst of the Great Depression, the Civilian Conservation Corps provided much of the labor to reconstruct the village. For more on the development of Lincoln's New Salem, see *Lincoln's New Salem: A Village Reborn* (Petersburg, IL: New Salem Lincoln League, 1994).

27. ALPLM guests who take the time to read the full explanations for the "real" sites will see them described as "re-created" or "reconstructed" sites.

28. From undated promotional pamphlet and map issued by the Looking for Lincoln Coalition, Springfield, Illinois.

29. Details on the Ann Rutledge burial sites are taken from Steers, *Lincoln Legends*, 51–59.

30. Comment by ALPLM administrator during a site visit by Bradley University students and faculty, April 2008.

31. See Schwartz's Durkheimian analysis of Lincoln's place in the national imagination in *Abraham Lincoln and the Forge of National Memory* and his *Abraham Lincoln in the Post-Heroic Era.*

32. The restaurant was known simply as the Waffle Shop until it recently relocated to the Lincoln House Restaurant across from Ford's Theatre.

33. For a detailed account of the plot, see Thomas J. Craughwell, *Stealing Lincoln's Body* (Cambridge, MA: Belknap, 2007).

34. See George Ritzer, *The McDonaldization of Society*, rev. ed. (Thousand Oaks, CA: Pine Forge Press, 2004).

35. Baudrillard, *Simulacra and Simulation.*

36. Personal observation at the Louvre.

CHAPTER THREE

1. Robert N. Bellah, "Civil Religion in America," *Daedalus: Journal of the American Academy of Arts and Sciences* 96, no. 1 (1967): 1–21.

2. Croly quoted in Schwartz, *Abraham Lincoln and the Forge of National Memory*, 256.

3. In an analysis of 8,200 scholarly journals in the Academic Search Premier index from between 1988 and 2008, 1,114 articles contained Abraham Lincoln as a subject, compared with 634 articles focused on George Washington.

4. Schwartz, *Abraham Lincoln in the Post-Heroic Era*, 152.

5. Based on a search of publications with "Abraham Lincoln" in the subject field in www.worldcat.org. Accessed July 1, 2011. Figure 3.1 shows the number of books published in each five-year period from 1870 to 2010.

6. James G. Randall, "Has the Lincoln Theme Been Exhausted?" *American Historical Review* 41 (1936): 270–94.

7. Robert D. Hormats, "Abraham Lincoln and the Global Economy," *Harvard Business Review* 81, no. 8 (2003); George McKenna, "On Abortion: A Lincolnian Perspective," *Atlantic Monthly*, September 1995. Available at http://www.theatlantic.com/issues/95sep/abortion/abortion.htm (accessed September 12, 2008); Ronald S. Fishman and Adriana Da Silveira, "Lincoln's Craniofacial Microsomia: Three-Dimensional Laser Scanning of 2 Lincoln Life Masks," *Archives of Ophthalmology* 125, no. 8 (2007); Donna D. McCreary, *Lincoln's Table: A President's*

Culinary Journey from Cabin to Cosmopolitan (Charlestown, IN: Lincoln Presentations, 2008).

8. Vera Kaikobad, "Acupuncture Diagnosis of Abraham Lincoln," *Medical Acupuncture* 19, no. 4 (2007): 187.

9. Due to the vast number of Lincoln biographies available, I was forced to be quite selective in compiling my sample. I chose to analyze twenty texts from a neat 140-year period (1866 to 2006), concentrating on those volumes that generated marked public and scholarly attention. I concluded my analysis with Doris Kearns Goodwin's (2006) *Team of Rivals*, arguably the highest-profile Lincoln biography of the last ten years. This sample should not be interpreted as a list of the "best" or most definitive Lincoln biographies. I leave such judgments to my esteemed colleagues in the Lincoln academy. Those volumes analyzed for this study are detailed in table 3.1 below.

10. Peterson, *Lincoln in American Memory*, 7.

11. Barry Schwartz, "Collective Memory and History: How Abraham Lincoln Became a Symbol of Racial Equality," *Sociological Quarterly* 38, no. 3 (1997): 469–96; Barry Schwartz and Howard Schuman, "History, Commemoration, and Belief: Abraham Lincoln in American Memory, 1945–2001," *American Sociological Review* 70, no. 2 (2005): 183–203.

12. Because Joshua Wolf Shenk's biography, *Lincoln's Melancholy*, focuses almost exclusively on Lincoln's depression, it was excluded from this statistical analysis in order to avoid skewing the averages.

13. Hogan, *Gender, Race and National Identity*.

14. For an incisive discussion of America's struggles against real and imagined threats, see Richard Slotkin, *Gunfighter Nation: The Myth of the Frontier in Twentieth-Century America* (New York: Atheneum, 1992).

15. Josiah Holland, *The Life of Abraham Lincoln* (Springfield, MA: Gurdon Bill, 1866), 8, 544.

16. Ida M. Tarbell, *The Life of Abraham Lincoln*, 2 vols. (New York: McClure, Phillips, 1900), 17.

17. William M. Thayer, *From Pioneer Home to White House: Life of Abraham Lincoln, Boyhood, Youth, Manhood, Assassination, Death* (New York: Hurst, 1882), 157.

18. Tarbell, *Life of Abraham Lincoln*, 46.

19. Of course, some anecdotes and quotations do not appear in the earlier works because they had not yet been discovered. However, each of these examples did appear in at least one nineteenth-century source.

20. While the term *me generation* has been used by different authors in a variety of ways, it is generally used to designate those who came of age during the 1970s, 1980s, or 1990s. It is said to be characterized by a heightened concern with self, bordering on narcissism.

21. Elizabeth Wurtzel, *Prozac Nation: Young and Depressed in America* (New York: Penguin, 1994).

22. Joshua Wolf Shenk, *Lincoln's Melancholy* (New York: Mariner Books, 2005).

23. The incident is included in many recent biographies, among these, Doris Kearns Goodwin, *Team of Rivals: The Political Genius of Abraham Lincoln* (New York: Simon and Schuster), 174–76; and Donald, *Lincoln*, 186–87.

Table 3.1. Lincoln Biographies

Author	Year	Title	Period
Josiah Holland	1866	*The Life of Abraham Lincoln* (Springfield, MA: Gurdon Bill)	Nineteenth Century
William M. Thayer	1882	*From Pioneer Home to the White House: Life of Abraham Lincoln, Boyhood, Youth, Manhood, Assassination, Death* (New York: Hurst)	
William O. Stoddard	1884	*Abraham Lincoln: The True Story of a Great Life* (New York: Fords, Howard and Hubert)	
Isaac N. Arnold	1887	*The Life of Abraham Lincoln* (Chicago: A. C. McClurg)	
William H. Herndon and Jesse W. Weik	1889	*Herndon's Lincoln: The True Story of a Great Life*, 3 vols. (Springfield, IL: Herndon's Lincoln Publishing Company)	
Ida M. Tarbell	1900	*The Life of Abraham Lincoln*, 2 vols. (New York: McClure, Phillips)	Early–Mid Twentieth Century
Ward Hill Lamon	1911	*The Life of Abraham Lincoln* (Washington, DC: Dorothy Lamon Teillard)	
Benjamin P. Thomas	1952	*Abraham Lincoln* (New York: Knopf)	
Carl Sandburg	1954	*The Prairie Years and the War Years* (New York: Harcourt, Brace and World)	
J. G. Randall and Richard N. Current	1957	*Mr. Lincoln* (New York: Dodd, Mead)	
Stephen B. Oates	1977	*With Malice toward None* (New York: HarperPerennial)	Late Twentieth Century
Mark Neely	1993	*The Last Best Hope* (Cambridge: Harvard University Press)	
Michael Burlingame	1994	*The Inner World of Abraham Lincoln* (Urbana: University of Illinois Press)	
David H. Donald	1995	*Lincoln* (New York: Simon and Schuster)	
Allen Guelzo	1999	*Abraham Lincoln: Redeemer President* (Grand Rapids, MI: Eerdmans)	
William Lee Miller	2002	*Lincoln's Virtues: An Ethical Biography* (New York: Vintage)	
C. A. Tripp	2005	*The Intimate World of Abraham Lincoln* (New York: Avalon)	
Joshua Wolf Shenk	2005	*Lincoln's Melancholy* (New York: Mariner Books)	
Richard Carwardine	2006	*Lincoln: A Life of Purpose and Power* (New York: Vintage)	
Doris Kearns Goodwin	2006	*Team of Rivals: The Political Genius of Abraham Lincoln* (New York: Simon and Schuster)	

Table 3.2. Lincoln Quotations in All Biographies

Quotation	Context
"The institution of slavery is founded on both injustice and bad policy."	Lincoln's written protest to the Illinois state legislature, 1837.
"[I]t is a great piece of folly to attempt to make anything out of my early life. It can all be condensed into a single sentence . . . you will find in Gray's *Elegy*: 'The short and simple annals of the poor.'"	Lincoln's response to John Locke Scripps's request for biographical details, 1860.
"If [the Union] can't be saved upon that principle [of the Declaration of Independence], I was about to say I would rather be assassinated on this spot than to surrender it."	Lincoln's speech at Independence Hall, Philadelphia, 1861.
"Without the assistance of that Divine Being, who ever attended him, I cannot succeed. With that assistance I cannot fail."	Lincoln's farewell speech, Springfield, Illinois, 1861.
"I am naturally anti-slavery. If slavery is not wrong, nothing is wrong. I cannot remember when I did not so think, and feel."	Lincoln's letter to Albert Hodges, 1864.
"Remember to call upon, and confide in, our great, and good, and merciful Maker; who will not turn away from him in any extremity. He notes the fall of a sparrow, and numbers the hairs of our heads; and He will not forget the dying man who puts his trust in Him."	Lincoln's words to his ailing father in a letter to his step-brother, John Johnston, 1851.
"The purposes of the Almighty are perfect and must prevail, though we erring mortals may fail to accurately perceive them in advance. . . . Surely He intends some great good to follow this mighty convulsion, which no mortal could make, and no mortal could stay."	Lincoln's letter to Eliza P. Gurney of the Society of Friends, 1864.

(continued)

Table 3.2. (*continued*)

Quotation	Context
"I am not, nor ever have been in favor of bringing about in any way the social and political equality of the white and black races. . . . There is a physical difference between the white and black races which I believe will for ever forbid the two races living together on terms of social and political equality."	Lincoln's statement during the 1858 debate with Stephen Douglas, in Charleston, Illinois.
"It isn't a pleasant thing to think that when we die that is the last of us."	Lincoln's reported statement to Parthena Hill, New Salem, ca. 1835.
"I am not a Christian. God knows, I would be one, but I have carefully read the Bible, and I do not so understand this book."	Lincoln's reported statement to Newton Bateman, Springfield, Illinois, 1860.
"You and we are different races. We have between us a broader difference than exists between almost any other two races." He added that it was "better for us both, therefore, to be separated."	Lincoln's statement in support of colonization to a group of freedmen, 1862.
Christ was a "bastard."	Lincoln's reported comment to Methodist minister James Matheny, cited in W. E. Barton, *The Soul of Abraham Lincoln* (New York: George H. Doran Company, 1920), 344.

24. For a discussion of changing human-animal relations, see Adrian Franklin, *Animals and Modern Cultures: A Sociology of Human-Animal Relations in Modernity* (London: Sage, 1999).

25. Peterson, *Lincoln in American Memory*, 70–77.

26. The phrases in figure 3.6 are paraphrases of Lincoln quotations. The full quotations and the original context of each quotation are listed in table 3.2 above.

27. William Lee Miller, *Lincoln's Virtues: An Ethical Biography* (New York: Vintage, 2002), 256. Miller goes on to present an extended defense of Lincoln's comments on race, 353–63.

28. I use the term *men* intentionally here. In most cases, Lincoln's assertions about freedom and equality applied specifically to men. Women only made their way into widespread national discourses of equality in the second half of the twentieth century.

29. Thomas DiLorenzo, *Lincoln Unmasked: What You're Not Supposed to Know about Dishonest Abe* (New York: Crown Forum, 2006), 150.

30. DiLorenzo, *Lincoln Unmasked*, 49, 50.

31. DiLorenzo, *Lincoln Unmasked*, 170.

32. In the early twentieth century, the idea that language influences cognition was put forth by Edward Sapir. It was later championed by Sapir's student Benjamin Whorf and tested by Roger Brown and Eric Lenneberg. Today this notion is widely known as the Sapir-Whorf hypothesis.

33. Lera Boroditsky, "How Does Our Language Shape the Way We Think?" in *What's Next: Dispatches on the Future of Science*, ed. Max Brockman (New York: Vintage, 2009).

34. Boroditsky, "How Does Our Language Shape the Way We Think?"

35. Erving Goffman, *Frame Analysis: An Essay on the Organization of Experience* (New York: Harper and Row, 1974).

36. See, for example, Robert M. Entman, "Framing: Toward Clarification of a Fractured Paradigm," *Journal of Communication* 43, no. 4 (1993): 51–58.

37. Entman, "Framing," 52.

38. In fact, social theorist Liah Greenfeld has called nationalism "*the* cultural framework of modernity." Liah Greenfeld, "Is Nation Unavoidable? Is Nation Unavoidable Today?" in *Nation and National Identity: The European Experience in Perspective*, ed. Hanspeter Kriesi, Klaus Armigeon, Hannes Siegrist, and Andreas Wimmer (Chur and Zürich: Rüegger, 1999), 39, emphasis added.

39. See the discussion of frames in Erika G. King and Mary deYoung, "Imag(in) ing September 11: Ward Churchill, Frame Contestation, and Media Hegemony," *Journal of Communication Inquiry* 32, no. 2 (2008): 123–39.

40. See, for instance, Carragee and Roefs's argument about the importance of analyzing the power relations that shape the production and reception of frames, in Kevin M. Carragee and Wim Roefs, "The Neglect of Power in Recent Framing Research," *Journal of Communication* 54, no. 2 (2004): 214–33.

41. See James Bradley, *The Imperial Cruise: A Secret History of Empire and War* (New York: Little, Brown, 2009).

CHAPTER FOUR

1. Seth Grahame-Smith, *Abraham Lincoln: Vampire Hunter* (New York: Grand Central Publishing, 2008), 53.

2. Gore Vidal, *Lincoln: A Novel* (New York: Vintage, 2000), originally published in 1984; John Ford, *Young Mr. Lincoln* (Twentieth Century Fox, 1939).

3. Grahame-Smith, *Abraham Lincoln: Vampire Hunter*; *Star Trek*: "The Savage Curtain" (Paramount Studios, 1969); Shawn Levy, *Night at the Museum: Battle for the Smithsonian* (Twentieth Century Fox, 2009); Aaron Loeb, *Abraham Lincoln's Big Gay Dance Party* (2010).

4. Analysis of listings (excluding documentaries) on the Internet Movie Database, available at www.imdb.com (accessed January 6, 2011).

5. James Tackach, "Abraham Lincoln in Recent American Fiction," *Lincoln Herald* 110, no. 4 (2008): 238.

6. As detailed here, my terminology differs somewhat from the formal genres used by scholars of film and literature. *Biographical fiction/biopic*: I classify as biographical fiction/biopic those works grounded strongly in the historical record, often closely following the documented events of Lincoln's life. These works are generally aimed at bringing Lincoln and his time alive by blending historical evidence with invented dialog and fictional characters. *Period suspense*: The period suspense genre includes works set in the Civil War era and focusing on perilous intrigue, particularly espionage and conspiracy. Stories in this genre are rife with anxiety, tension, and danger. *Contemporary suspense*: Likewise, in the contemporary suspense genre, modern-day characters face threats that arise out of Lincoln's life and legacy. This often centers on explosive Civil War–era secrets that the innocent main character stumbles upon. *Romance*: The Lincoln romance centers on the amorous, often sexually charged relationship between Lincoln and real or fictional women. (Despite ongoing debates regarding Lincoln's sexual orientation, I have been unable to find any fictional works depicting Lincoln in a sexual/romantic relationship with a man.) *Science fiction/fantasy*: In the science fiction/fantasy genre are those works featuring supernatural and extraterrestrial characters, time travel, cyborgs, and other fantastical elements. This is a broad genre, with works ranging from the romantic to the philosophical to the downright gory.

7. Ivan Reitman, *Kindergarten Cop* (Universal Studios, 1990); Spike Lee, *Bamboozled* (New Line Cinema, 2000); Thomas Dixon, *The Clansman: An Historical Romance of the Ku Klux Klan* (New York: Doubleday, Page, 1905); D. W. Griffith, *The Birth of a Nation* (David W. Griffith Corp., 1915); Stephen Herek, *Bill and Ted's Excellent Adventure* (De Laurentiis Entertainment Group, 1989).

8. U.S. Scouting Service Project, available at http://usscouts.org/advance/boyscout/bsoathlaw.asp (accessed January 7, 2011). The one exception here is the trait of cheerfulness. Although biographical novels and biopics usually represent Lincoln as good humored, many also show his melancholy side.

9. Richard Slotkin, *Abe: A Novel* (New York: Henry Holt, 2000), 16.

10. Slotkin, *Abe*, 416, 11, 68, 275.

11. Slotkin, *Abe*, 165, 125, 383.

12. Slotkin, *Abe*, 383.

13. Slotkin, *Abe*, 151, 136.

14. Slotkin, *Abe*, 58–60, 68.

15. Slotkin, *Abe*, 197–99, 317–27, 419.

16. Slotkin, *Abe*, 419.

17. Slotkin, *Abe*, 383–412.

18. Slotkin, *Abe*, 72–73, 224–25.

19. Slotkin, *Abe*, 358–59.

20. Slotkin, *Abe*, 469–70.

21. Vidal, *Lincoln*, 342, 105.

22. William Safire, *Freedom: A Novel of Abraham Lincoln and the Civil War* (New York: Avon, 1988), 743.

23. Vidal, *Lincoln*, 289–90.

24. Vidal, *Lincoln*, 356.

25. Anna Myers, *Assassin* (New York: Walker Books, 2005), 136.

26. Myers, *Assassin*, 199, 178–79, 112.

27. Ann Rinaldi, *An Acquaintance with Darkness* (Boston: Graphia, 1999), 29–30, 57.

28. Gary Blackwood, *Second Sight* (New York: Penguin, 2005), 202.

29. David Robertson, *Booth: A Novel* (New York: Doubleday, 1997), 256, 161.

30. Robertson, *Booth*, 278.

31. Robertson, *Booth*, 280.

32. Robertson, *Booth*, 181.

33. Steven Wilson, *President Lincoln's Spy* (New York: Kensington, 2008), 133–34.

34. Wilson, *President Lincoln's Spy*, 314.

35. Myers, *Assassin*, 86.

36. Rinaldi, *An Acquaintance with Darkness*, 104–5, 123.

37. Blackwood, *Second Sight*, 35.

38. Wilson, *President Lincoln's Spy*, 27.

39. Robertson, *Booth*, 216.

40. John A. McKinsey, *The Lincoln Secret* (Dixon, CA: Martin Pearl Publishing, 2008), 12.

41. Although most literary and film critics would not place *Busted Flush* and *National Treasure* in the suspense genre, they share enough commonalities with the other texts in this section to be placed in that genre for the purposes of this particular analysis.

42. McKinsey, *The Lincoln Secret*, 43.

43. Brad Smith, *Busted Flush: A Novel* (New York: Henry Holt, 2005), 304.

44. Smith, *Busted Flush*, 47.

45. Smith, *Busted Flush*, throughout the book.

46. McKinsey, *The Lincoln Secret*, 13, 80, 37.

47. Smith, *Busted Flush*, 92; McKinsey, *The Lincoln Secret*, 37; Jon Turteltaub, *National Treasure: Book of Secrets* (Walt Disney Pictures, 2007).

48. Barbara Hambly, *The Emancipator's Wife: A Novel of Mary Todd Lincoln* (New York: Bantam Dell, 2006), 196.

49. Hambly, *The Emancipator's Wife*, 217, 591, 229.

50. Irving Stone, *Love Is Eternal: A Novel about Mary Todd and Abraham Lincoln* (New York: Bantam Doubleday Dell, 1954), 80–81.

51. Hambly, *The Emancipator's Wife*, 454, 587.

52. Hambly, *The Emancipator's Wife*, 162, 189; Stone, *Love Is Eternal*, 38.

53. Stone, *Love Is Eternal*, 76.

54. Tony Wolk, *Abraham Lincoln: A Novel Life* (Portland, OR: Ooligan Press, 2004), 40, 70, 50.

55. Wolk, *Abraham Lincoln*, 136, 23.

56. Wolk, *Abraham Lincoln*, 23, 66.

57. Wolk, *Abraham Lincoln*, 77, 104.

58. Stone, *Love Is Eternal*, 28.

59. Hambly, *The Emancipator's Wife*, 317, 319, 412, 250.

60. This theme will sound familiar to those who have either read Dick's 1968 novel *Do Androids Dream of Electric Sheep?* or seen the 1982 film *Blade Runner*, which was based on the novel. Philip K. Dick, *Do Androids Dream of Electric Sheep?* (Toronto: Del Rey, 1968); Ridley Scott, *Blade Runner* (Warner Brothers, 1982).

61. Philip K. Dick, *We Can Build You* (New York: Vintage, 1994), 177. Originally published in 1972.

62. Dick, *We Can Build You*, 185, 118, 164.

63. Scout McCloud, *The New Adventures of Abraham Lincoln* (La Jolla, CA: Homage Comics, 1998), unnumbered pages.

64. McCloud, *The New Adventures of Abraham Lincoln*, 118–121.

65. Although the author of the Harry Potter series, J. K. Rowling, is British and the first books of the series were published before September 11, 2001, the post-9/11 novels turn increasingly toward conspiracy, social breakdown, and apocalyptic battles between good and evil. For a thought-provoking discussion of the zombie as a narrative device, see Jen Webb and Sam Byrnand, "Some Kind of Virus: The Zombie as Body and as Trope," *Body & Society*, 14, no. 83 (2008).

66. Stephen Lindsay, *Jesus Hates Zombies, Featuring Lincoln Hates Werewolves*, vols. 2–4 (Levittown, NY: Alterna Comics, 2009–2010), unnumbered page.

67. Lindsay, *Jesus Hates Zombies*.

68. Grahame-Smith, *Abraham Lincoln: Vampire Hunter*, 215.

69. For a succinct overview of the place of psychoanalytical principles in contemporary critical theory, see Lois Tyson, *Critical Theory: A User-Friendly Guide*, 2nd ed. (New York: Routledge, 2006).

70. Blackwood, *Second Sight*, 277.

71. Slotkin, *Abe*, 136.

72. Dick, *We Can Build You*, 164; Lindsay, *Jesus Hates Zombies*; McKinsey, *The Lincoln Secret*, 80; Stone, *Love Is Eternal*, 262; Rinaldi, *An Acquaintance with Darkness*, 104–5; Vidal, *Lincoln*, 342.

73. Wolk, *Abraham Lincoln*, 25, 66, 77, 104; Hambly, *The Emancipator's Wife*, 317, 454, 587.

74. Stone, *Love Is Eternal*, 459.

75. Schwartz, *Abraham Lincoln in the Post-Heroic Era*, 157–59.

76. Schwartz, *Abraham Lincoln in the Post-Heroic Era*, 178.
77. Schwartz, *Abraham Lincoln in the Post-Heroic Era*, 189.
78. Schwartz, *Abraham Lincoln in the Post-Heroic Era*, 190.
79. Maurice Halbwachs, *The Collective Memory*, trans. Francise J. Ditter Jr. and Vida Yazdi Ditter (New York: Harper Colophon, 1980).
80. Halbwachs, *The Collective Memory*, 72–73.
81. For an informative overview of the production of culture literature, see Richard A. Peterson and N. Anand, "The Production of Culture Perspective," *Annual Review of Sociology* 30 (2004): 311–34.
82. Richard A. Peterson and N. Anand, "The Production of Culture Perspective."

CHAPTER FIVE

1. David Donald, "Getting Right with Lincoln," in *Lincoln Reconsidered: Essays on the Civil War* (New York: Knopf, 1956).
2. This question is asked so frequently, in fact, that author David Accord recently used it as the title of his self-help book *What Would Lincoln Do? Lincoln's Most Inspired Solutions to Challenging Problems and Difficult Situations* (Naperville, IL: Sourcebooks, 2009), which offers advice on such everyday challenges as how to respond to rumors, how to deal with difficult coworkers, and how to decline a relative's request.
3. The Republican Party has held Lincoln banquets since 1887. See Donald, "Getting Right with Lincoln."
4. Frank J. Williams, "Abraham Lincoln and Civil Liberties in Wartime," available at http://www.heritage.org/research/nationalsecurity/hl834.cfm (accessed May 20, 2009).
5. Interview with Charlie Gibson of ABC News, September 11, 2008, available at http://abcnews.go.com/Politics/Vote2008/story?id=5778018&page=1 (accessed September 12, 2008).
6. Walt Handelsman, "Too Lincolny?" 2009, available at http://www.gocomics.com/walthandelsman/2009/01/15/ (accessed June 25, 2009).
7. "A Presidential Portrait in Pastry," available at www.npr.org/templates/story/story.php?storyId=100719176 (accessed May 25, 2008).
8. Barack Obama's victory speech, Grant Park, Chicago, November 4, 2008, emphasis added.
9. Harold Holzer, *Lincoln at Cooper Union: The Speech That Made Abraham Lincoln President* (New York: Simon and Schuster, 2004).
10. "Obama on Renewing the American Economy," March 27, 2008, available at http://www.nytimes.com/2008/03/27/us/politics/27text-obama.html?pagewanted=print (accessed June 16, 2010).
11. "Remarks by the President on Wall Street Reform," April 22, 2010, available at http://www.whitehouse.gov/the-press-office/remarks-president-wall-street-reform (accessed June 16, 2010).

12. Obama opened the much-anticipated official announcement of his candidacy in Springfield, Illinois, on February 10, 2007, with this phrase.

13. Donald, *Lincoln*, 48–49; Carwardine, *Lincoln: A Life of Purpose*, 36; Guelzo, *Abraham Lincoln: Redeemer President* (Grand Rapids, MI: Eerdmans, 1999), 21.

14. Peterson, *Lincoln in American Memory*, 81.

15. Craughwell, *Stealing Lincoln's Body*, 13–14.

16. Donald, *Lincoln*, 20–21; Peterson, *Lincoln in American Memory*, 218–31; Guelzo, *Abraham Lincoln: Redeemer President*, esp. 21, 152–53.

17. Peterson, *Lincoln in American Memory*, 219.

18. Peterson, *Lincoln in American Memory*, 231.

19. Carwardine, *Lincoln: A Life of Purpose*, 33.

20. Assertions by Lincoln impersonators in Ottawa, IL (August 2008), and Pekin, IL (September 2008).

21. "All Things Lincoln," offered by Illinois Community College, Peoria, IL (October 2008).

22. Holland, *The Life of Abraham Lincoln*, 455, 541–42; J. G. Randall and Richard N. Current, *Mr. Lincoln* (New York: Dodd, Mead, 1957), 385.

23. Ward Hill Lamon, *The Life of Abraham Lincoln* (Washington, DC: Dorothy Lamon Teillard, 1911).

24. Randall and Current, *Mr. Lincoln*, 385.

25. Randall and Current, *Mr. Lincoln*, 388.

26. I gratefully borrow this turn of phrase from Charles E. Morris III, whose article is essential reading for those interested in the construction of the gay Lincoln. See Charles E. Morris III, "My Old Kentucky Homo: Abraham Lincoln, Larry Kramer, and the Politics of Queer Memory," in *Queering Public Address: Sexualities in American Historical Discourse*, ed. Charles E. Morris III (Columbia: University of South Carolina Press, 2007).

27. Tripp himself rejects the term *gay* as a synonym for *homosexual* because it implies "lightness and frivolity" (Tripp, *The Intimate World*, xxvii). When discussing Tripp's position, I therefore use the term *homosexual*, while in more general discussion I employ the now more common term *gay*.

28. Shenk, *Lincoln's Melancholy*, 30–31.

29. Tripp, *The Intimate World*, 20.

30. James Kepner's work is excerpted in *From the Closet of History*, self-published by Kepner in 1984.

31. Tripp, *The Intimate World*, xxviii–xxxi.

32. For a detailed discussion of the controversy, see Morris, "My Old Kentucky Homo."

33. *State Journal-Register* (Springfield, IL), May 20, 1999, 6.

34. Barry Locher, "Claims about Lincoln Deserved Investigation," *State Journal-Register* (Springfield, IL), May 20, 1999, 7.

35. One antiabortion group, Life Decisions International, claims to have forced 214 companies to withdraw their donations to Planned Parenthood; available at http://www.fightpp.org/ (accessed May 29, 2009).

36. For an overview of such arguments, see Earl M. Maltz, "Roe v. Wade and Dred Scott," *Widener Law Journal* 17, no. 1 (2007).

37. George McKenna, "On Abortion: A Lincolnian Position," *The Atlantic*, September 1995, available at http://www.theatlantic.com/issues/95sep/abortion/abortion.htm (accessed September 12, 2008); Republican National Coalition for Life, available at http://www.rnclife.org/brochure/rprolife.html (accessed May 29, 2009); Steven Brizek, "Abortion: Heading the Way of Slavery?" NorthJersey.com, 2009, available at http://www.northjersey.com/opinion/moreviews/45374322.html (accessed June 1, 2009).

38. Ronald Reagan, "Abortion and the Conscience of the Nation," *Human Life Review*, Spring 1983.

39. David Volk, "On Lincoln, Obama and Evil," *Peoria Journal Star*, November 29, 2008.

40. Althea Hatfield, "Take Note of Obama's Actions on Abortion," *Peoria Journal Star*, February 22, 2009.

41. W. E. B. Du Bois, "Again, Lincoln," *The Crisis*, September 1922. See also Philip B. Kunhardt, Peter W. Kunhardt, and Peter W. Kunhardt Jr., *Looking for Lincoln: The Making of an American Icon* (New York: Knopf, 2008), 455.

42. 1858 debate with Stephen A. Douglas in Ottawa, IL.

43. Holland, *The Life of Abraham Lincoln*, 121.

44. Frederick Douglass, "Oration Delivered on the Occasion of the Unveiling of the Freedmen's Monument in Memory of Abraham Lincoln," Frederick Douglass Papers at the Library of Congress, 1876, available at http://memory.loc.gov/cgibin/ampage?collId=mfd&fileName=23/23004/23004page.db&recNum=17&itemLink=/ammem/doughtml/dougFolder5.html&linkText=7 (accessed June 22, 2009).

45. Michele Steinbacher, "Infamous 1908 Race Riot Sparked by Secret Move to Bloomington," *Pantagraph*, August 9, 2008, available at http://www.pantagraph.com/articles/2008/08/09/news/doc489dbc52e34d8112745755.txt (accessed June 23, 2009).

46. Kunhardt et al., *Looking for Lincoln*, 410.

47. Kunhardt et al., *Looking for Lincoln*, 454–55.

48. Kunhardt et al., *Looking for Lincoln*.

49. Malcolm X, "God's Judgment of White America," commonly known as "the chickens come home to roost" speech, New York City, December 4, 1963.

50. Lerone Bennett, "Was Abe Lincoln a White Supremacist?" *Ebony*, February 1968.

51. Lerone Bennett, *Forced into Glory: Abraham Lincoln's White Dream* (Chicago: Johnson Publishing, 2007), 42.

52. Doris Kearns Goodwin, *Team of Rivals*, 207.

53. *Looking for Lincoln*, PBS Home Video, 2008.

54. David Blight, *Race and Reunion: The Civil War in American Memory* (Cambridge, MA: Belknap, 2001); George M. Fredrickson, *Big Enough to Be Inconsistent: Abraham Lincoln Confronts Slavery and Race* (Cambridge, MA: Harvard University Press, 2008); Henry Louis Gates Jr., ed., *Lincoln on Race and Slavery* (Princeton, NJ: Princeton University Press, 2009); James Oliver Horton and Lois Horton, *Slavery and the Making of America* (New York: Oxford University Press, 2005).

55. Ku Klux Klan, "Abraham Lincoln on Race," available at http://www.kkk.bz/aberace.htm (accessed June 15, 2009).

56. Donald, "Getting Right with Lincoln."

57. Edward Herman and Noam Chomsky, *Manufacturing Consent: The Political Economy of the Mass Media* (New York: Pantheon, 1988).

58. Karl Marx and Friederich Engels, *The German Ideology* (London: Lawrence and Wishart, [1845] 1970); and Theodor Adorno and Max Horkheimer, *The Dialectic of Enlightenment* (New York: Herder and Herder, 1972).

59. See, for instance, Stuart Hall, "Cultural Studies: Two Paradigms," *Media, Culture and Society* 2 (1980): 57–72; and Ruth Wodak, Rudolf de Cillia, Martin Reisigl, and Karin Liebhart, *The Discursive Construction of National Identity*, trans. Angelika Hirsch and Richard Mitten (Edinburgh: Edinburgh University Press, 1999).

60. Herman and Chomsky, *Manufacturing Consent*.

61. See Gary Alan Fine, *Difficult Reputations: Collective Memories of the Evil, Inept, and Controversial* (Chicago: University of Chicago Press, 2001); and "Reputational Entrepreneurs and the Memory of Incompetence: Melting Supporters, Partisan Warriors, and Images of President Harding," *American Journal of Sociology* 101, no. 5 (1996): 1159–93.

62. For analyses of the historical reputations of other prominent public figures, see Ari Adut, "A Theory of Scandal: Victorians, Homosexuality, and the Fall of Oscar Wilde," *American Journal of Sociology* 111, no. 1 (2005): 213–48; Fine, "Reputational Entrepreneurs and the Memory of Incompetence"; Barry Schwartz, *George Washington: The Making of an American Symbol* (Ithaca, NY: Cornell University Press, 1990).

63. Fine, *Difficult Reputations*, 5.

64. Lincoln Prize acceptance speeches by Doris Kearns Goodwin (2006), Richard Carwardine (2004), Alan Guelzo (2000), and Douglas Wilson (1999), available at http://www.gettysburg.edu/civilwar/prizes_andscholarships/lincoln_prize/previous-winner-speeches/ (accessed June 22, 2010).

65. Fine, *Difficult Reputations*, 11.

66. *Team of Rivals: Lincoln's Cabinet at the Crossroads of War* opened October 14, 2010, at the ALPLM; press release available at http://www.alplm.org/events/team_of_rivals.html# (accessed June 16, 2010).

67. B. Child, "Spielberg's Abraham Lincoln Project to Go Ahead Despite Competition," *Guardian*, September 15, 2009, available at http://www.guardian.co.uk/film/2009/sep/15/abraham-lincoln-spielberg-redford (accessed June 16, 2010).

68. Fine, *Difficult Reputations*, 8, 21.

CHAPTER SIX

1. Donald, *Lincoln*, 51.

2. The earliest edition of Mason L. Weems's *Life of George Washington; with Curious Anecdotes, Equally Honorable to Himself, and Exemplary to His Young Countrymen* was published in 1800 and was reissued in more than eighty editions.

3. I met more than two hundred participants at educator workshops and conducted interviews via e-mail with twenty of these teachers, six men and fourteen

women. They came from ten states: Georgia, Illinois, Indiana, Kansas, Kentucky, Missouri, New Jersey, New York, North Carolina, and Washington. This is a small, nonrepresentative sample, so it cannot be generalized to the entire population of American schoolteachers. Nonetheless, in the tradition of qualitative research, I assert that such material provides insights into broader trends, in this case, classroom priorities and practices.

4. *Time for Kids*, News Scoop Edition, vol. 14, no. 17 (February 6, 2009).

5. "The Fight for Equal Rights: Black Soldiers in the Civil War," available at http://www.archives.gov/education/lessons/blacks-civil-war/ (accessed July 8, 2009).

6.

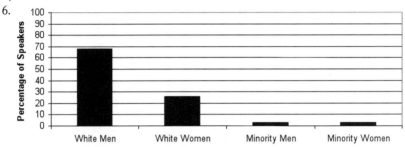

Figure 6.5. Speakers at Lincoln Events (2008–2009)

7. Horatio Alger, *The Backwoods Boy, or the Boyhood and Manhood of Abraham Lincoln* (Philadelphia, PA: David McKay, 1883).

8. Among many others, see Betty Carson Kay, *The Lincolns from A to Z* (Bloomington, IN: Author House, 2008); Tanya Lee Stone, *Abraham Lincoln: A Photographic Story of a Life* (New York: DK Publishing, 2005); Betty Carson Kay, *Americans of Character: Abraham Lincoln* (San Diego, CA: Young People's Press, 2000); Kay Winters and Nancy Carpenter, *Abraham Lincoln: The Boy Who Loved Books* (New York: Simon and Schuster, 2003); Ellen Jackson and Doris Ettlinger, *Abe Lincoln Loved Animals* (Morton Grove, IL: Albert Whitman, 2008); Saton Rabin, *Mr. Lincoln's Boys* (New York: Viking, 2008); Robert Burleigh and Wendell Minor, *Abraham Lincoln Comes Home* (New York: Henry Holt, 2008); Martha Brenner and Donald Cook, *Abe Lincoln's Hat* (New York: Random House, 1994); Karen B. Winnick, *Mr. Lincoln's Whiskers* (Honesdale, PA: Boyds Mills Press, 1996).

9. Based on an analysis of thirty recent children's picture books detailed in table 6.1 below. This is not a statistically representative sample but rather a collection of all the recent Lincoln children's books available at a single local library. As such, the patterns described here cannot be generalized in statistically reliable ways to the whole corpus of Lincoln children's books. Nonetheless, I argue that the patterns identified here provide insights into conventions of Lincoln representation in children's books.

10. Wil Mara, *Abraham Lincoln* (New York: Children's Press, 2002), 22–23.

11. Malcah Zeldis and Edith Kunhardt, *Honest Abe* (New York: Greenwillow, 1993), unnumbered pages.

12. Zeldis and Kunhardt, *Honest Abe*.

Table 6.1. Lincoln Picture Books

Author	Title
David A. Adler, John Wallner, and Alexandra Wallner	A Picture Book of Abraham (New York: Lincoln Holiday House, 1989)
Jim Aylesworth and Barbara McClintock	Our Abe Lincoln (New York: Scholastic, 2009)
Raymond Bial	Where Lincoln Walked (New York: Walker Publishing, 1998)
Sonia Black and Carol Heyer	Let's Read about Abraham Lincoln (New York: Scholastic, 2002)
Louise Borden and Ted Lewin	A. Lincoln and Me (New York: Scholastic, 1999)
Martha Brenner and Donald Cook	Abe Lincoln's Hat (New York: Random House, 1994)
Jen Bryant and Amy June Bates	Abe's Fish: A Boyhood Tale of Abraham Lincoln (New York: Sterling, 2009)
Robert Burleigh and Wendell Minor	Abraham Lincoln Comes Home (New York: Henry Holt, 2008)
Amy Cohn and Suzy Schmidt	Abraham Lincoln (New York: Scholastic, 2002)
Justine Fontes and Ron Fontes	Abraham Lincoln: Lawyer, Leader, Legend (New York: Dorling Kindersley, 2001)
Jean Fritz and Charles Robinson	Just a Few Words, Mr. Lincoln: The Story of the Gettysburg Address (New York: Grosset and Dunlap, 1993)
Nikki Giovanni and Bryan Collier	Lincoln and Douglass: An American Friendship (New York: Henry Holt, 2008)
Carol Greene	Abraham Lincoln: President of a Divided Country (Chicago: Children's Press, 1989)
Cheryl Harness	Abe Lincoln Goes to Washington, 1837–1865 (Washington, DC: National Geographic Society, 1997)
Ellen Jackson and Doris Ettlinger	Abe Lincoln Loved Animals (Morton Grove, IL: Albert Whitman, 2008)
Wil Mara	Abraham Lincoln (New York: Children's Press, 2002)

Kay Melchisedech Olson and Otha Zachariah Edward Lohse — *The Assassination of Abraham Lincoln* (Mankato, MN: Capstone Press, 2005)

Ingri Parin D'Aulaire and Edgar Parin D'Aulaire — *Abraham Lincoln* (New York: Bantam Doubleday, [1939] 1993)

Patricia A Pingry and Stephanie McFetridge Britt — *Discover Abraham Lincoln: Storyteller, Lawyer, President* (Nashville, TN: Ideals Children's Books, 2005)

Staton Rabin and Bagram Ibatoulline — *Mr. Lincoln's Boys, Being the Mostly True Adventures of Abraham Lincoln's Trouble-Making Sons, Tad and Willie* (New York: Viking, 2008)

Doreen Rappaport and Kadir Nelson — *Abe's Honest Words: The Life of Abraham Lincoln* (New York: Hyperion, 2008)

Mike Reiss and David Catrow — *The Boy Who Looked Like Lincoln* (New York: Puffin, 2003)

Jane A Schott — *Abraham Lincoln* (Minneapolis: Lerner, 2002)

Judith St. George and Matt Faulkner — *Stand Tall, Abe Lincoln* (New York: Philomel Books, 2008)

Sarah Thomson and James Ransome — *What Lincoln Said* (New York: HarperCollins, 2009)

Ann Turner and Wendell Minor — *Abe Lincoln Remembers* (New York: HarperCollins, 2001)

Elizabeth Van Steenwyk and Bill Farnsworth — *When Abraham Talked to the Trees* (Grand Rapids, MI: Eerdmans, 2000)

Kay Winters and Nancy Carpenter — *Abe Lincoln: The Boy Who Loved Books* (New York: Aladdin, 2003)

Andrew Woods and Pat Schories — *Young Abraham Lincoln: Log Cabin President* (New York: Troll Associates, 1992)

Malcah Zeldis and Edith Kunhardt — *Honest Abe* (New York: Greenwillow, 1993)

13. See especially Cheryl Harness, *Abe Lincoln Goes to Washington, 1837–1865* (Washington, DC: National Geographic Society, 1997).

14. Justine Fontes and Ron Fontes, *Abraham Lincoln: Lawyer, Leader, Legend* (New York: Dorling Kindersley, 2001), 41.

15. "Writing for Children," roundtable discussion at the ALPLM, Springfield, IL, February 12, 2009.

16. "Writing for Children," roundtable discussion.

17. Raymond Bial, *Where Lincoln Walked* (New York: Walker Publishing, 1998), 23, 29.

18. Schwartz, *Abraham Lincoln in the Post-Heroic Era*; Barry Schwartz, "Postmodernity and Historical Reputation: Abraham Lincoln in Late Twentieth-Century American Memory," *Social Forces* 77, no. 1 (1998): 63–103.

19. Schwartz, *Abraham Lincoln in the Post-Heroic Era*, 210.

20. Schwartz, *Abraham Lincoln in the Post-Heroic Era*, 210.

21. Schwartz, *Abraham Lincoln in the Post-Heroic Era*, 216.

22. Schwartz, *Abraham Lincoln in the Post-Heroic Era*, 211.

23. I analyzed the Civil War chapters of ten recent secondary school history textbooks. This is not a statistically representative sample, so I make no claims as to statistical significance. Rather, these are the ten history textbooks from the 1990s onward that were available to undergraduate education majors at one midsized university library in Illinois during the period of my analysis. I therefore contend that this is a relatively accurate reflection of the secondary textbooks used in the state of Illinois today. The texts were as follows: Thomas Bailey, David M. Kennedy, and Lizabeth Cohen, *The American Pageant* (Boston: Houghton Mifflin, 1998); Carol Berkin, Alan Brinkley, Clayborne Carson, Robert W. Cherry, Robert A. Divine, Eric Foner, Jeffrey B. Morris, Arthur Wheeler, and Leonard Wood, *American Voices* (Glenview, IL: Scott Foresman, 1995); Daniel J. Boorstin and Brooks Mather Kelley, *A History of the United States* (Needham, MA: Prentice Hall, 1999); Andrew Cayton, Elisabeth Perry, Linda Reid, and Allan M. Winkler, *America: Pathways to the Present* (Needham, MA: Prentice Hall, 2005); Gerald A. Danzer, J. Jorge Klor de Alva, Larry S. Krieger, Louis E. Wilson, and Nancy Woloch, *The Americans* (Evanston, IL: McDougal Little, 2000); James West Davidson, *America: History of Our Nation, Beginnings through 1877* (Upper Saddle River, NJ: Pearson, 2009); John Mack Faragher, Mari Jo Buhle, Daniel Czitron, and Susan H. Armitage, *Out of Many: A History of the American People* (Upper Saddle River, NJ: Prentice Hall, 2002); John A. Garraty, *The American Nation: A History of the United States* (New York: Longman, 1998); Emma J. Lapsansky-Werner, Peter B. Levy, Randy Roberts, and Alan Taylor, *United States History* (Upper Saddle River, NJ: Pearson, 2010); Joanne Suter, *Fearon's United States History* (Paramus, NJ: Globe Fearon, 1994).

24. Individuals whose gender or race could not be discerned were excluded from analysis, as were images of children and crowd scenes.

25. Cayton et al., *America: Pathways to the Present.*

26. Berkin et al., *American Voices*, 239; Faragher et al., *Out of Many*, 479; Boorstin and Kelley, *A History of the United States*, 364.

27. Brenner and Cook, *Abe Lincoln's Hat.*

28. Giovanni and Collier, *Lincoln and Douglass: An American Friendship* (New York: Henry Holt, 2008).

29. Bial, *Where Lincoln Walked*, 5.

30. Fine, *Difficult Reputations*, 5.

31. Fine, *Difficult Reputations*, 5-6.

32. Louis Althusser, "Ideology and Ideological State Apparatuses," in *Lenin and Philosophy and other Essays* (New York: Monthly Review Press, [1971] 2001).

33. Pierre Bourdieu, *Outline of a Theory of Practice* (London: Cambridge University Press, 1977).

34. Samuel Bowles and Herbert Gintis, *Schooling in Capitalist America* (London: Routledge and Kegan Paul, 1976); Samuel Bowles and Herbert Gintis, "Schooling in Capitalist America Revisited," *Sociology of Education* 75, no. 1 (2002): 1–18.

35. Caroline Persell and Peter Cookson Jr. *Preparing for Power: America's Elite Boarding Schools* (New York: Basic Books, 1985). See also Caroline Persell and Peter Cookson Jr., "Chartering and Bartering: Elite Education and Social Reproduction," *Social Problems* 33, no. 2 (1985): 114–29; and Ivor Goodson, Peter Cookson Jr., and Caroline Persell, "Distinction and Destiny: The Importance of Curriculum Form in Elite American Private Schools," *Discourse* 18, no. 2 (1997): 173–83.

36. Myra Sadker and David Sadker, *Failing at Fairness: How Our Schools Cheat Girls* (New York: Scribner, 1994); and David Sadker and Karen Zittelman, *Still Failing at Fairness: How Gender Bias Cheats Girls and Boys and What We Can Do about It* (New York: Scribner, 2009).

37. Jonathon Kozol, *Savage Inequalities* (New York: Harper Perennial, 1991).

38. Dale Spender, *Learning to Lose* (London: Women's Press, 1980).

CHAPTER SEVEN

1. Roy Rosenzweig and David Thelen, *The Presence of the Past: Popular Uses of History in American Life* (New York: Columbia University Press, 1998).

2. See, for instance, Robert Lumley, ed., *The Museum Time-Machine* (London: Routledge, 1988).

3. Gerard Benjamin Fleet Hallock, "The Homiletic Year—February," *Expositor* 21, no. 241 (1919).

4. Peter Pels, "The Spirit of Matter: On Fetish, Rarity, Fact, and Fancy," in *Border Fetishisms: Material Objects in Unstable Spaces*, ed. Patricia Spyer (New York: Routledge, 1998).

5. For an insightful discussion of the ways that museums reflect and shape regional and national identities, see John M. Mackenzie, *Museums and Empire: Natural History, Human Cultures and Colonial Identities* (Manchester: Manchester University Press, 2009).

6. "Edgier" in the customary sense of being new and discomfiting, but also in the sense of bringing to light the stories of those on the "edges" or margins of society. See Warwick Frost, "Making an Edgier Interpretation of the Gold Rushes: Contrasting

Perspectives from Australia and New Zealand," *International Journal of Heritage Studies* 11, no. 3 (2005): 235–50.

7. Bob Thompson, "Histrionics and History: Lincoln Library's High-Tech Exhibits Have Scholars Choosing Sides," *Washington Post*, February 15, 2005, C1.

8. Thompson, "Histrionics and History."

9. "The Newest Exhibit at the Abraham Lincoln Presidential Museum," *State Journal-Register*, Springfield, IL, November 30, 2004.

10. "Newest Exhibit at the Abraham Lincoln Presidential Museum."

11. Comments by ALPLM staff during April 2008 workshop for Bradley University students and faculty.

12. On the issue of gender bias in "heritage" sites, see Briavel Holcomb, "Gender and Heritage Interpretation," in *Contemporary Issues in Heritage and Environmental Interpretation: Problems and Prospects*, ed. David Uzzell and Roy Ballantyne (London: Stationery Office, 1998), 37–55.

13. Discussed in detail in chapter 3 of this volume.

14. A national traveling exhibit sponsored by the Gilder Lerhman Institute for American History, the National Endowment for the Humanities, the Abraham Lincoln Bicentennial Commission, and the Huntington Library of San Marino, California. I analyzed the exhibit while it was on display at the Hardin County Library in Elizabethtown, Kentucky.

15. Of course, this is only true if we consider each change of residence within Illinois to be a move to a "different place."

16. Nicole Bauer, chair of the Lincoln-Douglas Debate Sesquicentennial Committee, Freeport, IL, at the Debate Square dedication, August 2008.

17. "Gov. Blagojevich Announces Museum Exhibit National Tour in Honor of the Abraham Lincoln Bicentennial: One-of-a-Kind 'Abraham Lincoln: Self-Made in America' Mobile Exhibit Debuts April 30 in Denver," April 29, 2008, available at http://www.illinois.gov/pressreleases/ShowPressRelease.cfm?SubjectID=2&RecNum=6783.

18. Letter to John M. Brockman, September 25, 1860.

19. William Herndon quoted in Waldo W. Braden, *Abraham Lincoln, Public Speaker* (Baton Rouge: Louisiana State University Press, 1988), 98.

20. Lincoln's speech at Peoria, October 16, 1854.

21. Video in the SNMAH's *Abraham Lincoln: An Extraordinary Life.*

22. *Confronting Democracy's Boundaries: The Lincoln-Douglas Debates*, traveling exhibit of the ALPLM on display at the Freeport Public Library.

23. Galleries of the Lincoln Home National Historic Site.

24. Lincoln's speech at Peoria, October 16, 1854: "If the negro is a *man*, why then my ancient faith teaches me that 'all men are created equal' and that there can be no moral right in connection with one man's making a slave of another," quoted in introductory video to the Lincoln Home National Historic Site.

25. *America's New Birth of Freedom*, SNMAH in cooperation with the ALPLM.

26. "Interpreting Lincoln: From Memorialization to Active Involvement," a panel discussion of the Lincoln Institute for Teachers, June 18, 2009, University of Southern Indiana, Evansville, IN.

27. Schwartz, *Abraham Lincoln and the Forge of National Memory*, 33.
28. Schwartz, *Abraham Lincoln and the Forge of National Memory*, 49.
29. See David Lowenthal, *The Heritage Crusade and the Spoils of History* (Cambridge, UK: Cambridge University Press, 1998). Lowenthal describes heritage tourism as a "secular religion" that gives us faith in "who we are, where we came from, and to what we belong" (xvii).
30. Based on my counts of adult visitors during one- to two-hour observation intervals at the SNMAH's *America's New Birth of Freedom* and *Abraham Lincoln: An Extraordinary Life* exhibits, the National Portrait Gallery's *One Life: The Mask of Lincoln* exhibit, the ALPLM's traveling *Abraham Lincoln: Self-Made in America* exhibit, and the Ford's Theatre Museum. Ethnoracial categories were determined based on visual cues; however, I make no claims about how these visitors identify themselves. Counts are as follows:

Table 7.1. Attendance at Lincoln Exhibits by Gender and Ethnicity

	White men	White women	Nonwhite men	Nonwhite women	Totals
America's New Birth of Freedom	44	25	8	6	83
One Life: The Mask of Lincoln	57	54	9	2	122
Self-Made in America	35	38	1	2	76
An Extraordinary Life	75	92	4	8	179
Ford's Theatre Museum	42	27	1	4	74
Totals*	253 (47%)	236 (44%)	23 (4%)	22 (4%)	534

*Percentages total less than 100 due to rounding.

31. Specifically, according to the 2010 U.S. Census, 72 percent of American residents identified themselves as "white" alone. Moreover, non-Hispanic whites constituted only 64 percent of the American population.
32. Schwartz, *Abraham Lincoln in the Post-Heroic Era*, 168–69.
33.

Table 7.2. Named Individuals in ALPLM Exhibits

	White Men	White Women	Nonwhite Men	Nonwhite Women	Total
The Early Years	41	11	5	2	59
The White House and Start of War	33	8	1	3	45
The Civil War	68	18	8	2	96
The War Ends and Funeral	28	13	0	0	41
Total*	170 (71%)	50 (21%)	14 (6%)	7 (3%)	241

*Total exceeds 100 percent due to rounding.

34. For details on these historical figures, see especially James Oakes, *The Radical and the Republican: Frederick Douglass, Abraham Lincoln, and the Triumph of Antislavery Politics* (New York: Norton, 2007); Nell Irvin Painter, *Sojourner Truth: A Life, a Symbol* (New York: Norton, 1994); Elizabeth Keckley, *Behind the Scenes in the Lincoln White House: Memoirs of an African-American Seamstress* (Mineola, NY: Dover, [1868] 2006); and Jennifer Fleischner, *Mrs. Lincoln and Mrs. Keckly: The Remarkable Story of the Friendship between a First Lady and a Former Slave* (New York: Broadway Books, 2003).

35.

Table 7.3. Attendance at Washington, D.C. Lincoln Exhibits by Gender and Ethnicity

	White Men	White Women	Nonwhite Men	Nonwhite Women	Totals
National Museum of American History	119	117	12	14	262
National Portrait Gallery	57	54	9	2	122
Ford's Theatre Museum	42	27	1	4	74
Lincoln Memorial Educational Center	26	26	14	20	86
TOTAL*	244 (45%)	224 (41%)	36 (6%)	40 (7%)	544

*Percentages total less than 100 due to rounding.

36. George Orwell, *Nineteen Eighty-Four* (New York: Signet Classic, 1950).

37. For a critical perspective on museums and "heritage tourism," see especially Lowenthal, *The Heritage Crusade*; Robert Hewison, *The Heritage Industry: Britain in a Climate of Decline* (London: Methuen, 1987); Barbara Kirshenblatt-Gimblett, *Destination Culture: Tourism, Museums and Heritage* (Berkeley: University of California Press, 1998); Dallen J. Timothy and Stephen W. Boyd, *Heritage Tourism* (Harlow, UK: Prentice Hall, 2003); and David Uzzell and Roy Ballantyne, eds., *Contemporary Issues in Heritage and Environmental Interpretation: Problems and Prospects* (London: Stationery Office, 1998). Thought-provoking case studies of the place of history and identity in heritage and cultural tourism include Bruner, *Culture on Tour*; Millie Creighton, "Spinning Silk, Weaving Selves: Nostalgia, Gender, and Identity in Japanese Craft Vacations," *Japanese Studies* 21, no. 1 (2001); Greg Dickinson, Brian L. Ott, and Eric Aoki, "Memory and Myth at the Buffalo Bill Museum," *Western Journal of Communication* 69, no. 2 (2005); Frost, "Making an Edgier Interpretation"; Nuala C. Johnson, "Where Geography and History Meet: Heritage Tourism and the Big House in Ireland," *Annals of the Association of American Geographers* 86, no. 3 (1996); and Scott Magelssen, "Remapping American-ness: Heritage Production and the Staging of the Native American and the African American as Other in 'Historyland,'" *National Identities* 4, no. 2 (2002).

38. Hogan, *Gender, Race and National Identity*, chap. 11.

39. Bruner, *Culture on Tour*, chap. 8.

40. Johnson, "Where Geography and History Meet," 551–66.

41. Hogan, *Gender, Race and National Identity*, chap. 11.

42. The one notable exception is that some museums include exhibits on the United States Colored Troops (USCT). However, these tend to be relatively small.

43. Speech to the 166th Ohio Regiment, August 22, 1864.

44. Such scenes are found mainly in Lincoln fiction, however, rather than in museum exhibits.

45. Holcomb, "Gender and Heritage Interpretation."

46. The domination of Lincoln scholarship by white males shows little sign of significant change. For example, since the establishment of the Lincoln Prize in 1990, just 15 percent (four out of twenty-six) laureates have been women, and virtually all of the prizewinners have been white.

47. Quoted in Kearns Goodwin, *Team of Rivals*, xv.

48. As Barry Schwartz notes, attendance at Lincoln "shrines" has declined since the 1960s (*Abraham Lincoln in the Post-Heroic Era*, 153–54). With the advent of digital entertainment, megamalls, immersive edutainment products, and other competitors for our attention and money, it is hardly surprising that fewer people are visiting such sites in person today. However, decreased attendance figures do not necessarily equate to decreased esteem for Abraham Lincoln.

49. Lowenthal, *The Heritage Crusade*, 6.

50. There are many competing definitions of globalization. I derive mine from the work of Malcolm Waters, *Globalization* (New York: Routledge, 1995).

51. See, for instance, Stuart Hall, "The Question of Cultural Identity," in *Modernity and Its Futures*, ed. Stuart Hall, David Held, and Tony McGrew (Cambridge, UK: Polity Press, 1992), 273–326.

52. The leading proponent of such views was Jean Baudrillard. For insightful explication and criticisms of Baudrillard's work, see Douglas Kellner, *Jean Baudrillard: From Marxism to Postmodernism and Beyond* (Stanford, CA: Stanford University Press, 1989).

53. Lowenthal, *The Heritage Crusade*, 1–2.

54. John Urry, *The Tourist Gaze: Leisure and Travel in Contemporary Societies* (London: Sage, 1990).

55. David Lowenthal, *The Past Is a Foreign Country* (Cambridge, UK: Cambridge University Press, 1985), xvii.

CHAPTER EIGHT

1. Carl Sandburg, *The Prairie Years and the War Years* (New York: Harcourt, Brace and World, 1954), 257.

2. Donald, *Lincoln*, 317.

3. Guelzo, *Abraham Lincoln: Redeemer President*, 296.

4. Carwardine, *Lincoln: A Life of Purpose and Power*, 188.

5. Guelzo, *Abraham Lincoln: Redeemer President*, 298; Kearns Goodwin, *Team of Rivals*, 427.

6. William H. Herndon and Jesse W. Weik, *Herndon's Lincoln: The True Story of a Great Life*. 3 vols. (Springfield, IL: Herndon's Lincoln Publishing Company, 1889), 83.

7. Tarbell, *The Life of Abraham Lincoln*, 129.

8. Oates, *With Malice Toward None* (New York: Harper Perennial, 1977), 285.

9. Carwardine, *Lincoln: A Life of Purpose and Power*, 188.

10. Guelzo, *Abraham Lincoln: Redeemer President*, 300.

11. Kearns Goodwin, *Team of Rivals*, 418.

12. Donald, *Lincoln*, 339.

13. Guelzo, *Abraham Lincoln: Redeemer President*, 305.

14. Kearns Goodwin, *Team of Rivals*, 380.

15. Sandburg, *The Prairie Years and the War Years*, 553.

16. Oates, *With Malice Toward None*, 286.

17. Kearns Goodwin, *Team of Rivals*, 671–72.

18. Kearns Goodwin, *Team of Rivals*, 19; Guelzo, *Abraham Lincoln: Redeemer President*, 256; Oates, *With Malice Toward None*, 202; Carwardine, *Lincoln: A Life of Purpose and Power*, 290.

19. David Davis quoted in Kearns Goodwin, *Team of Rivals*, 605.

20. Guelzo, *Abraham Lincoln: Redeemer President*, 386.

21. Oates, *With Malice Toward None*, 390–91.

22. Guelzo, *Abraham Lincoln: Redeemer President*, 394.

23. Kearns Goodwin, *Team of Rivals*, 680.

24. Kearns Goodwin, *Team of Rivals*, 680.

25. Lincoln quoted in Guelzo, *Abraham Lincoln: Redeemer President*, 355.

26. Kearns Goodwin, *Team of Rivals*, 18; Sandburg, *The Prairie Years and the War Years*, 490.

27. Sandburg, *The Prairie Years and the War Years*, 490.

28. Ohio politician Thomas Corwin quoted in Sandburg, *The Prairie Years and the War Years*, 494.

29. Kearns Goodwin, *Team of Rivals*, 679–80.

30. Jean H. Baker, *Mary Todd Lincoln: A Biography* (New York: Norton, 1987), 132.

31. Baker, *Mary Todd Lincoln*, xiii.

32. Almost three-quarters of those biographies examined in chapter 3 carried such accounts.

33. Michael Burlingame, *The Inner World of Abraham Lincoln* (Urbana: University of Illinois Press, 1993), 313.

34. Daniel Mark Epstein, *The Lincolns: Portrait of a Marriage* (New York: Ballantine, 2008), 6.

35. Catherine Clinton, *Mrs. Lincoln: A Life* (New York: HarperCollins, 2009), 5, 17.

36. Epstein, *The Lincolns*, 16–17, 28, 31.

37. Baker, *Mary Todd Lincoln*, 88, 94.

38. Kearns Goodwin, *Team of Rivals*, 96–97.

39. William O. Stoddard, *Abraham Lincoln: The True Story of a Great Life* (New York: Fords, Howard and Hubert, 1884); Herndon and Weik, *Herndon's Lincoln*; Guelzo, *Abraham Lincoln: Redeemer President*; H. Donald Winkler, *The Women in Lincoln's Life:*

How the Sixteenth American President Was Shaped by Fascinating Women Who Loved, Hated, Helped, Charmed and Deceived Him (Nashville, TN: Rutledge Hill Press, 2001).

40. Stoddard, *Abraham Lincoln*, 121.

41. Herndon and Weik, *Herndon's Lincoln*, 132–45.

42. Guelzo, *Abraham Lincoln: Redeemer President*, 98–100.

43. Winkler, *The Women in Lincoln's Life*, 97–125.

44. Ruth Painter Randall quoted in Guelzo, *Abraham Lincoln: Redeemer President*, 268.

45. Epstein, *The Lincolns*, 95, 54.

46. Epstein, *The Lincolns*, 75, 103.

47. Clinton, *Mrs. Lincoln*, 84, 90.

48. Baker, *Mary Todd Lincoln*, 132.

49. Epstein, *The Lincolns*, 191. While it is unusual (and some might say inappropriate) to describe domestic abuse as "picturesque," such a description serves to downplay reports of Mary's violence.

50. Clinton, *Mrs. Lincoln*, 74–75.

51. Baker, *Mary Todd Lincoln*, xiv–xv.

52. Tripp, *The Intimate World*, 170–71, 213–24.

53. Guelzo, *Abraham Lincoln: Redeemer President*, 111–13.

54. Winkler, *The Women in Lincoln's Life*, 128.

55. Winkler, *The Women in Lincoln's Life*, 160–61; Burlingame, *The Inner World*, 292.

56. Burlingame, *The Inner World*, 270–326.

57. Burlingame, *The Inner World*, 358.

58. Guelzo, *Abraham Lincoln: Redeemer President*, 111; Winkler, *The Women in Lincoln's Life*, 127.

59. Baker, *Mary Todd Lincoln*, 120, 122.

60. Clinton, *Mrs. Lincoln*, 76–77.

61. Burlingame, *The Inner World*, 62; Guelzo, *Abraham Lincoln: Redeemer President*, 387.

62. Stoddard, *Abraham Lincoln*, 121; Kearns Goodwin, *Team of Rivals*, 384; Clinton, *Mrs. Lincoln*, 148.

63. Burlingame, *The Inner World*, 62; Winkler, *The Women in Lincoln's Life*, 129.

64. Clinton, *Mrs. Lincoln*, 100.

65. Baker, *Mary Todd Lincoln*, 132–44.

66. Epstein, *The Lincolns*, 114, 246, 266–67, emphasis in the original.

67. Herndon and Weik, *Herndon's Lincoln*, 262.

68. Winkler, *The Women in Lincoln's Life*, 122.

69. Burlingame, *The Inner World*, 325–26.

70. Burlingame, *The Inner World*, 358.

71. Winkler, *The Women in Lincoln's Life*, 213–22.

72. Baker, *Mary Todd Lincoln*, xiii.

73. Comment by General Grant's secretary, Adam Badeau, reflecting on Mary's jealous tirade against Mary Ord at City Point. The incident is frequently included in Lincoln biographies. Cited here in Sandburg, *The Prairie Years and the War Years*, 678.

74. Winkler, *The Women in Lincoln's Life*, 164.

75. Two of these names have spelling variations: Elizabeth Keckley or Keckly, and William de Fleurville or de Florville. Because of de Fleurville's humble station in life, few images of him remain.

76. Based on an analysis of index entries in the following biographies: Holland, *The Life of Abraham Lincoln*; Stoddard, *Abraham Lincoln*; Isaac N. Arnold, *The Life of Abraham Lincoln* (Chicago: A. C. McClurg, 1887); Herndon and Weik, *Herndon's Lincoln*; Tarbell, *The Life of Abraham Lincoln*; Carl Sandburg, *The Prairie Years and the War Years*; Oates, *With Malice Toward None*; Baker, *Mary Todd Lincoln*; Burlingame, *The Inner World*; Donald, *Lincoln*; Guelzo, *Abraham Lincoln: Redeemer President*; Winkler, *The Women in Lincoln's Life*; Miller, *Lincoln's Virtues*; Tripp, *The Intimate World*; Shenk, *Lincoln's Melancholy*; Jerrold M. Packard, *The Lincolns in the White House, Four Years That Shattered a Family* (New York: St. Martin's, 2006); Carwardine, *Lincoln: A Life of Purpose and Power*; Kearns Goodwin, *Team of Rivals*; Epstein, *The Lincolns*; Clinton, *Mrs. Lincoln*.

77. Sandburg, *The Prairie Years and the War Years*, 193.

78. Sandburg, *The Prairie Years and the War Years*, 395.

79. Burlingame, *The Inner World*, 334. The description is quoted from one of Mary's relatives.

80. Burlingame, *The Inner World*, 307.

81. Guelzo, *Abraham Lincoln: Redeemer President*, 346.

82. Frederick Douglass, "Oration Delivered on the Occasion of the Unveiling of the Freedmen's Monument."

83. Guelzo, *Abraham Lincoln: Redeemer President*, 350.

84. Oates, *With Malice Toward None*, 412.

85. Hall, "The Question of Cultural Identity," 293.

86. Benedict Anderson, *Imagined Communities* (London: Verso, 1983).

87. For more on the national identity literature, see my discussion in Hogan, *Gender, Race and National Identity*.

88. For a discussion of these everyday iterations of national identity, see also Michael Billig, *Banal Nationalism* (London: Sage, 1995); and Tim Edensor, *National Identity, Popular Culture and Everyday Life* (Oxford: Berg, 2002).

89. Baar, "Lincoln Focuses on Its Name," 2.

90. Peterson, *Lincoln in American Memory*; Schwartz, *Abraham Lincoln and the Forge of National Memory*; and Schwartz, *Abraham Lincoln in the Post-Heroic Era*.

Bibliography

Abraham Lincoln Presidential Library and Museum. ALPLM. "Governor Blagojev-ich Announces That Abraham Lincoln Presidential Museum Has Welcomed Its 1 Millionth Visitor," January 6, 2007. Available at http://www.alplm.org/news/jan06_07.html (accessed August 21, 2009).

Accord, David. *What Would Lincoln Do? Lincoln's Most Inspired Solutions to Challeng-ing Problems and Difficult Situations.* Naperville, IL: Sourcebooks, 2009.

Adler, David A., and Alexandra Wallner. *A Picture Book of Abraham.* New York: Lincoln Holiday House, 1989.

Adorno, Theodor, and Max Horkheimer. *The Dialectic of Enlightenment.* New York: Herder and Herder, 1972.

Adut, Ari. "A Theory of Scandal: Victorians, Homosexuality, and the Fall of Oscar Wilde." *American Journal of Sociology* 111, no. 1 (2005): 213–48.

Alger, Horatio, *The Backwoods Boy, or the Boyhood and Manhood of Abraham Lincoln.* Philadelphia, PA: David McKay, 1883.

Althusser, Louis. "Ideology and Ideological State Apparatuses." In *Lenin and Philoso-phy and other Essays.* New York: Monthly Review Press, [1971] 2001.

Anderson, Benedict. *Imagined Communities.* London: Verso, 1983.

Arnold, Isaac N. *The Life of Abraham Lincoln.* Chicago: A. C. McClurg, 1887.

Aylesworth, Jim, and Barbara McClintock. *Our Abe Lincoln.* New York: Scholastic, 2009.

Baar, Aaron. "Lincoln Focuses on Its Name." *Adweek, Midwest Edition* 43, no. 30 (2002).

Baker, Jean H. *Mary Todd Lincoln: A Biography.* New York: Norton, 1987.

Barton, W. E. *The Soul of Abraham Lincoln.* New York: George H. Doran, 1920.

Baudrillard, Jean. *Simulacra and Simulation.* Translated by Sheila Glaser. Ann Arbor: University of Michigan Press, 1995.

Bellah, Robert N. "Civil Religion in America." *Daedalus: Journal of the American Acad-emy of Arts and Sciences* 96, no. 1 (1967): 1–21.

Bennett, Lerone. *Forced into Glory: Abraham Lincoln's White Dream.* Chicago: Johnson Publishing, 2007.

———. "Was Abe Lincoln a White Supremacist?" *Ebony,* February 1968.

Bial, Raymond. *Where Lincoln Walked.* New York: Walker Publishing, 1998.

Billig, Michael. *Banal Nationalism.* London: Sage, 1995.

Black, Sonia, and Carol Heyer. *Let's Read about Abraham Lincoln.* New York: Scholastic, 2002.

Blackwood, Gary. *Second Sight.* New York: Penguin, 2005.

Blight, David. *Race and Reunion: The Civil War in American Memory.* Cambridge, MA: Belknap, 2001.

Borden, Louise, and Ted Lewin. *A. Lincoln and Me.* New York: Scholastic, 1999.

Boroditsky, Lera. "How Does Our Language Shape the Way We Think?" In *What's Next: Dispatches on the Future of Science,* ed. Max Brockman. New York: Vintage, 2009.

Bourdieu, Pierre. *Outline of a Theory of Practice.* London: Cambridge University Press, 1977.

Bowles, Samuel, and Herbert Gintis. *Schooling in Capitalist America.* London: Routledge and Kegan Paul, 1976.

———. "Schooling in Capitalist America Revisited." *Sociology of Education* 75, no. 1 (2002).

Braden, Waldo W. *Abraham Lincoln, Public Speaker.* Baton Rouge: Louisiana State University Press, 1988.

Bradley, James. *The Imperial Cruise: A Secret History of Empire and War.* New York: Little, Brown, 2009.

Brenner, Martha, and Donald Cook. *Abe Lincoln's Hat.* New York: Random House, 1994.

Brizek, Steven. "Abortion: Heading the Way of Slavery?" NorthJersey.com. Available at http://www.northjersey.com/opinion/moreviews/45374322.html (accessed June 1, 2009).

Bruner, Edward M. *Culture on Tour: Ethnographies of Travel.* Chicago: University of Chicago Press, 2005.

Bryant, Jen, and Amy June Bates. *Abe's Fish: A Boyhood Tale of Abraham Lincoln.* New York: Sterling, 2009.

Bunker, Gary L. *From Rail-Splitter to Icon: Lincoln's Image in Illustrated Periodicals, 1860–1865.* Kent, OH: Kent State University Press, 2001.

Burkhimer, Michael. *100 Essential Lincoln Books.* Nashville, TN: Cumberland Publishing, 2003.

Burleigh, Robert, and Wendell Minor. *Abraham Lincoln Comes Home.* New York: Henry Holt, 2008.

Burlingame, Michael. *The Inner World of Abraham Lincoln.* Urbana: University of Illinois Press, 1994.

Carragee, Kevin M., and Wim Roefs. "The Neglect of Power in Recent Framing Research." *Journal of Communication* 54, no. 2 (2004).

Carwardine, Richard. *Lincoln: A Life of Purpose and Power.* New York: Vintage, 2007.

Child, Ben. "Spielberg's Abraham Lincoln Project to Go Ahead Despite Competition." *Guardian*, September 15, 2009. Available at http://www.guardian.co.uk/film/2009/sep/15/abraham-lincoln-spielberg-redford (accessed June 16, 2010).

Clinton, Catherine. *Mrs. Lincoln: A Life*. New York: HarperCollins, 2009.

Cohn, Amy, and Suzy Schmidt. *Abraham Lincoln*. New York: Scholastic, 2002.

Cornelius, James. "Abe's Day: What's New in the Annals of Lincolnology." *Newsweek*, February 12, 2008. Available at http://www.newsweek.com/id/110794 (accessed September 12, 2008).

Craughwell, Thomas J. *Stealing Lincoln's Body*. Cambridge, MA: Belknap, 2007.

Creighton, Millie. "Spinning Silk, Weaving Selves: Nostalgia, Gender, and Identity in Japanese Craft Vacations." *Japanese Studies* 21, no. 1 (2001).

Dick, Philip K. *Do Androids Dream of Electric Sheep?* Toronto: Del Rey, 1968.

———. *We Can Build You*. New York: Vintage, 1994.

Dickinson, Greg, Brian L. Ott, and Eric Aoki. "Memory and Myth at the Buffalo Bill Museum." *Western Journal of Communication* 69, no. 2 (2005).

DiLorenzo, Thomas. *Lincoln Unmasked: What You're Not Supposed to Know about Dishonest Abe*. New York: Crown Forum, 2006.

Dixon, Thomas. *The Clansman: An Historical Romance of the Ku Klux Klan*. New York: Doubleday, Page, 1905.

Donald, David H. *Lincoln*. New York: Simon and Schuster, 1995.

———. "Getting Right with Lincoln." In *Lincoln Reconsidered: Essays on the Civil War Era*. New York: Knopf, 1956.

Douglass, Frederick. "Oration Delivered on the Occasion of the Unveiling of the Freedmen's Monument in Memory of Abraham Lincoln." The Frederick Douglass Papers at the Library of Congress, 1876. Available at http://memory.loc.gov/cgibin/ampage?collId=mfd&fileName=23/23004/23004page.db&recNum=17&itemLink=/ammem/doughtml/dougFolder5.html&linkText=7 (accessed June 22, 2009).

Du Bois, W. E. B. "Again, Lincoln." *The Crisis*, September 1922.

Edensor, Tim. *National Identity, Popular Culture and Everyday Life*. Oxford: Berg, 2002.

Entman, Robert M. "Framing: Toward Clarification of a Fractured Paradigm." *Journal of Communication* 43, no. 4 (1993).

Epstein, Daniel Mark. *The Lincolns: Portrait of a Marriage*. New York: Ballantine, 2008.

Ferguson, Andrew. *Land of Lincoln: Adventures in Abe's America*. New York: Atlantic Monthly Press, 2007.

Fine, Gary Alan. *Difficult Reputations: Collective Memories of the Evil, Inept, and Controversial*. Chicago: University of Chicago Press, 2001.

———. "Reputational Entrepreneurs and the Memory of Incompetence: Melting Supporters, Partisan Warriors, and Images of President Harding." *American Journal of Sociology* 101, no. 5 (1996): 1159–93.

Fishman, Ronald S., and Adriana Da Silveira. "A Lincoln's Craniofacial Microsomia: Three-Dimensional Laser Scanning of 2 Lincoln Life Masks." *Archives of Ophthalmology* 125, no. 8 (2007).

Fleischner, Jennifer. *Mrs. Lincoln and Mrs. Keckly: The Remarkable Story of the Friendship between a First Lady and a Former Slave.* New York: Broadway Books, 2003.

Fontes, Justine, and Ron Fontes. *Abraham Lincoln: Lawyer, Leader, Legend.* New York: Dorling Kindersley, 2001.

Ford, John. *Young Mr. Lincoln.* Twentieth Century Fox, 1939.

Franklin, Adrian. *Animals and Modern Cultures: A Sociology of Human-Animal Relations in Modernity.* London: Sage, 1999.

Fredrickson, George M. *Big Enough to Be Inconsistent: Abraham Lincoln Confronts Slavery and Race.* Cambridge, MA: Harvard University Press, 2008.

Fritz, Jean, and Charles Robinson. *Just a Few Words, Mr. Lincoln: The Story of the Gettysburg Address.* New York: Grosset and Dunlap, 1993.

Frost, Warwick. "Making an Edgier Interpretation of the Gold Rushes: Contrasting Perspectives from Australia and New Zealand." *International Journal of Heritage Studies* 11, no. 3 (2005).

Gates, Henry Louis, Jr., ed. *Lincoln on Race and Slavery.* Princeton, NJ: Princeton University Press, 2009.

Giovanni, Nikki, and Bryan Collier. *Lincoln and Douglass: An American Friendship.* New York: Henry Holt, 2008.

Goffman, Erving. *Frame Analysis: An Essay on the Organization of Experience.* New York: Harper and Row, 1974.

Goodson, Ivor, Peter Cookson Jr., and Caroline Persell. "Distinction and Destiny: The Importance of Curriculum Form in Elite American Private Schools." *Discourse* 18, no. 2 (1997).

Grahame-Smith, Seth. *Abraham Lincoln: Vampire Hunter.* New York: Grand Central Publishing, 2008.

Grayson, Richard. *Lincoln's Doctor's Dog & Other Stories.* Lincoln, NE: iUniverse. com, 2001.

Greene, Carol. *Abraham Lincoln: President of a Divided Country.* Chicago: Children's Press, 1989.

Greenfeld, Liah. "Is Nation Unavoidable? Is Nation Unavoidable Today?" In *Nation and National Identity: The European Experience in Perspective,* ed. Hanspeter Kriesi, Klaus Armigeon, Hannes Siegrist, and Andreas Wimmer. Chur and Zürich: Rüegger, 1999.

Griffith, David W. *The Birth of a Nation.* David W. Griffith Corp., 1915.

Guelzo, Allen. *Abraham Lincoln: Redeemer President.* Grand Rapids, MI: Eerdmans, 1999.

Gustason, Harriett. "Echoes of History." *Journal-Standard,* Debate Reunion Tour insert, August 17, 2008, 2.

Halbwachs, Maurice. *The Collective Memory.* Translated by Francise J. Ditter Jr. and Vida Yazdi Ditter. New York: Harper Colophon, 1980.

Hall, Stuart. "Cultural Studies: Two Paradigms." *Media, Culture and Society* 2 (1980).

———. "The Question of Cultural Identity." In *Modernity and Its Futures,* ed. Stuart Hall, David Held, and Tony McGrew. Cambridge, UK: Polity Press, 1992.

Hallock, Gerard Benjamin Fleet. "The Homiletic Year—February." *Expositor* 21, no. 241 (1919).

Hambly, Barbara. *The Emancipator's Wife: A Novel of Mary Todd Lincoln.* New York: Bantam Dell, 2006.

Handelsman, Walt. "Too Lincolny?" Available at http://www.gocomics.com/walthandelsman/2009/01/15/ (accessed June 25, 2009).

Harness, Cheryl. *Abe Lincoln Goes to Washington, 1837–1865.* Washington, DC: National Geographic Society, 1997.

Hatfield, Althea. "Take Note of Obama's Actions on Abortion." *Peoria Journal Star,* February 22, 2009.

Herek, Stephen. *Bill and Ted's Excellent Adventure.* De Laurentiis Entertainment Group, 1989.

Herman, Edward, and Noam Chomsky. *Manufacturing Consent: The Political Economy of the Mass Media.* New York: Pantheon, 1988.

Herndon, William H., and Jesse W. Weik. *Herndon's Lincoln: The True Story of a Great Life.* 3 vols. Springfield, IL: Herndon's Lincoln Publishing Company, 1889.

Hewison, Robert. *The Heritage Industry: Britain in a Climate of Decline.* London: Methuen, 1987.

Hogan, Jackie. *Gender, Race and National Identity: Nations of Flesh and Blood.* New York: Routledge, 2009.

Holcomb, Briavel. "Gender and Heritage Interpretation." In *Contemporary Issues in Heritage and Environmental Interpretation: Problems and Prospects,* ed. David Uzzell and Roy Ballantyne. London: Stationery Office, 1998.

Holland, Josiah. *The Life of Abraham Lincoln.* Springfield, MA: Gurdon Bill, 1866.

Holzer, Harold. *Lincoln at Cooper Union: The Speech That Made Abraham Lincoln President.* New York: Simon and Schuster, 2004.

Hormats, Robert D. "Abraham Lincoln and the Global Economy." *Harvard Business Review* 81, no. 8 (2003).

Horton, James Oliver, and Lois Horton. *Slavery and the Making of America.* New York: Oxford University Press, 2005.

Illinois Heritage Corridor Convention and Visitor's Bureau. *2008–2009 Heritage Corridor Visitor's Guide.* Joliet, IL: Heritage Corridor Convention and Visitor's Bureau.

Iskowitz, Marc. "Don't Blame DTC for Dismal Rozerem Sales." *Medical Marketing and Media,* June 15, 2007. Available at http://www.mmm-online.com/Dont-blame-DTC-for-dismal-Rozerem-sales/article/24186/ (accessed December 9, 2008).

Jackson, Ellen, and Doris Ettlinger. *Abe Lincoln Loved Animals.* Morton Grove, IL: Albert Whitman, 2008.

Johnson, Nuala C. "Where Geography and History Meet: Heritage Tourism and the Big House in Ireland." *Annals of the Association of American Geographers* 86, no. 3 (1996).

Kadinsky, Sergey, and Christina Boyle. "On Abraham Lincoln's 200th Birthday, Handwritten Speech Breaks Auction Record at Christie's." *New York Daily News,* February 12, 2009. Available at http://www.nydailynews.com/news/2009/02/12/2009-02-12_on_abraham_lincolns_200th_birthday_handw.html (accessed June 14, 2010).

Kaikobad, Vera. "Acupuncture Diagnosis of Abraham Lincoln." *Medical Acupuncture* 19, no. 4 (2007).

Kay, Betty Carson. *Americans of Character: Abraham Lincoln*. San Diego, CA: Young People's Press, 2000.

———. *The Lincolns from A to Z*. Bloomington, IN: Author House, 2008.

Kearns Goodwin, Doris. *Team of Rivals: The Political Genius of Abraham Lincoln*. New York: Simon and Schuster, 2006.

Keckley, Elizabeth. *Behind the Scenes in the Lincoln White House: Memoirs of an African-American Seamstress*. Mineola, NY: Dover, [1868] 2006.

Kellner, Douglas. *Jean Baudrillard: From Marxism to Postmodernism and Beyond*. Stanford, CA: Stanford University Press, 1989.

Kepner, James. *From the Closet of History*. Self-published by Kepner, 1984.

King, Erika G., and Mary deYoung. "Imag(in)ing September 11: Ward Churchill, Frame Contestation, and Media Hegemony." *Journal of Communication Inquiry* 32, no. 2 (2008).

Kirshenblatt-Gimblett, Barbara. *Destination Culture: Tourism, Museums and Heritage*. Berkeley: University of California Press, 1998.

Kozol, Jonathon. *Savage Inequalities*. New York: Harper Perennial, 1991.

Ku Klux Klan. "Abraham Lincoln on Race." Available at http://www.kkk.bz/aberace. htm (accessed June 15, 2009).

Kunhardt, Philip B., Peter W. Kunhardt, and Peter W. Kunhardt Jr. *Looking for Lincoln: The Making of an American Icon*. New York: Knopf, 2008.

Lamon, Ward Hill. *The Life of Abraham Lincoln*. Washington, DC: Dorothy Lamon Teillard, 1911.

Landis, Tim, and Natalie Morris. "Tourism Booming, Museum Seems to Be Boosting All Attractions." *State Journal Register* (Springfield, IL), July 21, 2005. Available at http://showcase.netins.net/web/creative/lincoln/news/boom.htm (accessed January 21, 2011).

Lee, Spike. *Bamboozled*. New Line Cinema, 2000.

Lethlean, Jane. "Untold Stories: Multimedia Exhibit on Display." *Journal-Standard*, October 16, 2008.

Levy, Shawn. *Night at the Museum: Battle for the Smithsonian*. Twentieth Century Fox, 2009.

Lincoln-Douglas Society. *The Stump: Publication of the Lincoln-Douglas Society* (Freeport, IL), no. 1 (Spring 2008).

Lincoln Heritage Coalition. *Looking for Lincoln*, pamphlet. Springfield, IL: Lincoln Heritage Coalition, 2005.

Lincoln Heritage Coalition. *Looking for Lincoln*, pamphlet. Springfield, IL: Lincoln Heritage Coalition, 2008.

Lincoln Heritage Coalition. *Looking for Lincoln*, map and pamphlet. Springfield, IL: Lincoln Heritage Coalition, n.d.

Lindsay, Stephen. *Jesus Hates Zombies, Featuring Lincoln Hates Werewolves*. Vols. 2–4. Levittown, NY: Alterna Comics, 2009–2010.

Locher, Barry. "Claims about Lincoln Deserved Investigation." *State Journal-Register* (Springfield, IL), May 20, 1999, 7.

Loeb, Aaron. *Abraham Lincoln's Big, Gay Dance Party.* Details available at http://www.abrahamlincolnsbiggaydanceparty.com/ (accessed January 30, 2011).

Loewen, James. *Lies across America: What Our Historic Sites Get Wrong.* New York: Touchstone, 1999.

Lowenthal, David. *The Heritage Crusade and the Spoils of History.* Cambridge, UK: Cambridge University Press, 1998.

———. *The Past Is a Foreign Country.* Cambridge, UK: Cambridge University Press, 1985.

Lumley, Robert, ed. *The Museum Time-Machine.* London: Routledge, 1988.

Mackenzie, John M. *Museums and Empire: Natural History, Human Cultures and Colonial Identities.* Manchester: Manchester University Press, 2009.

Magelssen, Scott. "Remapping American-ness: Heritage Production and the Staging of the Native American and the African American as Other in 'Historyland.'" *National Identities* 4, no. 2 (2002).

Maltz, Earl M. "Roe v. Wade and Dred Scott." *Widener Law Journal* 17, no. 1 (2007).

Mara, Wil. *Abraham Lincoln.* New York: Children's Press, 2002.

Marx, Karl, and Friederich Engels. *The German Ideology.* London: Lawrence and Wishart, [1845] 1970.

McCloud, Scout. *The New Adventures of Abraham Lincoln.* La Jolla, CA: Homage Comics, 1998.

McCreary, Donna D. *Lincoln's Table: A President's Culinary Journey from Cabin to Cosmopolitan.* Charlestown, IN: Lincoln Presentations, 2008.

McKenna, George. "On Abortion: A Lincolnian Perspective." *Atlantic Monthly,* September 1995. Available at http://www.theatlantic.com/issues/95sep/abortion/abortion.htm (accessed September 12, 2008).

McKinsey, John A. *The Lincoln Secret.* Dixon, CA: Martin Pearl Publishing, 2008.

Melchisedech, Kay Olson, and Otha Zachariah Edward Lohse. *The Assassination of Abraham Lincoln.* Mankato, MN: Capstone Press, 2005.

Miller, William Lee. *Lincoln's Virtues: An Ethical Biography.* New York: Vintage, 2002.

Morris, Charles E., III. "My Old Kentucky Homo: Abraham Lincoln, Larry Kramer, and the Politics of Queer Memory." In *Queering Public Address: Sexualities in American Historical Discourse,* ed. Charles E. Morris III. Columbia: University of South Carolina Press, 2007.

Myers, Anna. *Assassin.* New York: Walker Books, 2005.

National Public Radio. "Presidential Portrait in Pastry." Available at www.npr.org/templates/story/story.php?storyId=100719176 (accessed May 25, 2008).

Neely, Mark. *The Last Best Hope.* Cambridge, MA: Harvard University Press, 1993.

New Salem Lincoln League. *Lincoln's New Salem: A Village Reborn.* Petersburg, IL: New Salem Lincoln League, 1994.

Oakes, James. *The Radical and the Republican: Frederick Douglass, Abraham Lincoln, and the Triumph of Antislavery Politics.* New York: Norton, 2007.

Oates, Stephen B. *With Malice Toward None.* New York: Harper Perennial, 1977.

Orwell, George. *Nineteen Eighty-Four.* New York: Signet Classics, 1950.

Packard, Jerrold M. *The Lincolns in the White House: Four Years That Shattered a Family.* New York: St. Martin's, 2006.

Painter, Nell Irvin. *Sojourner Truth: A Life, a Symbol.* New York: Norton, 1994.

Parin D'Aulaire, Ingri, and Edgar Parin D'Aulaire. *Abraham Lincoln.* New York: Bantam, Doubleday, [1939] 1993.

PBS. *Looking for Lincoln.* PBS Home Video, 2008.

Pels, Peter. "The Spirit of Matter: On Fetish, Rarity, Fact, and Fancy." In *Border Fetishisms: Material Objects in Unstable Spaces,* ed. Patricia Spyer. New York: Routledge, 1998.

Persell, Caroline, and Peter Cookson Jr. "Chartering and Bartering: Elite Education and Social Reproduction." *Social Problems* 33, no. 2 (1985).

———. *Preparing for Power: America's Elite Boarding Schools.* New York: Basic Books, 1985.

Peterson, Merrill. *Lincoln in American Memory.* New York: Oxford University Press, 1994.

Peterson, Richard A., and N. Anand, "The Production of Culture Perspective." *Annual Review of Sociology* 30 (2004): 311–34.

Pingry, Patricia A., and Stephanie McFetridge Britt. *Discover Abraham Lincoln: Storyteller, Lawyer, President.* Nashville, TN: Ideals Children's Books, 2005.

Povse, Paul. "Closure of Illinois Historic House Garners Protest; It's Just One of 14." *St. Louis Beacon,* September 15, 2008. Available at http://www.stlbeacon.org/region/3194 (accessed January 21, 2011).

Rabin, Staton, and Bagram Ibatoulline. *Mr. Lincoln's Boys: Being the Mostly True Adventures of Abraham Lincoln's Trouble-Making Sons, Tad and Willie.* New York: Viking, 2008.

Randall, James G. "Has the Lincoln Theme Been Exhausted?" *American Historical Review* 41 (1936): 270–94.

Randall, J. G., and Richard N. Current. *Mr. Lincoln.* New York: Dodd, Mead, 1957.

Rappaport, Doreen, and Kadir Nelson. *Abe's Honest Words: The Life of Abraham Lincoln.* New York: Hyperion, 2008.

Reagan, Ronald. "Abortion and the Conscience of the Nation." *Human Life Review,* Spring 1983.

Reiss, Mike, and David Catrow. *The Boy Who Looked Like Lincoln.* New York: Puffin, 2003.

Reitman, Ivan. *Kindergarten Cop.* Universal Studios, 1990.

Rinaldi, Ann. *An Acquaintance with Darkness.* Boston: Graphia, 1999.

Ritzer, George. *The McDonaldization of Society.* Rev. ed. Thousand Oaks, CA: Pine Forge Press, 2004.

Robertson, David. *Booth: A Novel.* New York: Doubleday, 1997.

Rosenzweig, Roy, and David Thelen. *The Presence of the Past: Popular Uses of History in American Life.* New York: Columbia University Press, 1998.

Sadker, David, and Karen Zittelman. *Still Failing at Fairness: How Gender Bias Cheats Girls and Boys and What We Can Do about It.* New York: Scribner, 2009.

Sadker, Myra, and David Sadker. *Failing at Fairness: How Our Schools Cheat Girls.* New York: Scribner, 1994.

Safire, William. *Freedom: A Novel of Abraham Lincoln and the Civil War*. New York: Avon, 1988.

Sandburg, Carl. *The Prairie Years and the War Years*. New York: Harcourt, Brace and World, 1954.

Schott, Jane A. *Abraham Lincoln*. Minneapolis, MN: Lerner, 2002.

Schwartz, Barry. *Abraham Lincoln in the Post-Heroic Era: History and Memory in Late Twentieth-Century America*. Chicago: University of Chicago Press, 2008.

———. *Abraham Lincoln and the Forge of National Memory*. Chicago: University of Chicago Press, 2000.

———. "Postmodernity and Historical Reputation: Abraham Lincoln in Late Twentieth-Century American Memory." *Social Forces* 77, no. 1 (1998): 63–103.

———. "Collective Memory and History: How Abraham Lincoln Became a Symbol of Racial Equality." *Sociological Quarterly* 38, no. 3 (1997): 469–96.

———. *George Washington: The Making of an American Symbol*. Ithaca, NY: Cornell University Press, 1990.

Schwartz, Barry, and Howard Schuman, "History, Commemoration, and Belief: Abraham Lincoln in American Memory, 1945–2001." *American Sociological Review* 70, no. 2 (2005): 183–203.

Scott, Ridley. *Blade Runner*. Warner Brothers, 1982.

Shenk, Joshua Wolf. *Lincoln's Melancholy*. New York: Mariner Books, 2005.

Shoard, Catherine. "Daniel Day-Lewis Set for Steven Spielberg's Lincoln Film." *Guardian*, November 19, 2010. Available at http://www.guardian.co.uk/film/2010/nov/19/daniel-day-lewis-spielberg-lincoln (accessed January 21, 2011).

Slotkin, Richard. *Abe: A Novel*. New York: Henry Holt, 2000.

———. *Gunfighter Nation: The Myth of the Frontier in Twentieth-Century America*. New York: Atheneum, 1992.

Smith, Brad. *Busted Flush: A Novel*. New York: Henry Holt, 2005.

Spender, Dale. *Learning to Lose*. London: Women's Press, 1980.

Steers, Edward, Jr. *Lincoln Legends: Myths, Hoaxes and Confabulations Associated with Our Greatest President*. Lexington: University Press of Kentucky, 2007.

Steinbacher, Michele. "Infamous 1908 Race Riot Sparked by Secret Move to Bloomington." *Pantagraph*, August 9, 2008. Available at http://www.pantagraph.com/articles/2008/08/09/news/doc489dbc52e34d8112745755.txt (accessed June 23, 2009).

St. George, Judith, and Matt Faulkner. *Stand Tall, Abe Lincoln*. New York: Philomel Books, 2008.

Stoddard, William O. *Abraham Lincoln: The True Story of a Great Life*. New York: Fords, Howard and Hubert, 1884.

Stone, Irving. *Love Is Eternal: A Novel about Mary Todd and Abraham Lincoln*. New York: Bantam Doubleday Dell, 1954.

Stone, Tanya Lee. *Abraham Lincoln: A Photographic Story of a Life*. New York: DK Publishing, 2005.

Tackach, James. "Abraham Lincoln in Recent American Fiction." *Lincoln Herald* 110, no. 4 (2008).

Tarbell, Ida M. *The Life of Abraham Lincoln*. 2 vols. New York: McClure, Phillips, 1900.

Taylor, Jud. *Star Trek*: "Let That Be Your Last Battlefield." Paramount Television, 1969.

Thayer, William M. *From Pioneer Home to the White House: Life of Abraham Lincoln, Boyhood, Youth, Manhood, Assassination, Death*. New York: Hurst, 1882.

Thomas, Benjamin P. *Abraham Lincoln*. New York: Knopf, 1952.

Thompson, Bob. "Histrionics and History: Lincoln Library's High-Tech Exhibits Have Scholars Choosing Sides." *Washington Post*, February 15, 2005, C1.

Thomson, Sarah, and James Ransome. *What Lincoln Said*. New York: HarperCollins, 2009.

Time for Kids, News Scoop Edition, vol. 14, no. 17 (February 6, 2009).

Timothy, Dallen J., and Stephen W. Boyd. *Heritage Tourism*. Harlow, UK: Prentice Hall, 2003.

Tripp, C. A. *The Intimate World of Abraham Lincoln*. New York: Avalon, 2005.

Turner, Ann, and Wendell Minor. *Abe Lincoln Remembers*. New York: HarperCollins, 2001.

Turteltaub, Jon. *National Treasure: Book of Secrets*. Walt Disney Pictures, 2007.

Tyson, Lois. *Critical Theory: A User-Friendly Guide*. 2nd ed. New York: Routledge, 2006.

Urry, John. *The Tourist Gaze: Leisure and Travel in Contemporary Societies*. London: Sage, 1990.

U.S. Census. *Overview of Race and Hispanic Origin: 2010*. Available at http://www.census.gov/prod/cen2010/briefs/c2010br-02.pdf (accessed May 11, 2011).

Uzzell, David, and Roy Ballantyne, eds. *Contemporary Issues in Heritage and Environmental Interpretation: Problems and Prospects*. London: Stationery Office, 1998.

Van Steenwyk, Elizabeth, and Bill Farnsworth. *When Abraham Talked to the Trees*. Grand Rapids, MI: Eerdmans, 2000.

Vidal, Gore. *Lincoln: A Novel*. New York: Vintage, 2000.

Volk, David. "On Lincoln, Obama and Evil." *Peoria Journal Star*, November 29, 2008.

Waters, Malcolm. *Globalization*. New York: Routledge, 1995.

Webb, Jen, and Sam Byrnand. "Some Kind of Virus: The Zombie as Body and as Trope." *Body & Society* 14, no. 83 (2008).

Weems, Mason L. *Life of George Washington; with Curious Anecdotes, Equally Honorable to Himself, and Exemplary to His Young Countrymen*. Philadelphia, PA: Joseph Allen, 1800.

Williams, Frank J. "Abraham Lincoln and Civil Liberties in Wartime." Available at http://www.heritage.org/research/nationalsecurity/hl834.cfm (accessed May 20, 2009).

Wilson, Steven. *President Lincoln's Spy*. New York: Kensington, 2008.

Winkler, H. Donald. *The Women in Lincoln's Life: How the Sixteenth American President Was Shaped by Fascinating Women Who Loved, Hated, Helped, Charmed and Deceived Him*. Nashville, TN: Rutledge Hill Press, 2001.

Winnick, Karen B. *Mr. Lincoln's Whiskers*. Honesdale, PA: Boyds Mills Press, 1996.

Winters, Kay, and Nancy Carpenter. *Abe Lincoln: The Boy Who Loved Books*. New York: Aladdin, 2003.

Wodak, Ruth, Rudolf de Cillia, Martin Reisigl, and Karin Liebhart. *The Discursive Construction of National Identity*. Translated by Angelika Hirsch and Richard Mitten. Edinburgh: Edinburgh University Press, 1999.

Wolk, Tony. *Abraham Lincoln: A Novel Life*. Portland, OR: Ooligan Press, 2004.

Woods, Andrew, and Pat Schories. *Young Abraham Lincoln: Log Cabin President*. New York: Troll Associates, 1992.

Wurtzel, Elizabeth. *Prozac Nation: Young and Depressed in America*. New York: Penguin, 1994.

Zeldis, Malcah, and Edith Kunhardt. *Honest Abe*. New York: Greenwillow, 1993.

Index

About the Author

Jackie Hogan is the chair of sociology at Bradley University in Illinois, the "Land of Lincoln." She is the author of numerous scholarly articles and the 2009 book *Gender, Race and National Identity: Nations of Flesh and Blood.* With graduate degrees in both anthropology (M.A., University of Iowa) and sociology (Ph.D., University of Tasmania, Australia), and research interests in the United States, the United Kingdom, Australia, and Japan, Hogan crosses both disciplinary and national boundaries in her work. In addition to her ongoing research on national identity, she teaches a range of courses on social inequality and non-Western cultures. She is the chair of the Asian Studies Program, the founder and coordinator of the Body Project, and an enthusiastic participant in the university's Study Abroad Program.